Property links the economic, the political and the jural dimensions of social life. Anthropologists have traditionally argued that property relations are not relations between people and things, but social relations between people. Building on this definition and extending it to take more account of cultural diversity, the contributors to this volume emphasize the political and economic embeddedness of property relations. The contents include accounts of sharing among hunter-gatherers in Africa and ecological knowledge among reindeer herders in Siberia; 'inclusive' versus 'exclusive' property relations and rights of disposal among Melanesians; legal concepts of property and its transmission in England and Japan, the two island pioneers of industrial society; land appropriation from native Americans; property redistribution following recent social and political upheaval in Cyprus and Romania; the ability of English civil law to ensure adequate protection of the environment; and the devolution of property in modern Britain, with particular reference to changing family structures and unsustainable demands on public welfare provision.

Criticizing both the dominant Western liberal paradigm of property relations and its Marxist-Leninist counterpart, Professor Hann argues that a broader idea of property should once again become an integrating concept in anthropology and the social sciences. The collection will be of particular interest to economic anthropologists, who have conducted many studies of exchange, production and consumption, but have rather neglected property. It will also appeal to wider audiences: the basic issues of ownership, control and power are central to the lives of all citizens in all forms of society.

# Property relations

# Property relations

*Renewing the anthropological tradition*

*Edited by*

## C. M. Hann

*University of Kent at Canterbury*

PUBLISHED BY THE PRESS SYNDICATE OF THE UNIVERSITY OF CAMBRIDGE
The Pitt Building, Trumpington Street, Cambridge CB2 1RP, United Kingdom

CAMBRIDGE UNIVERSITY PRESS
The Edinburgh Building, Cambridge CB2 2RU, United Kingdom
40 West 20th Street, New York, NY 10011–4211, USA
10 Stamford Road, Oakleigh, Melbourne 3166, Australia

First published 1998

Printed in the United Kingdom at the University Press, Cambridge

Typeset in Plantin 10/12pt [CE]

*A catalogue record for this book is available from the British Library*

*Library of Congress cataloging in publication data*

Property relations: Renewing the anthropological tradition / edited
by C. M. Hann.
     p.   cm.
Includes bibliographical references and index.
ISBN 0 521 59389 1 (hb)
1. Property.   2. Economic anthropology.   3. Right of property.
I. Hann, C. M., 1953– .
GN449.P76   1998
306.3′2–dc21   97–35811   CIP

ISBN 0 521 59389 1 hardback
ISBN 0 521 59636 X paperback

# Contents

# Contributors

DAVID G. ANDERSON is Lecturer in Arctic Anthropology, University of Alberta.

JAMES G. CARRIER is Lecturer in Social Anthropology, University of Durham.

JACK GOODY is Emeritus Professor of Social Anthropology, University of Cambridge.

C. M. HANN is Professor of Social Anthropology, University of Kent at Canterbury.

WILLIAM HOWARTH is Professor of Environmental Law, University of Kent at Canterbury.

ALAN MACFARLANE is Professor of Anthropological Science, University of Cambridge.

JULIE SCOTT is Lecturer in Social Anthropology, University of the Eastern Mediterranean, Famagusta.

MARILYN STRATHERN is William Wyse Professor of Social Anthropology, University of Cambridge.

KATHERINE VERDERY is Eric R. Wolf Professor of Anthropology, University of Michigan.

PAULA L. WAGONER is a Doctoral Candidate, Department of Anthropology, Indiana University, and an Instructor at Juniata College.

JAMES WOODBURN is Senior Lecturer in Social Anthropology, London School of Economics.

# Acknowledgements

Most of the chapters in this book were originally read as seminar papers in Canterbury during the Lent Term 1995, and I am greatly indebted to all who participated in this series. I am also grateful to Chris Gregory and Keith Hart, Cambridge University Press's readers, for several helpful suggestions. Above all I wish to thank my colleagues and the support staff in the Department of Sociology and Social Anthropology at the University of Kent who, somewhat against the odds, manage to maintain a truly excellent research environment. Special thanks to Yana Johnson for assistance in the preparation of the typescript.

CMH
Canterbury, February 1997

# 1 Introduction: the embeddedness of property

## C. M. Hann

'With regard to external things, a man ought to possess them not as his own but as common, and always be ready to put them at the disposal of others who are in need' (St Thomas Aquinas; cited in Gill 1983: 126).

'In every society there are men who control more of the food, clothing and other forms of wealth produced in the society than do other men. The word *control* is used deliberately: from many points of view the control of wealth is more important than its mere possession' (Homans 1942: 339).

### People, things, words

New forms of property relations have come and gone as long as human societies have existed, but one particular cluster has achieved world dominance in the last two centuries. The rigorous specification of private property rights is nowadays almost everywhere thought to be a necessary condition not only for improved economic performance but also for healthy societies founded on civil and political liberties. The other key ideas in what I term the dominant liberal paradigm are free individuals, competitive markets, pluralistic civil societies and the 'rule of law'. Most of these have attracted more scholarly attention of late than property *per se*. The liberal paradigm is often traced back to Adam Smith. It is attractive to many, and it has certainly proved more powerful than its Marxist-Leninist challenger. A standardized model of private, exclusive ownership has now been disseminated to most societies, including in recent years to the former communist societies of Eastern Europe and Asia by their Western advisers. Liberals advocate this model as more efficient and more just than rival models in which, they allege, ownership is a matter of arbitrary dictate by powerholders. Liberals also frequently allege that communal forms necessarily give rise to the overexploitation of scarce natural resources. Following global dissemination of the model, private ownership has also been vigorously revived as an ideological principle in some of the countries where it originated.

1

For example, in Britain major industries that had been taken into state ownership in earlier generations have been privatized, and centuries-old principles of mutuality have been abandoned as building societies have rushed to convert themselves to commercial banks.

Yet the actual preeminence of private property and of the liberal paradigm of which it forms a central element has never been as complete as either its proponents or its critics like to claim. To a large extent it is a myth. There are powerful countercurrents, in Britain no less than in post-communist Russia, since in all societies the property rights of individuals are subject to political as well as legal regulation. In many parts of the world the private property model has been resisted by indigenous peoples, sometimes covertly when any form of overt opposition seemed impossible, but sometimes through well-organized campaigns. The 1992 Mabo Judgement in Australia was a landmark which overturned the legal edifice that had hitherto denied the Aborigines title to their land. The universality of the liberal model is called into question by some of the most advanced capitalist economies themselves, notably East Asian states which have given greater priority to careful governmental support and regulation than to the pursuit of 'pure competition', and to collectivities (starting with the family) rather than the individual. The private property component of the liberal model looks increasingly suspect throughout the capitalist world, as ownership of large enterprises continues to shift away from persons to institutions, and is increasingly detached from issues of control and management.

To speak of property, then, is to engage with a range of issues of global political economy in the contemporary world. However, other aspects of property may be more significant for anthropologists. Mrs Thatcher's governments did not restrict themselves to privatizing industries (what Marxists call the 'means of production') and the promotion of shareholding by individuals. They also cut back on public housing investment, initiated the large-scale sale of council houses to their tenants, and achieved a substantial increase in the number of households which own the property in which they live. Evidently many people in Britain support these policies. Most of the academics I know also gain pleasure and fulfilment from being 'owner occupiers', just as they do from the ownership of other objects and 'personal effects'. More generally, it is evident that the ways in which people relate to the objects in their environment play a vital role in forming their social identities. Here, too, the private property model seems to have become pervasive, at least in countries like Britain. If I ask my ten-year-old son to explain the meaning of the word 'property', he answers promptly that it has to do with owning things. If a thing is your property, it belongs to you. Others cannot take it from you. Assuming his response to be fairly typical of British children, what do his phrases reveal about property as an institution in British society and property in general? Does my son display an instinct to acquire objects and own them exclusively that is universal among humans? Or is he articulating a notion of possessive individualism that is the specific product of modern Western societies? How does a Trobriand Islander who seeks to possess items of value exchanged ceremonially in the complex system known as *kula* differ from a British entrepreneur who puts his personalized numberplates on to his new Mercedes, and aspires to own his town's football team and to pass it on in due course to his eldest son or grandson? If you have bought this book, do you write your name in it, to establish a relationship and maintain possession? Do you treat it differently if it is a library copy you have borrowed, or if you are just browsing in the bookstore? How does ownership of a book differ from the ownership of other kinds of objects, and from the relationship that is expressed when I speak of *my* son?

Most anthropologists will take it for granted that people's attitudes towards objects and the ways in which they are used to create meaning are culturally and historically variable. For example, slaves are by definition human beings who form the property of others, but they are marked off from other forms of property and although they are widely distributed in time and space it is rather difficult to make any further universal statements about this property relation (Watson 1980). At any one time within each culture concepts of ownership and possession, control and disposal, are likely to vary greatly for different categories of object. The identifications people have with the land on which a sacred shrine is located differ from their identifications with land that is just another parcel of suburban real estate – and when one enquires further into the market for this commodity, as every estate agent knows, a tremendous variety of sentiments is uncovered. Some items of personal hygiene were not taken into communal ownership in even the most extreme socialist systems, while even the most dedicated apostles of privatization generally refrain from applying their model to the national army. This point brings us back at once to questions of political economy. At the micro level, property relations form the myriad ways in which people build up their social identities through holding and using a variety of 'things' in their environment. At the macro level the anthropologist also needs to address issues of political power and control over the distribution of 'things' in society. These levels can be connected in analysis. For example, most Western countries are currently having to review their levels of welfare provision. In Britain the entitlement of single-parent families to claim welfare benefits has been called into question by some politicians. The high costs of terminal care have left some people with no choice but to sell the greater part of the personal property they have accumulated, which they had hoped to be able to pass on to their children. Such problems show that property distribution and transmission within families are in fact intimately connected to the policies of states – which seem increasingly unable to sustain the obligations they have assumed. When British politicians talk about the need for greater social 'inclusion' and a 'stakeholder society' they are raising explicit issues about property, just as surely as academics who moan in their common-room about the local housing market and the undermining of tenure, or their students who complain about their rents and the withdrawal of their state grants. Of course our 'nation-states' are themselves based on an extension of the principle of exclusive ownership. Some descendants of Adam Smith today support the cause of Scots nationalism, on the grounds that oil assets which belong to Scotland should not be appropriated for the benefit of a larger British public. In other parts of the world struggles for territory and other forms of property have been more violently contested. Often these struggles focus on the language spoken by a group, and the purity of its 'culture', which is considered to be its exclusive property.

Although anthropologists are likely to emphasize the cultural diversity and historical contingency of property relations, it is nonetheless helpful to retain some core definition. This is more difficult than might be supposed, since neither lawyers nor philosophers have come up with conclusive, universally accepted definitions. In contemporary ordinary language usage, property commonly refers to the 'thing' over which a person claims more or less exclusive rights of ownership. Sometimes this thing is in fact an activity, as in statements like 'he made his fortune from (buying and selling) property'. However, in established Western theoretical and academic usage property is not an activity or a thing at all, but the rights that people hold over things which guarantee them a future 'income stream'. They 'own' only incorporeal rights, not the thing itself. Property *relations* are consequently better seen as social relations between people. A textbook anthropological definition runs as follows:

> The essential nature of property is to be found in social relations rather than in any inherent attributes of the thing or object that we call *property*. Property, in other words, is not a thing, but a network of social relations that governs the conduct of people with respect to the use and disposition of things (Hoebel 1966: 424).

According to this definition, it would be incorrect to see the culturally variable ways in which people relate to 'things' as in themselves constituting property relations.[1] Property relations can only exist between people: as John Davis has put the point, 'you cannot sue an acre; a boundary dispute is not a dispute with a boundary. The study of property rules in general, and of land tenure in particular, is the study of relationships between people' (1973a: 157). In any case, the things to which Hoebel refers in his definition are by no means restricted to the material objects that a society produces. Things are construed much more broadly by anthropologists to include such intangibles as names, reputation and knowledge, personal and collective identities, not to mention intangibles such as currency holdings and shares in joint-stock companies. The liberal paradigm was formed in an age when the archetypal form of property was private land ownership, but it is important to question this paradigm in a world in which most quantifiable wealth items are not material things at all, and intellectual property rights attract more legal attention than land.

Useful though it is to be warned against generalization from the ordinary language usage of modern Western society, this anthropological definition in terms of social relations versus 'things' may be too restrictive. Apart from the special case of slavery, people have rights in other persons, such as those shared by a married couple in each other, which are not directly connected to 'things'. Moreover, since people everywhere do talk about the ties that bind them to all sorts of non-human entities, and since these are often crucial to social identities, these relationships need to be included in our definition. The boundaries between people and things, between human and non-human (even inanimate) persons, are not always sharply drawn. Even in Western societies people are often considered to have a special relationship with the objects they produce, and this has been the basis of many justifications for private ownership. It therefore seems desirable to stretch the definition of property beyond the conventional anthropological formula, which proclaims simply that property relations *are* social relations. The word 'property' is best seen as directing attention to a vast field of cultural as well as social relations, to the symbolic as well as the material contexts within which things are recognized and personal as well as collective identities made. This usage may seem abstruse and at variance with both ordinary language and academic usages. It might seem too loose and open-ended, making the study of property relations coextensive with the entire field of social anthropology. However, the main advantage of approaching property relations in this way is that it carries minimal ethnocentric baggage. It can therefore be used to facilitate comparative analysis in fields of social organization where economics, politics and law intersect.

Obviously I am here advocating the use of property as an analytic term at a high level of abstraction. It may not be readily translatable into other cultures and other eras. Nuances such as the distinction between 'own' and 'possess' are notoriously difficult to render in other languages; there may be significant difficulties even in translating between related European languages. The word 'property' itself is nowadays often used synonymously with exclusive ownership; but it seems preferable to specify ownership more precisely as 'the greatest possible interest in a thing which a mature system of law recognizes' (Honore 1961: 108; cited in Reeve 1986: 17–18). The contributors to this volume are concerned with both property and ownership. Their broad aim is to investigate both inequalities in the distribution of 'things' and historical and cultural variation in the ways that people 'hold' them and thereby create their social identities.

Some recent theoretical work in law has deconstructed the concept of property to the point where it vanishes altogether (Gray 1991). This conclusion can be averted if, parallel with cultural investigations, equal importance is attached to investigations of the realities of economic and political power and to the development of a general analytic framework. As Maurice Godelier has emphasized, 'a form of property only exists when it serves as a rule for the concrete appropriation of reality. Property only really exists when it is rendered effective in and through a process of concrete appropriation' (1986: 81). It is desirable, in the pursuit of this concreteness, to be alert to the similarities as well as the differences which exist between cultures, including the presence in most human communities of instrumental and exclusive ways of holding things that have some affinity with the dominant modern Western notions of property. Many pre-capitalist societies have allowed substantial forms of private property and ways of transferring it that resemble those used in modern market economies. Sometimes the things thus possessed are impersonal – objects that can be transacted as commodities in a market, without moral evaluation. In other cases, however, these things are treated as valuables or heirlooms, and their exchange is strictly circumscribed. Most societies provide many examples of both types of 'thing'; rather than forming two sharply opposed categories, they may be joined on a continuum.

All societies have property relations that transcend their individual members, i.e. they imply some sort of integrated collectivity. It is conventional for analysts to construct a continuum, from 'individual' (private) to 'communal' (public); again, this may be a continuum of many gradations, running from individual to family and on through various forms of cooperative or corporation to culminate in the state. A clear distinction is sometimes drawn between that which is the property of an entire people or their state and that which belongs to the members of a specified group, such as a collective farm. Despite the importance of many 'intermediate' forms of property-holding, the dichotomy between individual and communal has acquired particular salience in the context of the dominant Western liberal paradigm. This does not mean that these are the best terms with which to capture the actual realities of modern Western societies, and many anthropologists have urged caution in the application of this dichotomy to other forms of society.

Another striking feature of the liberal paradigm of property is the degree to which it requires that the holding of things be rendered formal and explicit. In most pre-capitalist societies property relations seem to be inchoate, only vaguely defined in law, and leaving much scope for interpretation and manipulation in concrete cases. For example, E. P. Thompson has commented on the 'petty and particular rights and usages which were transmitted in custom as the *properties* of the poor' (1991: 184). He also reminds us of Marx's comments on the '*indetermi-nate* aspect of property' for German peasants (Thompson 1977: 241). It is this aspect which, according to the liberal critique, is emulated in the 'property vacuum' of socialism. According to this view, the efficient organization of modern industrial economies is incompatible with such indeterminacy. I shall suggest below that the evidence on this point is less than conclusive. More generally, I argue that the focus on property must not be restricted to the formal legal codes which play a major role in our own society, but must be broadened to include the institutional and cultural contexts within which such codes operate. The concept of property has greater salience in capitalist society, but it can never be disembedded from these contexts. There is no anachronism in studying property relations in other forms of society where the economic and legal systems are very different. If we adopt a broad analytic concept of property in terms of *the distribution of social entitlements*, then it can be investigated anywhere in time and space. This usage will necessarily differ from specific local understandings of what constitutes property. For example, the right to a future stream of social security benefits may not be thought of as a property right in modern Britain, because it does not have sufficient 'thinginess'; but under the broad usage this should indeed be viewed as a property right, analogous to the rights of members of a hunting society to a share in the meat brought home by a successful hunter.

The intellectual origins of the currently hegemonic liberal paradigm of property have been the subject of many studies. Political theorists such as Macpherson (1962) have dated the rise of 'possessive individualism' to seventeenth-century England, and specifically to the writings of Thomas Hobbes and John Locke. But Western political theory and jurisprudential traditions are themselves rich and diverse. Locke did not follow the more restrictive Roman law definition of property, in terms of absolute and exclusive rights. Both his and later justifications for private ownership in terms of the work invested in land, and the improvements thereby accomplished, may be seen as reflecting powerful popular sentiments at the same time as they modify an evolving scholarly discourse. For centuries the discourse had ultimate roots in ideas of Divine Will, and private property in land was considered to be sacred. The ground for the later anthropological usages was laid in a more secular Victorian era by lawyers, notably Sir Henry Maine, who represented property as a 'bundle of rights' and understood that it defied 'exact circumscription'. For example, the right to use a particular thing might not coincide with the right to bequeath it to others, or to sell it to a stranger. When anthropologists emphasize social relations and criticize the tacit assumptions of possessive individualism that these rights should coincide, they should realize that they are in fact continuing to weave one of the enduring threads of the Western tradition.

The liberal (neo-classical) paradigm in economics draws selectively on several traditions, including those of the Physiocrats and the classical political economists, in adapting the logic of private property arguments for land to private ownership of the means of production more generally. This paradigm tends to emphasize the 'thinginess' of property. Yet the first country to complete the transition to capitalism and allow the liberal property paradigm to achieve its apogee was England, where the common law tradition emphasized the essentially relational, social character of property ownership. It was the continental systems which seemed to place greater weight on relationships with the *things,* rather than on the social webs within which they were held. This puzzle is explored further by Alan Macfarlane in chapter 5: it would seem that the sophisticated theory of the relational character of property expressed in the common law and upheld by intellectual elites had the flexibility that was required for the development of a uniquely individualist society, in which the dominant popular understanding of property relations came to be expressed in terms of exclusive private relations between people and things.

Of course anthropologists, like other scholars, have to be careful in distinguishing between the history of words and ideas and the history of the societies in which the ideas develop. The connections between private property as discussed by political theorists and the actual evolution of property relations in Britain, the world's first industrial

nation, are by no means self-evident. Anthropologists need to be aware
that they are themselves part of an evolving intellectual tradition; but
through their work with other people in other places they are well placed
to mount a critique of the dominant Western intellectual tradition. They
are able to explore how people outside the modern West deploy quite
different ideas and concepts to explain and legitimate distribution.
There are many who believe that the main currents of global political
economy are leading ever more certainly to crises of poverty, inequality
and unsustainability, and that modern concepts of private property are
at the heart of these crises. Anthropologists may play a vital role in
demonstrating that property relations do not *have* to follow the presently
dominant model. They can point to alternative ways of organizing social
life based on ideas of sharing, mutuality and inclusion that have
prevailed in most forms of social organization in the past – and which
survive in shadowy, attenuated forms in our own societies, and rather
more vigorously in some others. Analyses of other cultures can help
anthropologists to point out the inadequacies of the dominant private
property model as a description of how their own societies are organized, and to ask about the purposes that are served by such misleading
rhetoric.

My goal in this introduction is to approach property as a key category
in cross-cultural analysis with a view to restoring it to its nineteenth-
century role as a fundamental concept in anthropology. I suggest that it
can serve to integrate the separate disciplinary traditions in Western
scholarship, and also to expose the deepest problems posed by forms of
social organization rooted in misleading ideas about *separability*. In the
following section I review some of the ways in which property relations
have changed with the spread of capitalism, a mode of production
which promotes exclusive privately owned property in previously un-
precedented ways. I then move on to consider the history of discussions
of property in the anthropological literature and some recent developments in economic anthropology. Here I try to show that closer
attention to property could reinvigorate an area which has lately been
swinging between the poles of political economy and cultural studies.
Karl Polanyi was one of the founders of this sub-discipline. He was also
a giant among modern historians, whose mid-century assessment of
'the origins of our time' remains a classic (Polanyi 1944). Polanyi
adapted the concept of 'embeddedness' to draw attention to ways in
which pre-industrial economics differed from those of market capitalism: the latter had escaped from their political and social constraints.
I find this metaphor of embeddedness useful in a reappraisal of
property relations. The 'substantivist' school that Polanyi founded has

now faded, and his conception of industrial economies as 'disembedded' was exaggerated and perhaps largely illusory. Many historians no longer accept his view that in the course of the eighteenth century 'older, multiple use-rights to property were simply supplanted by a rise of absolute property rights' (Brewer and Staves 1995: 17). However, I shall suggest that Polanyi's notions of 'embeddedness' and a 'Great Transformation' may still prove fruitful. The modern welfare state, far from resolving the crisis that Polanyi identified, as some commentators have argued, seems to entail a new and more radical disjunction in property relations than anything witnessed in the emergence and heyday of market capitalism. In pursuing this line of thought, for us as for our predecessors a further goal in the analysis of property relations is to shed light on our own societies and the directions in which they are changing.

### Property in time and space

'belonging, private property in land, is itself a concept which has had a historical evolution. The central concept of feudal custom was not that of property but of reciprocal obligations' (Thompson 1991: 127).

Most of the contributions to this volume reflect the bias of modern anthropology toward detailed studies of specific social institutions observed synchronically through fieldwork. The emphasis on fieldwork enables the anthropologist to provide fine-grained analyses of the social consequences of different property systems, and of how exclusions and inequalities are legitimated. However, the anthropologist can also draw on a range of other sources – a body of past ethnographic work, a long tradition of theorizing about property in the context of human social evolution, and the contributions of archaeologists and historians to understanding how property relations have changed in the past. The difficulty with much of this work is that it proceeds either squarely within the liberal paradigm or within some sort of anti-liberal critique which is no less completely a product of the Western intellectual tradition. Despite the consequent difficulties of interpretation, it is worth attempting to sketch some of the large-scale changes that have taken place over time in the ways in which things have been held in human societies.

Arguments about the nature of property relations in early human societies are bound to be inconclusive. It is not possible to do fieldwork in the palaeolithic, and it is now recognized that accounts of the simplest societies known to anthropologists in the nineteenth and twentieth centuries cannot be assumed to have general validity for societies of hunters and gatherers in the distant past. They cannot be treated as isolated fossils: their contemporary property relations may well be the specific historical product of contacts with more powerful groups and economic marginalization. Having said this, archaeological evidence indicates that the picture of Hadza hunter-gatherers presented in this volume by James Woodburn has some plausibility for the hunter-gatherers of pre-history. Hadza society is characterized not by exclusive territorial rights and well-defined links between persons and specific objects, but by an emphasis upon sharing and social mechanisms to ensure that egalitarianism is maintained. A similar picture has been famously painted by Richard Lee following his fieldwork among the !Kung Bushmen of the Kalahari (1979). James Woodburn rejects Lee's use of the term 'primitive communism' on the grounds that both Hadza and !Kung also have clear notions of individual ownership. However, it does not follow from this that they can exclude others, for example from a share in the meat of an animal that has been killed. Woodburn has argued elsewhere that this egalitarianism is not characteristic of all hunter-gatherer societies, but only of those with 'immediate-return' economies (1980, 1982a). Societies with 'delayed-return' economies are those which require some investment in the production process, e.g. in the construction of traps and of storage facilities. These investments become the focus of exclusive claims, which subvert the principles of sharing and social equality within the group. Delayed-return societies are more likely to develop exclusive claims to territory (or perhaps to specific water holes). This argument suggests that patterns of structural inequality often associated with the emergence of agriculture in the neolithic actually have much earlier origins. Archaeological evidence suggests that members of palaeolithic societies did hold items of value and adornment as in some sense their personal property.[2]

Generalization about property relations among societies of cultivators is even more difficult. Jack Goody (e.g. 1977) has emphasized the need to distinguish between technologies based on the hoe (or digging stick), characteristic of sub-Saharan Africa and conducive to egalitarian social relations, and the technologies of the plough which predominated in Eurasia and provided a basis for more hierarchical social relations. The egalitarianism of 'tribal horticulturalists' differs sharply from that maintained by immediate-return hunter-gatherers. It is compatible with pronounced political stratification, in which offices such as that of chief or king may be inherited, and an aristocratic elite may demand deference from the mass of commoners. However, in other respects these societies remain societies of equals: there is comparatively little differentiation in terms of consumption standards, and everyone has the same fundamental entitlement to the resources necessary to earn a livelihood. In practice this means above all the guarantee to each member of the society of sufficient land to meet subsistence needs. Land tenure has consequently been a central focus of attention in studies of cultivating societies. An example is provided in this volume by James Carrier's description of how land is held on the Melanesian island of Ponam, New Guinea. The most important social unit is the collectivity of the kin group. It is within this collectivity that people build their houses and till their gardens. However, other things which Ponam Islanders hold may be transacted impersonally as commodities, thereby resembling privately owned commodities in the modern liberal paradigm.

According to Goody's dichotomy, Eurasia demonstrates greater individuation of property, inasmuch as rights to land typically pass through individual persons, both male and female, from one generation to the next, thereby creating the potential for a type of inequality that is not generated by the more corporate landholding and transmission arrangements found in other parts of the world. But what exactly is meant by greater individuation as far as land is concerned? The popular modern sense of property may be foreshadowed in Roman law, which allowed for the ownership of slaves as private property; but in fact the great bulk of land in the ancient world was farmed by peasant smallholders and transmitted within their communities according to custom. Most historians would argue that the same was true under feudalism. In a formal, legal sense the land was ultimately owned by the king, who granted land to lords or 'tenants-in-chief' in exchange for services. These in turn granted plots to 'mesne' tenants, who might or might not be the actual cultivators. At each level the tenant acknowledged obligations to provide services in return for the rights devolved to him. The peasants had exclusive rights to use particular plots of land and to transmit them to their heirs; but did English villagers of the thirteenth century view their land as a commodity that *individuals* could own and transact on a market? According to George Homans, the concept of private property in land was not yet a central principle of social organization. Villagers were a 'social organism' rather than an agglomeration of individuals; they 'acted as a community not only in the farming of 'champion' land and in dealing with the lord of the manor; they acted as a community in many of their dealings with the great world beyond the village bounds' (Homans 1942: 328). If this is correct, the position of villagers in late medieval England was not so different from that of other European peasants, or even that of shifting cultivators in tribal societies. The land, their principal productive resource, was not yet a focus of exclusive individual ownership claims. Beyond the formal, legal sense in which title lies with a political ruler, the substantive reality remained that land rights were exercised *inclusively*, according to the custom of the community.

Recently this image of late feudal England has been radically challenged by Alan Macfarlane. One of his central claims in *The Origins of English Individualism* (1978) is that, at least as far back as the thirteenth century, the English were implementing essentially modern models of property, i.e. the liberal conception according to which even land, the most fundamental productive resource, was held and transacted as exclusive private property. Macfarlane argued that:

This question of ownership is central to the notion of peasantry. The crux of the matter is *who* owned the land. It would be easy to assume that it was the family group; but if we look more closely at both the *de iure* and *de facto* situation – it will appear that this is a misinterpretation. Land did *not* belong to the family group but to an individual (1978: 102–3).

In his contribution to this volume he takes his argument further, without qualifying his original boldness. Adding the case of Japan, he suggests that not one but two suitably located island societies were able under feudalism to hold on to *relational* conceptions of *indivisible* property that were necessary for the emergence of industrial society. These arguments will no doubt continue to create controversy for a long time to come.

Other historians who assign a key role to the English in the spread of new forms of property relations all over the world have identified the onset of industrialization in the late eighteenth century as the critical period of change. This was when the enclosure movement reached its climax, and moral communities lost the last vestiges of their control. In the words of E. P. Thompson, 'Enclosure (when all the sophistications are allowed for) was a plain enough case of class robbery, played according to fair rules of property and law laid down by a Parliament of property owners and lawyers' (1968: 218). Karl Polanyi (1944) thought that the Speenhamland Decision of 1795 symbolized the end of the embedded moral community. It is clear that by the eve of the industrial revolution private property relations were the focus of ever more elaborate intellectual justifications. For example, one of the maxims of the Physiocrats was '*That the ownership of landed property and movable wealth should be guaranteed to those who are their lawful possessors*; FOR SECURITY OF OWNERSHIP IS THE ESSENTIAL FOUNDA-TION OF THE ECONOMIC ORDER OF SOCIETY' (Quesnay 1962: 232). In spite of the difficulty in demonstrating that the rents earned by a landlord class had any bearing on that class's willingness to invest and improve the production system, security of private ownership was given moral as well as economic justification by eloquent spokesmen for the secular liberal paradigm such as John Austin:

> Without security for property there were no inducement to save. Without habitual saving on the part of proprietors, there were no accumulation of capital. Without accumulation of capital, there were no fund for the payment of wages, no division of labour, no elaborate and costly machines: there were none of those helps to labour which augment its productive power and, therefore, multiply the enjoyments of every individual in the community. Frequent invasions of property would bring the rich to poverty; and, what were a greater evil, would aggravate the poverty of the poor (1954: 325–6).

Property ownership, and in particular the private ownership of land, was considered a basic human right and a precondition for full citizenship as more democratic societies emerged in the nineteenth century, notably in the United States.

The property relations which produced rents for a landlord class that seemed unrelated to that class's readiness to invest in the land were identified as an iniquitous problem by nineteenth-century critics as diverse as Marx, Proudhon and Henry George. Occupying the central political ground as capitalism expanded and land began to lose its central role, liberals such as John Stuart Mill accepted the general arguments for private property, but were concerned to impose limits on its application. Mill himself believed that land should be used for the advantage of the whole community and not treated as just another commodity. Yet that is exactly how it has been treated in the dominant neoclassical tradition in economics, which from the 1870s began to break decisively away from integrated analyses that linked property to social and moral issues of distribution. It was left to others to raise matters such as the moral rights of workers to the tools and products of their labour. Consider for instance the views of the Catholic artist–craftsman Eric Gill, who worked out a distinctive synthesis of Locke and Marx in which he urged *private* ownership as a precondition for moral *public* use:

> It is as artists, in the proper and broad sense of the word as used by the philosopher, it is as responsible workmen, that men must own; for it is only as owners that they can do to things as they should be done by, and that, and that alone, is the ground upon which it is said that men tend to look after their own property better than that which is owned in common – a very little consideration will suffice to show that it is in the order of *making* that ownership, individual appropriation, becomes necessary – while in the order of *doing*, of prudence, of service to one another, the use of things shall be in common, in the order of *making*, and for the sake of the good of the things made, ownership must be private (1937: 107–8).

This passage illustrates ideas about labour in the legitimation of private property that are deeply engrained in Western culture (cf. Schwimmer 1979).

The spread of the liberal model of property relations to other parts of the world preceded the spread of industry, but was everywhere fraught with implications for production and distribution. The chief agents were those European countries which established colonial empires and refused to recognize the rights of indigenous people where these did not expend labour on the land in the manner approved by Europeans. The manner in which Australia was claimed for the British crown by Captain Cook provides the most famous example. The appropriation of the land of American Indians, discussed in this volume by Paula Wagoner, is another. Large tracts of what is now Bennett County in the state of South Dakota were parcelled out for individualist tenure and allocated to European settlers, in flagrant contravention of the treaties which the federal authorities had signed with the native inhabitants. Later federal efforts to improve the position of the Indians have resulted in an unstable situation in which neither Indians nor settlers feel entirely secure in their property relations.

Analogous patterns of conquest were played out in most parts of the European empires. The British could not pretend that the intensively farmed territories they conquered in India were a wilderness, but they could and did try in the Bengal Permanent Settlement of 1793 to impose modern Western property relations, based on landlords and tenants, on to a much more complex structure of obligations and responsibilities (see also Neale 1962). The mistakes were not fully realized until much later. When the empire was entering its final phase C. K. Meek noted that:

a frequent source of error has been the presupposition that native conceptions of ownership must be basically the same as those of Europeans. English terms such as 'rent' or 'lease' have been employed to denote practices which bear only a superficial resemblance to those denoted by these terms. The gifts given to chiefs as administrators of land have been assumed to be 'rent' and the chiefs to be 'landlords' (1949: 11).

By this time the British colonial authorities had the benefit of anthropological advice. Meek cites the verdict of Lucy Mair on the Uganda agreement of 1900: 'A government which supposed itself to be confirming native rights turned the Chiefs by a stroke of the pen into landlords entitled to exact rent from their former subjects and to dispose of their land for cash' (1949: 13). But the alternative course sometimes followed: that of proclaiming native territories to be common land (understood as open-access land) was no less a misrepresentation of the pre-colonial reality. In most cultivating societies, individuals and families did have exclusive rights to *use* specific tracts of land, though very seldom to *own* them in the sense of English freehold, including the right to alienate.

The extension of the principle of private ownership continued to the end of the colonial empires and beyond their formal termination. This extension was inseparable from other interventions in tribal and peasant societies, including the introduction of new tax obligations, commercial crops, new forms of money, and possibilities of migration to highly commercialized urban environments where the domination of private property was unchallenged. New forms of ownership were often a basic requirement for other social and economic changes, but they were frequently resisted. Jack Goody (1980) has documented a case from Northern Ghana where a group of strangers needed to register land as private property in order to establish the security they needed to raise loans to finance new farming initiatives, involving the technology of the 'green revolution'. This registration was resented by members of the local acephalous society, who considered that they were the ultimate owners of the land in question. In their view no individual member of the group had authority to alienate to outsiders. The strangers' rice harvests were subsequently burned. However, in other cases the new property relations were readily accepted by indigenous communities, or at least by certain enterprising elites. As Lord Hailey pointed out in his introduction to Meek's survey volume:

in certain of the territories holders of native lands have made a conscious effort to assimilate their own traditional forms of land rights to those under which alienated lands are held by grant from the Crown. However strongly the native may be attached to the traditions and association which regulate his social life, it is inevitable that many individuals in the more progressive native communities should be increasingly attracted by the possibility of acquiring the more exclusive rights of possession or of transfer offered by modern English forms of tenure, in place of those which reflect in varying measure the tradition of collective landholding (Meek 1949: xv).

Whatever the exact combination of external pressures and local responses, no part of the world has entirely escaped the extension of the private property model in the twentieth century. Of course, large parts of the world have tried to do so, occasionally with some apparent degree of success. Property issues figured very prominently in the ideologies of Marxist-Leninist states, which according to their ideologies were supposed ultimately to recreate the egalitarian conditions of primitive communism. For this reason private property was severely restricted, and state-owned property was considered to be a 'higher' form than the collectively held property of an entity such as a small enterprise or collective farm. This approach to property relations, laying the same dogmatic emphasis on collective forms of property that the liberals laid upon private property, turned out in most variants to be far less conducive to efficient economic performance – exactly as liberals had always predicted.

However, the Marxist-Leninist regimes of the so-called Second World were no more a homogenous bloc than the capitalist societies of the First and Third Worlds. In a few places, such as Hungary after 1968, more respectable economic performances were achieved, thanks to the gradual introduction of aspects of market discipline and material incentives to economic actors at all levels. By the time I began fieldwork in Hungary in 1975, 'market socialism' was in its heyday and a new word was well established in Magyar. *Maszek* was a compound formed from *magán szektor,* meaning literally 'private sector'. *Maszek* farmers, traders and shopkeepers attracted many customers because of the quality of the goods and services they provided, though admiration for their skills was often tinged with jealousy and resentment, especially among veteran communists. Some younger people were oblivious to the origins of the term and the ideological controversies associated with it; they might use *maszek* as a synonym for 'cool', 'trendy'. The consequent widening of social inequalities in this period was largely restricted to the domain of consumption. Cars, second homes and other luxury goods became permissible items of private ownership and were the objects of feverish accumulation in the decades of 'mature socialism'. However, the means of production, the land and most urban housing remained in collective ownership.

Let me make the discussion more concrete with a brief outline of the property relations that I have investigated in fieldwork projects in Hungary and elsewhere, beginning with the Great Plain village of Tázlár (Hann 1980, 1993a, 1993b, 1996). It is widely acknowledged that Hungarian agriculture achieved notable successes in the era of market socialism. Its collective farms actually worked (Swain 1985), and they did so by promoting a symbiosis of large-scale, mechanized collective activities with the small-scale, labour-intensive activities that were focused on the 'private plot'. In Tázlár in the 1970s the collective sector was still only weakly established and most production was organized by rural households, assisted in various ways by their cooperative. Some villagers were angry when the cooperative sought to consolidate their family plots into large-scale fields, as part of the long-term strategy of collectivization. Formal title to land still lay for the most part with the villagers, but this was an irrelevance. They accepted that their socialist cooperative was the dominant local economic institution, with the power to allocate land as its leaders saw fit. But as long as it *de facto* guaranteed villagers as much land as they wanted to farm and supported them in their production activities, with guaranteed prices for agricultural produce, most villagers were reasonably content with their lot. The great majority were much more prosperous than their parents and grandparents had been, and the diminution of their formal private property rights was seldom raised as an issue, except by a few embittered members of the former well-to-do peasantry.

Property became a very prominent issue after the collapse of communism in the Soviet bloc in 1989–91. Most post-communist governments and their Western advisers were ideologically committed to a very pure version of the liberal model. They then found themselves in the awkward situation of having to design and enforce structures that were generally supposed to evolve 'naturally'. Ministries of Privatization were set up to expedite the transfer of ownership rights away from the state, a step seen as indispensable to 'systemic transformation'. In Tázlár as elsewhere villagers were given the opportunity to become full private owners once again. Complicated 'points' schemes were drawn up to compensate former owners (Julie Scott describes a comparable compensation scheme in Northern Cyprus in chapter 7). However, compared to the 1970s decollectivization has been implemented in an economic context that has been much less favourable for the farmers. Younger villagers capable of decision-taking on the basis of rational economic prognoses of the future for the agricultural sector have mostly refrained from investing in land. However, alongside those who take a rational or 'instrumental' approach to the land, there are some others, particularly in the oldest generation, who have felt impelled to regain ownership of land for sentimental, emotional reasons, more or less regardless of the economic consequences. Many other people have striven to ensure the survival of some vestiges of their cooperative, as a source of technical assistance and social benefits. Similar patterns have been reported from many other parts of Eastern Europe and they are explored further in chapter 8 of this volume by Katherine Verdery. They show the importance of attachments both to the land and to collective institutions for the self-identifications of rural families.

Support for the retention of long-established collective custom and resentment of the beneficiaries of the new private property model seem to be especially prominent in rural Russia. This is unsurprising in that, compared to the rest of Eastern Europe, the Russian countryside was subjected to communism over a longer period, and had been less exposed to capitalist market penetration in the pre-communist era. David Anderson's contribution in chapter 3 of this volume, which concerns the Evenki of Northern Siberia, shows how cultural ideas of 'knowing the land', which persisted throughout the era of the collective farm and were fundamental to social identity, have been undermined by recent privatization policies. Other work among Russian peasants by Myriam Hivon (in press) confirms some of the destructive effects of what might be called, in the spirit of Polanyi, a second Great Transformation. Contrary to some popular images, the old Soviet collective farm was an integrated community, underpinned by complex notions of responsibility and reciprocal obligations. Although land was held collectively, households had a guaranteed right to a private plot for subsistence production. Their rights to use this plot were exclusive, but if they no longer needed it, perhaps because the household had grown smaller, then they were expected to give up land for the benefit of those whose needs were greater. In this sense the collective farm, in addition to functioning as an institution of state power, also served as the vehicle of an older moral community, the successor to the peasants' commune, which had long practised periodic redistribution of plots according to household need in pre-communist days. Hivon reports on the social pressures faced by new private farmers. If an entrepreneur is sensible enough to divert some of his profits to a cause that commands popular moral support, such as refurbishing the village church, which is collective property, then his success can be accepted by his neighbours. However, if he offends against customary norms, for example by leaving good land untilled and using his new truck (obtained with cheap government credit) for other commercial purposes, then he will be branded a *spekuliant,* and his crops (if he has grown any) may be burned as a sanction. In most areas of Russia collective farming is persisting long after the formal individuation of land ownership. This is a neat reversal of the more typical situation in tribal societies, where cultivation is highly individualized but ownership is fundamentally collective.

There is, however, an alternative exit from communism which does not require a volte-face from an extreme collective property model to an equally extreme version of the liberal model. China under the leadership of Chairman Mao pursued the principle of communal property to extremes. The household ceased to be the main unit of consumption when even pots and pans were taken away to be used in collective kitchens. This policy proved on the whole to be unsuccessful economically, and China has been pursuing the course now officially described as 'socialist market economy' since the end of the 1970s. This has meant tremendous changes in economic organization, but the interesting point is that these have been accomplished without major changes in formal, legal property relations. Approximately three-quarters of the population remain villagers, and so once again the question of land tenure has the strongest claim on analysts' attention. The rural household has been restored as the main unit of production and consumption, and the lands previously cultivated collectively are now farmed once again by families. However, title is retained by the collective (the unit formerly known as the 'production brigade'), while the agricultural sector is still subject to close state regulation. The restoration of a relationship between family and land through the use of long-term leases, which can be inherited in the family but not alienated, has undoubtedly been conducive to much improved economic performance. The Chinese economy as a whole is showing very impressive rates of growth achieved *without* the rigorous specification of formal legal property rights that is central to the liberal paradigm and recommended by the World Bank (cf. Nolan 1994).

This Chinese experiment seems to confound the purists on all sides. On the one hand, liberal critics deplore the absence of civil and political liberties as well as the absence of private property. On the other, socialist critics allege the betrayal of collectivist ideals and speak of a 'great reversal' (Hinton 1990). How can an anthropological focus on property contribute to these debates? First, the anthropologist can explore concepts of ownership and wealth, and culturally appropriate ways of measuring living standards. In some respects, Chinese ideas conform to a standardized, exclusive model of property, above all in attitudes that see the territory of the 'nation state' as an indivisible unity belonging to the Chinese people. Recent changes have undoubtedly promoted Western patterns of consumerism. Rich can now own Japanese cars, when a generation earlier no one could own a bicycle or a television set. But measures of wealth also reflect many specifically local characteristics, which can be investigated ethnographically. Second, the anthropologist can conduct detailed empirical investigations of all the distributional consequences of recent changes in power relations, welfare entitlements and consumption practices. There is a considerable measure of agreement between academic authorities and villagers themselves that, by most objective criteria, the great majority are now significantly better off than in the Maoist era. Some elements of welfare provision have been weakened, and in this sense we can speak of a reduction in social entitlements. But in most places, for most people, capacities have been enlarged by the reforms, and not only in the realm of private consumption. Inequalities have increased, as they did under market socialism in Hungary, and there is much talk of 'corruption'. But the policy that still restricts private ownership of the means of production, including land, may also have limited the spread of social exclusion.

It is clear that China's present property relations create many problems.[3] At village level in Xinjiang some people seem to have a clear conception that private ownership should mean exclusive rights, but most villagers are unclear about what it is exactly that they own. Some families think that they own at least the plot of land on which their house is built, but others state (correctly, in a legal sense) that this is the property of the village. Others point to what they believe to be the most important fact – regardless of the formal legal position, the state can easily appropriate any plots it likes, whenever it wishes to do so. People often do not distinguish between the state and its local representatives, the village and township cadres; as in other socialist contexts, the formal distinction between state property and cooperatively held or communal property is in practice meaningless. Most rural people are well aware of the consequences of a policy which in effect freezes land use according to a pattern that was egalitarian when land was distributed around 1980, but which as a result of normal demographic fluctuations quickly gives rise to significant inequalities. The system is both inequitable and inefficient. Families with many children have insufficient land for subsistence purposes, while others have surpluses. Both might wish to expand acreage, but because there is no official land market neither is able to do so (in practice it is usually possible to secure at least some of one's objectives through 'informal' channels, such as private leasing, to which the authorities turn a blind eye; in some other parts of the country legal transfer of contracts is allowed – see Nolan 1988).

This situation in China is exceptional in the current global context, and many observers believe it to be unsustainable. Liberal economists argue that as China enters a further stage of economic development she will be forced into greater precision of property rights for reasons of economic efficiency. From their local angles, anthropologists may find that more and more villagers also clamour for security of title, and for the opportunity to expand their farms and their businesses as private owners. Entrepreneurship probably has a stronger cultural basis in most parts of China than in Russia. The modern liberal private property model, a source of fierce discontent in some cultures, seems in the case of China to be relatively easy to graft on to existing notions of property.

In some cases, however, the affinity may be more apparent than real. In some, people may have no illusions about the contrast between the new model and their traditional notions of property, and yet still find that it is in their interests to adopt the new. The Yolngu, an Aborigine Australian hunter-gatherer people, have recognized the force of Western notions of property in their struggle for collective social justice. They and the anthropologist who has conducted a most thorough investigation of their land tenure system have argued that, while rooted in ideas about kinship relations, myth and theology, this did amount to a system of law which gave them a 'proprietary interest' in their land (in contrast, for example, to the Hadza as documented in this volume by Woodburn). Others could use the land, but only after obtaining the permission of the Yolngu. These arguments were not accepted by an Australian judge, who was unwilling to acknowledge any system of land law that diverged from the exclusive individualist assumptions of the common law tradition (Williams 1986). In other words Aborigine claims were put forward in the courts in a language which approximated to the dominant Western idiom. Although at first rejected, a few years later the Mabo Judgement of 1992 represented a victory for this Aborigine perspective.

Meanwhile in most parts of the contemporary Western world the virtues of private property and the free market are continuously extolled by politicians of all parties. Hardly anyone questions the legitimacy of rents and the desirability of lowering taxes. Large sectors of public provision, including hospitals, schools and prisons, have been privatized, though some of the efficiency gains claimed seem open to doubt. (For example, in Britain it has been suggested that the privatization of water may have led consumers, who would have heeded calls for restraints on water use in a dry summer in the days of public ownership, to ignore such calls when they are issued by a private company.) Of course developments such as these may be good for the growth of the national economy. The logic of the liberal paradigm suggests that the manufacturers of domestic water meters will benefit from the new property relations. The makers of burglar alarms and every kind of private security equipment may also be long-term beneficiaries, for according to this paradigm it will be rational for each property owner to invest in additional protection up to the point at which the cost of doing so exceeds the value of the assets to be protected. In summary, long after the classical models of small-scale landed property have ceased to apply to all but a tiny fraction of the population, *private ownership* still seems to be central to ideals of citizenship and personal identity, and to provide the main driving force of national economies. Television soaps with global dissemination celebrate the ideal of dynastic families – and this ideal is not *entirely* divorced from realities, for despite all the trends toward impersonal bureaucratic organization in the management of large companies, families (such as the Sainsbury family in Britain) continue to figure prominently both as owners and managers, even in the largest companies of the most advanced capitalist countries (Marcus 1992).[4]

### Property in anthropology

'A mere property career is not the final destiny of mankind, if progress is to be the law of the future as it has been of the past' (Morgan 1877: 552).

Any starting point for anthropological discussions of property is to some degree arbitrary. What I have pretentiously termed the anthropological tradition is, of course, in large part derivative of a shared Western tradition, to which the most influential contributions have been made by political philosophers and legal theorists. The relative merits of individual and communal forms of property were debated by Aristotle and Plato. John Locke is widely acknowledged as the original source of modern ideas of possessive individualism, while David Hume had an anthropologist's appreciation of the importance of 'a sensible transference of the object' in facilitating what he termed 'the mysterious transition of the property' (1962: 218).[5] Adam Smith and Adam Ferguson were among the first to address property issues in a comparative anthropological way, by analysing the forms of property associated with different types of society in evolutionary ranking. In their fourfold schema, hunters formed the simplest kind of social organization, thought to be lacking any developed sense of property, though individuals might 'possess' their catch. Ownership of animals was important to pastoral peoples, and ownership of the land to agriculturalists. In what Smith and Ferguson called 'commercial society' the ownership of property was thought to be increasingly diffused, a healthy trend if one's goal was a just, non-authoritarian government. These thinkers, like most other contributors to Western intellectual debates about property, were quite clear that an ideal property system was not simply a technical matter pertaining to the maximization of economic efficiency. Property was thought to be vital to individual liberty and the health of civil society, and it depended upon good government. As we have already noted, the Western political theory tradition down to the present day contains a cacophony of voices. Those sharing the same view of liberty (whether positive or negative, in the terms of Berlin (1969)) may nonetheless differ sharply in their prescriptions for property.[6]

The writings of Marx and Engels deserve special attention, not only because of their formative influence on a twentieth-century social experiment which proved largely unsuccessful but also because of their influence on later scholarly work, including work in anthropology. In an early work, Marx and Engels endorsed the rather vague evolutionism of the great figures of the Scottish enlightenment and approached property relations in the same broad sense as we are using the term:

The various stages of development in the division of labour are just so many different forms of property; i.e. the stage reached in the division of labour also determines the relations of individuals to one another with respect to the materials, instruments and product of labour (Marx 1963: 126).

In his later work Marx is usually seen as elaborating a rigorous political economy in which all the emphasis falls on a critique of capitalism as a mode of production. The focus on production is often thought to be developed at the expense of an interest in legal and cultural forms such as ideas about property, which were part of superstructure, to be determined in all instances by the economic base. However, in a famous passage where he sums up his materialist philosophy of history, Marx makes it plain that he does not wish to separate *property relations* from *social relations of production*. These phrases for him are interchangeable:

At a certain stage of their development, the material forces of production in society come in conflict with the existing relations of production, or – what is but a legal expression for the same thing – with the property relations within which they had been at work before (1963: 67–8).

By the time European states began to colonize and administer native peoples they did so with one sharp dichotomy uppermost in their thinking: that between collective and private land tenure. As we noted in the preceding section, English administrators oscillated between the poles of their domestic dichotomy, identifying private landlords at one period, then recognizing communal ownership in the next. Although India in particular eventually received close attention from some fine scholars with a better awareness of the complexities of property relations in Europe, Sir Henry Maine among them, the apparent absence of private property in the Western sense led to enduring images of 'Oriental Despotism' and 'Asiatic' modes of production. It was against this back-cloth that anthropology began to establish itself as an academic discipline in the second half of the nineteenth century. Concepts of property were central to much of the theorizing of this period. Lewis Henry Morgan proclaimed that 'the history of property embodies the greater part of the mental history of mankind' (1877: 7), and sought to modify the ideal types of Smith and Ferguson in the light of new ethnographic evidence and reappraisals of the Western past. The driving spirit behind the work of Morgan, like that fuelling several of his contemporaries, was one that saw the predominance of private property as a threat to civilization. The state was the instrument which made the domination of private property possible, a message that was highly congenial to Marx and Engels. The latter (1972), emphasizing the negative effects of this domination upon women, incorporated Morgan's theories into a text which remained anthropological orthodoxy for Marxist regimes until their general demise more than a century later. More generally, the later nineteenth century saw the crystallization of the main anthropological approaches to property, above all the notion that property relations were to be understood in a social or community context. As T. E. Cliffe Leslie put it when introducing the translation of a French work:

Property has not its root in the love of possession. All living beings like and desire certain things, and if nature has armed them with any weapons are prone to use them in order to get and keep what they want. What requires explanation is not the want or desire of certain things on the part of individuals, but the fact that other individuals, with similar wants and desires, should leave them in undisturbed possession or allot them a share of such things. It is the conduct of a community, not the inclination of individuals, that needs investigation (Laveleye 1878: xi; cited in Herskovits 1965: 328).

If anthropological writing on property reached an early pinnacle with the appropriation of Morgan by Engels, this was by no means the end of anthropological interest. Attempts to relate more complex forms of property to economic activities, ecologies and political arrangements remained popular, particularly in America. Property relations (including 'incorporeal property') figured prominently in the work of Robert Lowie (1921). They formed part of the backcloth to the materialism of Leslie White and Marvin Harris. Ernest Beaglehole (1931) provided a wide-ranging classification of forms of property, though he was more interested in psychological aspects than in the sociological issues surrounding property relations. The subject was regularly allocated a chapter in textbooks. However, property gradually lost the dynamic central role assigned to it by the nineteenth-century pioneers.

In British social anthropology the evolutionist impulse was suppressed following the impact of the functionalism of Bronislaw Malinowski in the inter-war period. Malinowski made a major contribution towards taking the sub-field of economic anthropology beyond mere description of the natives' material culture, notably in his study of Trobriand exchanges, *Argonauts of the Western Pacific* (1922). (See the discussion of this and of the still more influential work of Marcel Mauss by James Carrier in chapter 4.) The new emphasis on fieldwork and grasping native categories led to the rejection of many earlier theories, including ideas about 'marriage by purchase'. Above all, the new methods contributed to a better understanding of the most salient form of property relations, land tenure. Malinowski stressed the need to move beyond 'the legal point of view' and to transcend the 'false antithesis' of the individual *versus* communal dichotomy (1935: 318–19). His discussion of Trobriand land tenure pays careful attention to webs of ideas, 'mythological foundations' and kin relations, notably the institution of *urigubu*. Far from being a narrow jural matter, the land tenure system is shown to be central to Trobriand conceptions of personhood and citizenship.

Yet Malinowski was simultaneously so preoccupied with the need to emphasize the individualistic character of Trobriand life that the very dualism he condemned intruded continuously into his analysis. Some of his students were more successful in avoiding this trap. Raymond Firth thought that tribal economies such as the one he studied on the island of Tikopia could be investigated using the concepts of modern Western economies, and that many items of production were held as individual property. However, when he came to consider vital resources such as land and canoes he found that '"individual ownership" can only be expressed in degrees of responsibility for and enjoyment of the group property' (1965: 278). Max Gluckman adapted Sir Henry Maine's definition of property as a 'bundle of rights', and extended Maine's notion of 'estates of administration' in order to explain how tribal land might be farmed in highly individualist ways (in 'estates of production'), and yet subject to several nesting levels of control and ownership, the details of which would correspond to the social structure of the group. For example, among the Barotse, cultivators of fertile mounds in the Zambesi valley, land was allocated on the basis of need by the village headman to household heads. It would revert back to the headman for reallocation when no longer needed by the household. Sometimes land might revert back to a higher level and the Lozi king was the 'ultimate owner'. This did not give him the right to sell land as a commodity, nor did it qualify his subjects' entitlement to as much land as they needed (Gluckman 1965a, 1968).

This framework was sufficiently flexible to deal with a wide variety of tribal societies. It was later ingeniously adapted to explain the property relations of a Soviet collective farm (Humphrey 1983). However, the anthropological work of this period, and in particular the 'structural-functionalism' of Radcliffe-Brown, still paid relatively little attention to non-Western concepts of property. These approaches were predisposed to identifying 'corporations' as the key jural entities of pre-capitalist societies, holding land and other property exclusively, with clearly demarcated boundaries. Edmund Leach (1961) did not really challenge this view in a polemical work based on fieldwork in Ceylon in which he claimed, contrary to his Cambridge colleagues, who placed kinship at the centre of their studies of social organization, that kinship relations were in fact determined by relations of property. As the colonial period came to a close the authorities had less reason to sponsor studies of 'native land law'. Only in the work of Jack Goody (1962) do we find a fieldworker of the late colonial period linking a detailed analysis of local transmission mechanisms for different types of property back to the nineteenth-century comparative concerns, and showing how they reproduce the social structures of the groups concerned. Goody followed up this study – an exemplar of the structural-functionalist approach, though he himself has not used this label – with further historical explorations of property relations and inheritance mechanisms in a range of European and Asian societies (1977; 1983; see also his discussion in this volume, chapter 10, and that of Alan Macfarlane in chapter 5).

One possible explanation for the decline in the attention that has been paid to property in anthropology lies in the increased fragmentation of the subject into sub-disciplines, no single one of which (economic, political or legal) provides an adequate framework for a topic that so clearly straddles both disciplinary and sub-disciplinary boundaries. The revised editions of Herskovits (first published in 1940), which was the first of several works to bear the title *Economic Anthropology*, still carried a whole section on ownership and property. This was followed by the grand debate between 'formalists' (basically, those who argued that all economies could be analysed using the modern economist's toolkit, founded on assumptions of scarcity and rational utility maximization) and 'substantivists' (those followers of Karl Polanyi who argued that pre-capitalist economies were embedded in social and political contexts, and could only be analysed with their own, quite distinct set of tools – reciprocity and redistribution were put forward as alternative principles of societal integration). Paul Bohannan (e.g. 1963) was the substantivist scholar who showed most sensitivity to the dangers of imposing Western conceptions of ownership where they did not belong.

Some critics have alleged that both the formalists and the substantivists were preoccupied with analyses of *exchange,* and rather narrow analyses at that. This charge was levelled by neo-Marxists such as Godelier (1972) and Clammer (1978). Inconsistencies in the stance of the substantivists were also pointed out by Raymond Firth: for example, recognizing a wide range of valuables as a form of 'primitive money', but finding the term 'brideprice' inadmissible because of the strong market associations of 'price' (1972: 472). It is true that a large part of the formalist-substantivist controversies concerned what could or could not be counted as money, the presence or absence of markets, and the merits of the concepts of reciprocity and redistribution for understanding pre-capitalist societies. However, George Dalton, for long the most trenchant defender of the substantivist approach, pointed out with some justification that Karl Polanyi's use of these terms was never intended to refer solely to the phenomena of exchange. They designated 'modes of integration' that, in Dalton's view, were intended to encompass productive systems and, in the broad sense that I am using the term, property relations as well (see Dalton 1981).

The neo-Marxists were explicit about the priority they attached to the study of production, but they too tended to neglect property. A major exception is Maurice Bloch's incisive article contrasting representations of property among the Merina and Zafimaniry of Madagascar (1975). Bloch locates property relations in the 'superstructure' among the Merina, who are rice cultivators with notions of exclusive ownership that resemble those of the English. In contrast, he argues that property relations are entwined with kinship and form an inseparable part of the economic 'base' among the neighbouring Zafimaniry. Bloch offers a rigorous materialist explanation for the difference he identifies, while remaining squarely within the anthropological tradition by upholding its central contention that property relations are to be understood as social relations. The Merina mystify the representation of property relations as relationships between people and things because they have invested labour in irrigated rice terraces, and they wish to exclude others from sharing the benefits of this asset. However, the Zafimaniry are shifting cultivators with a relative abundance of land who readily welcome strangers into their kin groups. They have a 'correct' representation of property relations as embedded in social relations, because their mode of production does not lead them to exclude others and reify their ties to territory. The contrast is convincingly established: property relations are fundamentally exclusive, separated out and mystified among the Merina, but they are inclusive and overtly embedded among the Zafimaniry. In this same article Bloch was dismissive of Leach's claims (1961) to the effect that kinship could ultimately be reduced to property relations – these were not seen by Bloch as advancing Marxist analysis at all (it was hardly Leach's intention to do so).

By the end of the 1970s there was increasing dissatisfaction with the imposition of a universal Marxist grid that included the concepts of alienation, exploitation, the labour theory of value, etc. The strongest trend in economic anthropology in recent decades has been to assert the importance of grasping indigenous understandings of economic life: 'local models', in the terminology of Stephen Gudeman (1986). The universalism of the Marxists, with their bias toward production, was felt to be no more satisfactory than formalist insistence on reducing all exchanges to the rational decision-taking of individual utility maximizers. Gudeman also criticized the substantivist paradigm, arguing that its general types were of little value in grasping the insider's model, the metaphors by which economic life is structured in particular places. His is a fundamentally idealist approach which provides little material historical contextualization. For example, his interesting analysis of the models of the Physiocrats explores their Lockean epistemology, their imagery and their assumptions about agency, but it makes little reference to the concrete conditions of different social groups or to the ideological role played by this intellectual elite in justifying highly unequal entitlements on the eve of the industrial revolution.

During this most recent period, relatively few anthropologists have made property a main focus of enquiry. Of course there are some exceptions, and I would identify several partly overlapping areas where older concerns have persisted and some innovative contributions have been made. First there is land tenure, and the role that anthropologists have continued to play in the documentation of native systems of tenure. This has led some, especially in Australia and North America, into active involvement in the legal claims brought forward by indigenous peoples. Many significant successes have been achieved, though in some cases the problems of cultural translation have proved insurmountable (for an overview of the Australian situation see Maddock 1983). Nancy Williams (1986), in the work noted in the preceding section, showed how Western concepts of property impeded recognition of the nature of the Yolngu system. While allowing for flexibility and fluidity, as emphasized in other recent studies of property and territoriality among hunter-gatherers, she sought to show that this was clearly a proprietary system, expressed in precise jural rules and sanctions as well as in the domains of myth and religion. Many land tenure disputes are extremely complex and do not present a clear-cut conflict between indigenous peoples and white settlers. In some cases conflicts may arise between two or more indigenous groups and political and ethical dilemmas inevitably arise when anthropologists become drawn into the pragmatics of land claims and resettlement schemes.

In a closely related field of investigation, anthropologists have recently undertaken numerous studies into common property arrangements and shown that liberal fears about the 'tragedy of the commons' (i.e. overexploitation of resources in the absence of rigorous private property rights) are frequently exaggerated. Communal arrangements *can* be environmentally viable, indeed superior to private systems for both marine and land resources (for examples see McCay and Acheson 1987).

Another notable exception to the pattern of anthropological neglect of property is the rediscovery of Engels by feminist scholars. Hirschon

(1984) is a collection which focuses on property and gender. The editor makes some important general points about property in her introduction, but the general message of this volume is a highly relativist one: the possibilities for cross-cultural comparison seem limited, even on specific gender issues. The most radical contribution to this volume is a chapter by Marilyn Strathern that sets out to deny the applicability of a Western concept of property in the Mount Hagen area of the New Guinea Highlands. Strathern reports a situation in which women seem to exercise little or no control over the products of their labour, while only men seem to be 'acting subjects' according to Western ideas of personhood. However, though Hagen men speak of themselves as 'owners' of the land and equate women to 'wealth', Strathern denies the 'western corollary', that Hagen women are objects. If indigenous concepts are correctly understood, neither women nor wealth items can be considered as property in the sense of alienable commodities. In this cultural logic, first explored by Marcel Mauss (1925), things 'cannot be *opposed* to persons, as our own subject-object matrix postulates' (1984b: 165, emphasis in original). Strathern therefore urges caution in using a concept of property. Her argument is developed more fully in a later study (1988), in which she elaborates how the Hagen notion of the person differs from the Western notion. This material provides convincing justification for not imposing a particular 'western paradigm of property ownership which is itself so very much bound up with a special view of the person' (1984b: 178). Hageners, it seems, do not own things in anything like the Western private property sense, although they clearly do hold, use and dispose of things in other ways – as Strathern demonstrates in chapter 11 of this volume.

A fourth area of research which has been opened up in recent years marks a return to the study of incorporeal property. Another Melanesianist, Simon Harrison, has followed up some of Strathern's ideas in the context of 'ritual as intellectual property'. His general perspective is that the study of property necessarily combines the study of the production and consumption of goods with the study of cultural meanings; consequently 'property is actually a form of sociality' (1992: 235). (Some recent work by Harrison on the ownership and management of knowledge is discussed by Strathern in chapter 11.) From a rather different angle, Darrell Posey has pursued the theme of intellectual property rights in environmental knowledge (e.g. 1990; Posey and Dutfield 1996). He argues that anthropologists should play a role in ensuring that knowledge which has commercial applications, e.g. of rainforest vegetation, should generate commercial benefits for the original 'owners' of that knowledge. Posey seems to assume that such knowledge will be widely shared in a group. However, the work of Harrison and others suggests that in practice it will sometimes be the exclusive property of a small minority, a fact which seems certain to complicate the political and ethical agenda for applied anthropology in this field.[7]

These recent contributions to the study of property must be set in the context of more general trends in economic anthropology. The most important loss consequent upon the jettisoning of the substantivist and neo-Marxist approaches is the loss of their attention to historical transformation. Each of these approaches saw a 'great divide' between traditional and modern, market-integrated societies. Many of their critics can see no gulf at all. The emphasis has come to rest once again on exchanges, corresponding to the dominant emphasis in neoclassical economics over the last 130 years. There is also a renewed interest in material culture, in the things which people make and then circulate, which provides an echo of the first descriptive phase in the emergence of economic anthropology, except that nowadays this is combined with a sophisticated interest in consumption, in how the things consumed contribute to identities, personal and social. A key concept is once again that of *value*; a primary task of the anthropologist is to document and explore the preferences that motivate economic action, which most economists simply take as given (Douglas and Isherwood 1978; Appadurai 1986; Humphrey and Hugh-Jones 1992). In his introduction to perhaps the most influential volume of recent years, Arjun Appadurai returns to Malinowski's *kula* material and reinterprets the competitive struggle to raise one's reputation as a 'tournament of value'. The art market is said to present a comparable tournament in our own societies. Appadurai is concerned with how commodities, loosely defined, pass between spheres and between cultures, in patterns governed by social knowledge and the criteria of good taste. Although he and most followers of these new approaches also emphasize the need to attend to power relations, it seems that the most consistent outcome of these recent approaches is the privileging of ideas and metaphors about the economy, rather than material constraints on consumption choices. The stress is placed on questions of 'authenticity', symbolic codes and the 'politics of culture', rather than on changing divisions of labour and the politics of class struggle. These new interests in commodities may be a reflection of increasing 'globalization'. But in focusing on forms of circulation and consumption, there is a danger that anthropologists may overlook the fact that many things (notably land – 'real property' as it is termed by the lawyers) do not circulate so readily. Many patterns of ownership demonstrate important continuities which provide effective stabilizing anchors in even the most rapidly changing, 'post-modern' societies.

If all people transact and consume according to their specific cultural repertoires, then it is hardly surprising that some anthropologists have reached the conclusion that exchanges have basically the same rich levels of meaning involved whatever the social context. For example, John Davis rejects Mauss's postulated evolutionary trajectory from the 'total prestation' of archaic Oceania to the impersonal, contract-dominated world of our own industrial age. For Davis, the symbolic content of gifting in contemporary Britain is no less rich than that of any primitive society: 'the amount of meaning carried by exchanges is a constant, is uniformly thick' (1992: 79). Such conclusions, denying the contrasts drawn by Mauss, Polanyi and other 'great divide' theorists, seem inevitable as long as economic anthropologists continue to approach value with an excessive emphasis on symbols and meaning, as revealed in exchange and consumption practices, rather than on the sociological factors and power relations which are necessarily foregrounded in investigations of property. We may agree that value is a critical concept, but the analysis of value cannot be an end in itself: it must lead on to analyses of the political and social conditions which determine access to scarce goods – in other words to the analysis of distribution and property relations.

A partial exception and notable milestone in the recent development of economic anthropology is the collection on money edited by Jonathan Parry and Maurice Bloch (1989). Popular attitudes to money offer an interesting parallel to perceptions of private property. Like property, money is seen in Western thought both negatively, as 'the root of all evil', and positively, as a source of autonomy and liberty. Most of the contributors to the Parry and Bloch volume tend to follow a particularizing approach, looking at the significance of various forms of money in the locations of their fieldwork. In their introduction the editors explicitly reject Paul Bohannan's well-known substantivist argument, which attributed the dislocation of a Central Nigerian economy in the late colonial period to the impact of Western money. They argue persuasively that money cannot in itself be the cause of radical social changes: it must be placed in a wider context of expanding market opportunities and colonial administrative and tax policies (all of which I would prefer to see as facets of changing property relations). Parry and Bloch go on to outline a general framework for analysis. They suggest that the older notion of a great divide must be rejected, since many pre-industrial societies, such as those of South Asia, were characterized by intensive forms of monetized, marketized exchange well before the impact of capitalism and industrialism. Instead, they propose that all societies are characterized by an *internal* divide between a short-term transactional order, in which impersonal, competitive individualistic behaviour is the norm, and a long-term order in which the stakes are the reproduction of the moral values of the society. Parry and Bloch have little to say about the relative importance of the two transactional orders in modern capitalist society. They do, however, raise the Polanyi-like possibility that we may inhabit a unique form of human society, in which the values of the short-term order have expanded to colonize and efface the long-term order (1989: 29). This possibility is apparently rejected, but the authors do not probe it very far. The notion of a 'great divide' between traditional and modern societies seems as unacceptable to them as it does to most other contemporary anthropologists.

In terms of property relations, it may be similarly useful to see a general divide pertaining *within* societies, rather than *between* them. This, in effect, is what James Carrier does in chapter 4 of this volume. According to this view, alienable and inalienable things, gifts and commodities, are to be found in all societies. But have the discontinuity arguments been given sufficient consideration? The most frequently cited theorists of discontinuity in the recent economic anthropology literature are Marx and Mauss (cf. Hart 1982). However, Polanyi's original analysis of *The Great Transformation* (1944), which pre-dated his direct engagement with economic anthropology and his launching of the 'substantivist' school, may still have something to offer. Both Marx and Polanyi saw capitalism as a radical force that destroyed embedded social forms, including the established forms of property. If the breakthrough to 'possessive individualism' took place in the seventeenth century, as Macpherson and others argue, or much earlier still if Alan Macfarlane is correct, then new ideas about private property can hardly be a consequence of the industrial revolution. They might instead be seen as one of its causes, which would introduce an awkward idealist element into materialist philosophies of history. Indeed, Marx does seem inconsistent in the role he attaches to property, which would seem to be fully 'superstructural' under capitalism, yet a part of the economic base in explaining the transition from feudalism to capitalism. Polanyi, however, is less committed to materialist modes of explanation. Consequently, he has no difficulty in allowing new attitudes to property to play an enabling role in capitalism's emergence, while institutions and moral communities only undergo radical changes ('disembedding') following the full impact of the Great Transformation. The later ideological predominance of private property in capitalist society is emblematic of 'disembedding'. Public and 'moral' aspects of property relations atrophy, and considerations of short-term gain overwhelm long-term values. Surely this train of thought retains some plausibility in our late twentieth-century world?

The reintroduction of property issues into economic anthropology that I am proposing, not in economistic or legalistic ways, but paying careful attention both to cultural sense and power relations, is perhaps consistent with the sense in which Stephen Gudeman called for greater attention to be paid to 'distribution' (1978); but this call has by and large gone unheeded on the material and sociological side. In comparison with the attention paid to money and to markets, property has not attracted the attention it deserves from economic anthropologists. A concern with property relations requires investigations into the total distribution of rights and entitlements within society, of material things and of knowledge and symbols. It requires examination of practical outcomes as well as ideals and moral discourses, and an appreciation of historical processes, both short-term and long-term. I now turn to further discussion of the ways in which the chapters in this volume contribute to these goals.

### Contents of this volume

'[W]hatever absolute criteria of property may be set up, *the ultimate determinant of what is property and what is not is to be sought in the attitude of the group from whose culture a given instance of ownership is taken*' (Herskovits 1965: 326; emphasis in original).

Although theories about primitive communism have been influential in anthropology since the writings of Morgan and Engels, it is only comparatively recently that property concepts and practices in foraging societies have attracted sustained anthropological investigation (Barnard and Woodburn 1988). In chapter 2 James Woodburn focuses on the concept of sharing, which he argues to be the dominant form of property relations among hunters and gatherers with 'immediate-return' economies. Supporting his analysis primarily with data from his own work among the Hadza of Tanzania. Woodburn criticizes the view which understands sharing to be a form of 'generalised reciprocity', a term put forward by Sahlins (1974). It is not the case that Hadza share the products of their labour because they think that they may need the products of other group members in the future. On the contrary, argues Woodburn, we should move beyond the 'exchange' focus that underpins Sahlins' typology. Sharing is above all a *political* achievement that stresses the equal *entitlements* of group members. It is best seen as a pervasive ideology, a community value or ethos, which cannot be reduced either to individual maximizing behaviour or to group ecological adaptation. Sharing does not mean generosity, and ideal forms of property relations are by no means consistently respected in practice.

The principal mechanism for reinforcing the ideal of sharing is gambling. Hadza put great pressure on all group members to share, and very few of their possessions are exempted from what Woodburn terms 'demand sharing'. The items that are 'ring fenced' are those essential for life, yet these are not given high cultural valuation. In terms of the substantivist categories, Woodburn follows Polanyi in seeing sharing as a form of redistribution rather than of reciprocity: it is analogous to the tax and welfare system of a modern industrial society, a kind of public, political regulation. However, it does not seem to afford the Hadza much protection against the outsiders who are encroaching on to their land, and whose incursions are now forcing Hadza to adopt new concepts of exclusive ownership hitherto entirely foreign to them.

Woodburn's analysis of sharing as a political achievement is conducted within the traditional anthropological framework which defines property relations as social relations. In chapter 3 David Anderson extends the cast beyond the usual range of human actors by approaching property as knowledge in terms of a 'sentient ecology' which allows no sharp distinction between humans and non-humans. As suggested by Mauss, objects too may have personalities and enter into relationships. The Evenki and their neighbours in the Taimyr Peninsula of Northern Siberia inhabit a part of the world which has held out against modern notions of private property longer than almost any other. Anderson describes how native hunters 'appropriate' their environment and demonstrate their personalized knowledge in their performances. Contrary to some models of other hunter-gatherers which emphasize a 'giving' environment, the experienced Evenki hunter is the man who knows how and when to 'take'. Evenki local knowledge differs radically from the modes of appropriation of newcomers to the region and of communist officials, based on 'intelligence-gathering' and surveillance. Evenki themselves, like Woodburn's Hadza, do not have an indigenous concept to signify the exclusive aspects of property, but the outside world has intruded dramatically upon them in two moments of twentieth-century history. The imposition of territorial boundaries and communist institutions under Stalin seems to have left the established bases of community life largely intact. It was possible to reconcile the collectivist ethic of the state farm with the cultural norms of Evenki life. In contrast, post-communist policies of decollectivization have threatened the very core of this embedded economy. Their response to the recent imposition of market economy and new, highly exclusive models of property has been fierce resistance. Evenki hunters and herders, like former collective farm members elsewhere in Russia, have placed a higher value on the substantive social entitlements they enjoyed under communism than on the formal property rights they now enjoy as sovereign individual citizens of a post-communist state.

James Carrier's analysis in chapter 4 takes us to Melanesia, a location of special interest for economic anthropology ever since Malinowski's studies among the Trobriand Islanders, which epitomized the achievements of his functionalist school. These studies presented real, flesh-and-blood human beings in their 'coral gardens', and the declared aim was to understand the 'native point of view'. However, later scholars have tended to see Malinowski as wedded to the 'individualist' pole of a dichotomy with 'communal' that is inappropriate to Melanesian thought. The point has been driven home in recent years in what Carrier sees as the exaggerated adoption of a model derived from Mauss. According to this 'essentialist' model, Melanesia can be understood only through an understanding of the Melanesian person and Melanesian categories, which do not include the idea of alienable things. Yet Carrier's Melanesians turn out not to be so alien after all. In his careful analysis, which builds on the arguments of his earlier work on exchange (1995a, b) and also on the work of Parry and Bloch (1989), Carrier argues that some aspects of property relations on the island of Ponam are effectively identical to the exclusive rights of private property in modern Western societies. Other aspects, however, are very different. The land on this island, which is of poor quality and formed a sort of wilderness until its recent settlement from the mainland, is held and used according to a complex pattern determined by kinship and relations to original owners, periodically brought to the fore in ceremonial exchanges that highlight and reinforce a 'web of social relations'. Carrier suggests that we see property relations of this latter kind as 'inclusive', while other property relations (by no means all of them associated with commodities transacted in modern markets) are preeminently 'exclusive'. In the latter cases, people do not identify with objects: they transact them as impersonal commodities for maximum advantage, much as any liberal neoclassical economist would predict. Carrier illustrates this with an example of how a man can engage in 'free trade' for sago.

Exclusive private property, it seems to me, corresponds quite closely to the notion of a short-term transactional order, as outlined by Parry and Bloch in their edited volume on money discussed in the preceding section, while an analysis of inclusive social relations is the equivalent of an enquiry into what Parry and Bloch call the long-term order. The analogy with money is not exact: property is a broader concept which requires that more attention be paid to political and legal dimensions, alongside the economic. But, as with money, people may wax eloquent on the inclusive, relational aspects of their social arrangements, and yet *behave* in ways that indicate the force of more exclusive, pragmatic considerations. Carrier's contribution suggests that this may well be the case for Melanesians. He is critical of 'Orientalist' constructions of Melanesia, and also of their counterparts, 'Occidentalist' views of the modern West. An idealist preoccupation with the seductive logic of Mauss's model of 'the gift' has prevented some anthropologists from recognizing that, in terms of their material practices, Melanesian property relations are not, after all, so radically different from those found in modern Western societies. The practical outcomes on Ponam depend very heavily on political skill and power. As Carrier concludes (p. 103), 'Melanesians have commodities and exclusive property just as surely as Westerners have gifts and inclusive property'.

Alan Macfarlane's complex historical argument in chapter 5 contrasts sharply with Carrier's implication of equivalence across time and space. His primary puzzle is how far the property concept in England's common law tradition can be seen as one of the causes of industrial capitalism. Private property is vital to the legitimating ideology of capitalism, and yet there is a paradox here which the liberal paradigm has been unable to explain. The English tradition emphasizes the indivisible and *relational* character of property, which would seem close to what Carrier terms its *inclusive* aspect. It is the derived forms of Roman law found elsewhere in continental Europe that approach property in terms of the *exclusive* ownership of things, rather than social relations between people. These, rather than the English conception, which also resembles the general anthropological definition of property, would seem at first sight to have a greater affinity with the capitalist mode of production. However, Macfarlane suggests that, thanks to its unique development of a state that was strong enough to avoid fragmentation and a property vacuum, but not so strong as to undermine the rights of a highly egalitarian citizenry, England was successful in preserving an older, Germanic notion of property. England's property system evolved organically, in the common law, from its Germanic origins. In contrast, absolutist governments on the continent were able to re-impose key elements of Roman law, including notions of property as a divisible 'thing'. These notions were antithetical to an ethos of alienability and capitalist accumulation, whereas English ideas of individual ownership remained very strong until eventually, under the secure protection of a state that was effective without being oppressive, they proved conducive to the emergence of the world's first industrial society.

Macfarlane has long argued that the crucial indicators of modernity, as specified by the classical social theorists, were present in England as far back as records allow us to delve. His contribution to this volume extends the argument in two main ways. First, he inserts legal concepts of property at the centre of his analysis, documents them in the history of ideas, and assesses what causal weight they can bear. Second, he introduces a fascinating comparison with Japan, seen as the other prime example of a successful, original path to industrialization. At the heart of the comparison lies an element of geographical determinism: both these island societies were relatively protected from the depredations of foreign armies and the threat of a large standing army at home. Although Tokugawa authoritarianism provided a less optimal framework than the balance achieved in England, he argues that the countries developed similar structures for holding and transmitting property. These included primogeniture, the location of the 'controlling interest' in a lord rather than in a family, and the widespread use of adoption to emphasize that the family is, in any case, an artificial corporation rather than a descent group. The argument will surprise those who associate Japan with a collectivist ethic that stands sharply opposed to the individualism of the English: but Macfarlane seeks to show that in the actual workings of their property relations, the Japanese structures were in fact highly individualistic in very much the English sense. Contract was more important than birth, and the 'nexus between family and land' was broken. Like Carrier, Macfarlane stresses the need to distinguish the level of practices from an ideal legal or cultural logic. Like Marx, he emphasizes that property relations are necessarily *political* relations, and that the liberal individualist paradigm can only function when the state provides the stable framework for it to do so.

Whatever the continuities in the English legal tradition, by the eighteenth century England was exporting a modern conception of private property all over the world. Lands were appropriated from native peoples who, because they did not work the soil as farmers, were not considered to have sustainable claims of ownership. Paula Wagoner in chapter 6 chronicles the crucial phases of the history of land appropriation in one county of South Dakota, where the natives have to this day failed to find a secure place for themselves in the American Dream. European settlers had a radically different relationship to the land from the spiritual bonds which were vital to Indian identities. Since the end of the nineteenth century people's legal relationships to the land on which they lived have undergone numerous changes as a result of changing state policies. Wagoner describes the factors which have caused economic conflicts to be perceived in terms of blood and race. Nowadays 'mixedbloods' are in the best situation to strategize, claiming Indian identity as, for tax reasons, they remove their land from deeded status into trust. 'Fullbloods' fear losing control of their reservation to wealthy mixedbloods who are phenotypically and culturally non-Indian. However, non-Indian farmers and ranchers also fear losing their land as a result of government policies that have moved away from assimilationist thinking to endorse ideas of self-determination for indigenous people.

The British colonization of Cyprus after 1878 undermined the complex indigenous system of property relations that had developed while the island was part of the Ottoman empire. Land was increasingly commodified in the colonial period, and modern English notions of proprietorship were introduced in 1945 through legislation that was designed to promote the consolidation of private landholdings by independent farmers according to the standard precepts of the liberal property paradigm. Yet, as Polanyi argued in general terms and as many other ethnographers of Cyprus have confirmed, land is always more than just another commodity, its 'markets' rather more complicated than the market for lemons (one of Cyprus's principal contemporary exports). Migrants frequently hang on to the village plots they have left behind, or inherited from parents and grandparents, because they see them not as parcels of real estate but as their patrimony – an essential part of their personal and familial identities. Julie Scott's analysis of property issues in chapter 7 focuses on the dislocation caused by the *de facto* partition of the island in 1974. Many members of both the Turkish and the Greek communities were obliged to flee their homes and move to the other side of the island following military action which is presented by the Turkish side as a 'peace operation' and by the Greeks as an invasion. The government of the Turkish Republic of Northern Cyprus has drawn up complicated schemes to compensate refugees as fairly as possible; but the provision of secure title is no easy task for the authorities of an internationally illegitimate state. Scott's material brings out the importance of competing ethical justifications for landed property, and also of the political context, both internationally and locally. The 'legitimizing systems' include a macro level where Turkish and Greek historiographies of the island highlight different phases of the past, and micro levels where rights earned through labour may clash with the realities of political clout. Property claims in Northern Cyprus can be taken to legal tribunals for resolution, but access to informal social and political networks (*torpil*) is often more effective. The operation of the land markets (including the related markets for 'points', and payments for 'goodwill') is largely consistent with the predictions of a modern economist (or, for that matter, a pre-modern philosopher): for example, it is confirmed that people who do not hold secure title are less likely to invest in their property to improve it. But this logic tells us little about how the meanings of land in the context of previous social relations, together with ideas about 'the other world', continue to affect economic behaviour in ways that cannot be reduced to an economist's 'rational choice' model.

In chapter 8, Katherine Verdery examines new forms of property relations in a Transylvanian village that she has been studying since the 1970s. Her data show that, in the chaos and confusion that exist at local level, members of the old communist elite are in a good position to maintain their dominance. Their former political power, as leaders of collective farms and local councils, now has to be converted into economic power based on the ownership of land. The extent to which they can succeed in this conversion of power depends to some extent on their ability to hijack the moral sentiments of villagers in debates over the legitimacy of competing property claims. When Verdery suggested to a Romanian judge (in classic liberal fashion) that further 'disambiguating' of property would be in the overall interest of society, she was told that, while this might be true in theory, in practice the conditions for this liberal blueprint were not met. Legal decisions inhibiting the emergence of exclusive private property have strong support in popular opinion, which does not approve of resources that were accumulated by the collective labour of large numbers of villagers passing into private ownership. These are the moral debates that have raged throughout Eastern Europe. Verdery finds that sharper definitions of private property rights are favoured by some of the less powerful as well as the powerful. There is a strong aspiration to private ownership, but at the same time most villagers seem to favour maintaining the security and social entitlements of the old regime. The eventual outcomes will be the result of complex local social relations and political processes, and Verdery emphasizes the futility of legislating exclusive private property rights in land when almost everything in the political environment mitigates against the effective exercising of such rights.

In chapter 9 William Howarth contributes a valuable non-anthropological perspective to this volume. He is a specialist in environmental law who, like Verdery, has worked recently in Romania. He begins, however, by offering intriguing glimpses of how the law operated in environmental cases in earlier periods of English history and in contemporary East Anglia. The historical precedents for environmental protection in the English common law tradition are based on the demonstration of private property interests. The continuous development of civil law remedies has been impressive, but Howarth argues that this tradition has been insufficient and is incapable of meeting the challenges posed by environmental protection today. This deficiency can be made good only through supplementing *private* remedies, for which it is necessary to establish a 'property interest', with effective *public* regulation. If remedies require the establishment of a property interest and take only quantifiable private liabilities into account, then the wider public interest will not be served. Preventability can be achieved only through proactive regulation, the use of licences and the criminalization of offences. In modern European legislation the '*activity* orientation of the criminal law is in marked contrast to the *property* qualification of the civil law of nuisance' (p. 193).

Howarth then reaches a similar conclusion, namely the desirability of some combination of private rights and public regulation, from a consideration of the very different case of Romania. Here a system ostensibly committed to public regulation through state ownership, along with all its other deficiencies, did little to avert serious pollution of the natural environment. It is therefore understandable that many Romanians, enthusiastic about land privatization, should look to a strong system of private rights as the effective antidote. But Howarth's analysis of England persuades him that the private, civil law tradition does not have all the answers. Ideas of 'ecological proprietorship', based on extreme doctrines of private ownership, are unhelpful in practice. Some convergence to achieve an appropriate balance of public, political regulation and private, individual rights is the best strategy for improved environmental protection. This need to strike the right balance between statutory intervention and 'freedom of contract' can also be understood as a modern variant of the balance between the inclusive and the exclusive aspects of property, as these terms are used by Carrier.

Jack Goody opens chapter 10 with a review of the tradition of anthropological writing about property and of the paths he himself has followed in a lifetime of pioneering research. He then proceeds to explore how the intergenerational transmission of property is currently affected by a range of social changes in modern Britain where rapid increases in divorce rates and the high incidence of single parenthood are bringing a revolution in family life. People are understandably reluctant to devolve their property to their children if there is a strong likelihood that a large part of it will be lost to in-laws following the dissolution of a union. Absent parents have been notoriously unwilling to contribute to child maintenance, and the overall consequence has been to generate massive demands on public funding. The claims of single parents might be seen as a modern form of 'demand sharing', but Goody points to the strength of popular and political reaction to these claims: they are not seen as legitimate. He argues that these dilemmas could be significantly alleviated if the property that persons brought into a union could remain attached to them, as in traditional dowry systems. He also recommends maintaining precise property inventories during a union, as a means of avoiding expensive recourse to formal litigation when unions break up. Far from reducing women to the status of 'thing', Goody suggests that sex-linked, individualized transmission of property offers women rights and entitlements superior to those they enjoy in practice in modern Western societies. He poses the question whether non-Western models of the family, in which close attention to property transmission has not been displaced (at least superficially) by an ideology of romantic love, might have more to offer the world than the contemporary Western model.

Goody has done more than any other contemporary anthropologist to draw attention to the importance of the ownership and transmission of material property in human social life. The material he presents in this chapter brings us back again to the questions of historical transformation that preoccupied Marx, Mauss and Polanyi. All of these scholars, in their different ways, drew distinctions between predominantly inclusive systems of property relations and the exclusive systems that they saw as originating in the early modern West and then spreading to the rest of the world. Whereas Karl Polanyi posited a great transformation at the onset of capitalist market societies, and published his major work just before Britain's commitment to the establishment of a welfare state, the implication of Goody's argument is that this much expanded role of the state is itself the cause of a further, more radical disembedding of economic life from previously established personal and group contexts. The problems that Goody addresses are a consequence not so much of the rise of the principle of *exclusive* private property, but of the expansion of *inclusive* property relations by the welfare state to remedy the defects of possessive individualism. To phrase the problem in concrete human terms, in a society of high divorce rates, why should I be willing to make *inter vivos* transfers of property to my children? But if I do not, my retention of one form of property may jeopardize my benefiting from another, e.g. it may limit my entitlements to welfare provision, including hospital care in my old age. The proposal to reinstate dowry payments would alleviate such dilemmas, and also the burden on the anonymous public of taxpayers. This would amount to a *reintegration of the personal:* the closer specification of exclusive, individual property would seem to be a form of re-embedding appropriate to a mature industrial society.

This argument suggests a rethinking of the theories that link the Great Transformation to the industrial revolution and to the rise of private property. Polanyi's problem was an economy that had escaped from the social and political controls in which it had been embedded prior to the emergence of the self-regulating markets of industrial capitalism. This disembedding of the economy can be understood as the triumph of the 'short term transactional order', in the terms of Parry and Bloch (1989), or of 'exclusive' property relations, in the terms of Carrier's dichotomy. But Goody's problem is an intolerable and unsustainable form of *inclusive* property relations. The state's assumption of sweeping welfare responsibilities has neither undermined the ideological predominance of the liberal paradigm, nor led to the desired re-embedding, to the effective replication of a hunter-gatherer ideal in late capitalist society. Instead it has contributed to an erosion of fundamental interpersonal responsibilities and to the weakening of social cohesion at the micro, familial level, a level to which the earlier Great Transformation did not fully penetrate. For Goody, it would seem that a more exclusive form of property, tying material objects to particular individuals, is needed in order to bring us back to an embedded economic system. A renewed emphasis on individuation can be variously seen as a renewal of the traditions of agrarian society, as the culmination of Polanyi's Great Transformation, or as the beginning of a new trajectory of evolution.

In the final chapter, Marilyn Strathern juxtaposes some specifically modern problems of property in America with contemporary ethnography from the New Guinea Highlands and predicts a more general 'explosion of concern with ownership'. She opens with a discussion, based on a recent legal case in Tennessee, of the difficulties involved in determining whether cryopreserved embryos can be considered as property or as persons, and links this to a consideration of intellectual property rights and the ownership of knowledge. Strathern dissociates herself from the 'Maussian model' criticized by Carrier, and is in turn critical of the way her fellow Melanesianist simplifies relationships between people and objects. In her view, his story about free trade in sago does not sustain the claims he makes for it, if due attention is paid to local cultural meanings and we refrain from imposing Western ideas about exclusive possession. For Strathern, following Annette Weiner, a better place to start in developing a comparative analytic model of property is with models of reproduction and bodily procreation. Melanesian systems are 'geared to producing persons through the production of things'. Pigs are raised jointly by men and women, and only a culturally inappropriate Western preoccupation with a narrow conception of production could lead to the conclusion that female effort is exploited by men. In the story Strathern tells about a woman called Kanapa, whether a particular pig will be sold as a commodity or exchanged as a gift depends upon how local beliefs about ghosts and sickness together with concepts of motherhood are brought into play. This then forms the basis for a comparison with the would-be mother in Tennessee.

Strathern uses this material to express a more general concern that anthropologists should be self-conscious about their vocabulary when they use terms such as 'property' and 'ownership'. It is important to historicize our conceptual tools as well as the societies we study, and selecting particular items of vocabulary from another era may prove fruitful. She finds an unlikely affinity between Melanesian ideas about persons and some of the quasi-legal tools now being developed in late twentieth-century Euro-American societies to deal with new life forms, traffic in body parts, and the management of knowledge. 'Generative' Melanesian models are more appropriate to the post-industrial Western world than outdated models of private ownership and possession. Strathern is here not merely challenging one powerful analytic construction, the Western liberal paradigm of property, with a relativist argument that the specific Hagen case does not fit this model. She moves from this case to propose an alternative analytic framework altogether. In contrast to Carrier's use of the inclusive/exclusive dichotomy, for her the term 'inclusive' refers to a radical sense of 'self-propriety'. She is also critical of those feminist responses to new reproductive technologies which remain constrained by Western dualisms. Strathern stops short, however, of rejecting the construct of property. Her work is consistent with the approach to property relations that I have followed in this introduction and her conclusions, that 'dispositional control', rights in other people, and (non-commodity) rights in one's own body are all to be considered as forms of property, are innovative extensions of the anthropological tradition. Like David Anderson in chapter 3, Strathern is drawing attention to the different ways in which things may be conceptualized, owned and used by a non-Western people in the course of constructing personal and collective identities. The argument that some aspects of contemporary property relations in the West may be better understood through a Melanesian model provides a stimulating conclusion to this volume and one which opens up many avenues for further research. I would only add that I see the concern with cultural differences and the rigorous questioning of Western models as complementing, and not invalidating, the efforts of other anthropologists to prioritize issues of distribution and political economy, and thereby to sustain traditional concerns with sharing and exclusion, equality and hierarchy, power and social justice. Whatever the languages used to express them, these are the universal concerns of property and they are shared by the people we study.

## Conclusions

'A man's property is some object related to him. The relation is not natural, but moral, and founded on justice. It is very preposterous, therefore, to imagine that we can have any idea of property, without fully comprehending the nature of justice, and showing its origin in the artifice and contrivance of men' (Hume 1962, II: 196).

I have tried to argue in this introduction for the renewal of anthropological approaches to property relations. The approaches followed in this volume are wide-ranging, but they have some unifying characteristics. Above all, they show that some very powerful models of property relations in the modern world are too simplistic. This applies both to the dominant liberal paradigm, which asserts the virtues of exclusive private ownership, and its Marxist rival, which claims that state ownership can provide a viable alternative. Both paradigms elevate a property doctrine into a fundamental principle of social organization. In each case adherents of the paradigm believe that their property doctrine offers the optimum reconciliation of liberty with economic efficiency, and of both of these with 'justice' in David Hume's sense.

The liberal paradigm is predicated on a separation of political, economic and legal spheres. This is a separation which analysts must take seriously: property rights in an advanced capitalist economy with a well-developed legal system certainly differ greatly from property rights in post-colonial or post-communist societies, where the institutional context is entirely different. The arguments put forward by economists for closer specification of property rights, for the elimination of ambiguity, also demand to be taken seriously. Yet the contributions to this volume draw attention to the sense in which this separation is fictitious – a myth which has real, material consequences, but nonetheless remains a myth. Real societies are functionally diffuse, and the apparent rigor of the liberal emphasis on separation must also be seen as a thin disguise for unequal power relations. Critics of the liberal paradigm may reciprocate the call for rigor, emphasizing not separate social spheres but the need for precision and transparency in the actual distribution of social entitlements. They can argue that the rigor espoused by economists and lawyers of the 'free markets and pure private property' persuasion leads to obfuscation and blurring of these distributional issues. In any case, no matter how far a society commits itself to implementing the liberal or the communist doctrine in all their purity, some 'ambiguities' are bound to remain, because the very concept of property continues to defy exact circumscription. At the end of the day, every liberal lawyer must acknowledge that juridical concepts are necessarily bound up with questions of embedded cultures and political economies. It is one thing (and a very significant one) to achieve a legal ruling such as the Mabo Judgement, but quite another to follow this up with concrete steps in the modern Australian polity to ensure that Aborigine claims are met across the full range of their entitlements. It is one thing to emancipate slaves and turn native Americans into allotment-holders, but quite another to create the conditions in which blacks and Indians can enjoy the conditions of democratic citizenship in the United States of America. It is one thing for post-communist states to legislate the return of collectivized farmland to private peasant ownership but quite another to implement this legislation, and something else again to empower those peasants in other domains of property in which, as they are increasingly aware, their rights and capacities were greater under the *ancien régime*.

As they have done for a long time, anthropologists will continue to trespass in neighbouring fields and to borrow ideas and vocabulary (including talk of 'rights', 'capacities' and 'entitlements') from adjacent disciplines. Perhaps in future anthropologists will come to draw more on traditions other than the Western, but most borrowings to date have been from this one broad stream. There is scope here for still more cross-fertilization. The most cogent modern contribution to debates about property to my mind remains that of the political theorist C. B. Macpherson (1962, 1978) who has argued for an updating of liberalism in terms of a 'new paradigm', based not on Locke and an individual's right to exclude others, but on the right *not to be excluded* from what he terms the 'means of labour'. This guarantee of access can be understood theoretically as a political problem of democratic control. Anthropologists can explore this problem ethnographically in terms of both concepts and practices in every type of collectivity, from families and small groups through all kinds of workplaces and associations, public and private institutions, to the 'sovereign nation-state' and beyond. Whatever the focus, the concrete empirical nature of modern anthropological research affords a closer understanding of human needs and of the property aspirations of real, flesh and blood individuals. The exact mix of inclusive and exclusive forms will continue to evolve. Calls for a 'reintegration of the personal' in contemporary societies may require the strengthening, at some levels, of exclusive links between people and things; but this need not be inconsistent with the call for democratic control at other levels.

Finally, in an elegant formulation, the historian Perry Anderson has described property as 'the nodal intersection between law and economy', linking the two in all social formations:

juridical property can never be separated either from economic production or politico-ideological power: its absolutely central position within any mode of production derives from its linkage of the two, which in precapitalist social formations becomes an outright and official fusion                    (1974: 404–5).

There is no doubt that the modern attempt at fusion known as Marxism-Leninism failed to achieve socially acceptable levels of economic performance or freedoms. Yet the contributions to this volume suggest that aspirations to fusion are unlikely to disappear. As the 'thinginess' of property gives way to a broader conception of the entitlements of citizens, it seems likely that there will be more pressure to abandon liberal chimeras and to recognize explicitly that the distribution of property is necessarily a function of the overall political organization. Anthropologists have always understood this and emphasized the interconnectedness of social phenomena. Linking their analyses of the political economy of property with investigations into culturally specific relationships and values, they are well placed to chart the fusions of our common, post-liberal, post-capitalist futures.

## 2   'Sharing is not a form of exchange': an analysis of property-sharing in immediate-return hunter-gatherer societies

*James Woodburn*

The sharing of the meat of large game animals is a much-stressed characteristic of many hunter-gatherer societies. The hunter-gatherers themselves stress it and so do anthropologists. They and we are right to do so. Unquestionably sharing is of central importance in the operation of these societies. It is politically central. In this chapter I shall make the case that we should give particular attention to the *politics* of sharing.

A particular difficulty in dealing with this topic is that our preconceptions badly obstruct our understanding of it. They have much influenced many analyses. Rather than engage in the unproductive task of criticizing the analyses of other named ethnographers and anthropologists, I shall set up a straw man, or rather a straw person, to represent a composite view which is rather widely held in whole or in part by people who are not straw people. Here is the kind of representation of hunter-gatherer sharing that I want to challenge:

Having killed a large game animal with bow and arrow, a hunter cuts it up and, because there is more meat than he can use before it would rot, he generously gives it out to his relatives and friends so that, when they in turn kill animals, he can claim meat back from them. He insures himself against the unpredictability of his own future hunting success by acting as a donor and benefits by accumulating claims on other hunters who may make kills when he does not.

For some hunter-gatherer societies this representation of how sharing operates may not be too far from the truth. But it certainly is *not* true for the society I am going to be focusing on – the Hadza of Tanzania – nor, I believe, for many other hunter-gatherers with what I call an immediate-return system.[1]

Let us look, then, at what is wrong with this representation of immediate-return hunter-gatherer sharing:

1. Sharing is not a product of the practical need to dispose of meat before it rots. The Hadza and other African hunter-gatherers, such as the !Kung and the Mbuti, well understand how to cut meat into

strips and to dry it. When dried, it keeps for months. The fact that they do not dry much meat is because they are obliged to share it, just as they have to share most other things for which they have no immediate need.

2. In these societies the hunter has very limited control over who gets the meat. Often he neither dismembers nor hands out the raw meat. If he does have some measure of control over the initial distribution of the raw meat, he is very unlikely to be able to control secondary distribution of the raw meat or further distribution once it has been cooked. The meat cannot, in general, be directed to past donors or potential future donors. It has to be given to everybody in the camp, whether or not they are effective hunters with the capacity to give in future.

3. Generosity is not stressed. We often think of sharing as deriving from generosity. The emphasis in these societies is quite different. Shares are asked for, even demanded. We have what can appropriately be called demand sharing.[2] People believe that they are entitled to their share and are not slow to make their claims. The whole emphasis is on donor obligation and recipient entitlement. The donor has no choice over whether the meat is shared and little influence over who gets what. In this context to describe the act of the donor in providing whatever should be shared as an act of generosity seems inappropriate. In ordinary English usage, we describe giving as generous when it is not obligatory[3] or when more is given than is expected. Giving something which has first been requested or demanded when the request or demand is locally seen as a reasonable entitlement, is hardly an act of generosity. Typically the donor is not thanked. This is consistent with the notion that the donor is doing no more than he should do.

4. Receiving meat does not bind the recipient to reciprocate. Many men are ineffective hunters because they are lazy or lack the necessary abilities or skills. They never, or almost never, reciprocate with meat or in other ways. Women who receive meat do not seek meat or anything else with which to reciprocate. This does not affect their entitlement. Meat yields do not balance out and are not balanced in other ways. Donors tend to remain on balance donors over long periods. Recipients tend to remain on balance recipients over long periods.

5. Success in hunting provides little insurance for the future. Donation establishes no significantly greater claims on future yields than would be the case without donation. Where much hunting is carried out individually and where hunting success is variable, the obligation to

share cannot be said to enhance significantly the access of successful hunters to meat and to other resources. Their overall access to meat of their own and other kills and to other resources would be greater if they were permitted to control the use of the meat of large animals they kill – to decide whether to use it fresh or to dry and store it, to decide whether to exchange it for other goods or services or to use it to pay off past debts or to establish future claims. They are prevented from doing all of these things by the obligation to share, which is a product of a system of values, indeed a political ideology, backed by sanctions positive and negative. We should not be surprised that shares have to be demanded, as donors derive little advantage from sharing.

The system is one that restrains the individual hunter from maximizing and tends to restrict the amount of hunting carried out. The motor of the system is more political than nutritional. Equality is what matters and the threat of inequality is of more concern than the threat of hunger.

It follows from these basic points that to treat this type of sharing as a form of exchange or reciprocity seriously distorts our understanding of what is going on. Hunter-gatherer meat-sharing is manifestly not direct or balanced exchange or reciprocity and is usually described as indirect or generalized exchange or reciprocity. My argument is that to treat such sharing as any form of exchange or reciprocity is inappropriate when donation is obligatory and is disconnected from the right to receive. To describe such sharing as exchange or reciprocity does not accord with local ideology or local practice among the Hadza and most other hunter-gatherer societies with immediate-return systems.[4]

As John Price argued in a pioneer paper (1975: 3–27), sharing is 'the most universal form of human economic behaviour, distinct from and more fundamental than reciprocity'. In the present chapter I seek to develop Price's insight by analysing the nature and significance of sharing in some societies in which sharing is particularly stressed in ideology and in practice.[5]

## The practicalities of sharing among the Hadza

What, then, is going on? I shall examine some Hadza ethnography to show how sharing works and how it fits into the wider context of Hadza property rights and Hadza political relations.

Among the Hadza, the central focus for sharing is the killing of large game animals. Using bows and poisoned arrows, they frequently kill very large animals – zebra, buffalo, eland, giraffe, wildebeest, hartebeest, waterbuck and so on. When an animal is killed, the carcase is skinned and the meat divided up, usually by two or three of the older men. The hunter may take part but ideally should not do so. The meat is carefully divided into two categories. The first category consists of certain valued joints of meat, specific joints for each species of animal, which are termed *manako ma Epeme*, God's meat. This meat is strictly controlled by the initiated men, who take it to the men's meeting place and eat it together on an equal basis in strict secrecy. They deceive the women and young uninitiated men by strongly denying that they do eat *Epeme* meat. There are very strict sanctions governing this meat and its consumption. Most cases of serious illness are blamed on consumption of *Epeme* meat out of context, whether such consumption is deliberate or inadvertent. The meat is said not to belong to the hunter who has obtained it. If he were to consume any of it in any context outside the meeting of the initiated men, he might well be accused of theft and would be liable to be attacked as well as being in danger of serious illness. If the hunter is an initiated man, he has at every stage exactly the same rights in *Epeme* meat as every other initiated man in the camp. If he is not an initiated man, he has no rights in it, either initially or at any other time. No hunter who successfully kills a large animal can be a donor of this category of meat because in Hadza ideology it does not belong to him.

Paradoxically, although this meat is not given away and is consumed in strict secrecy, and although it provides for a sectional interest – the interest of most of the adult men – the fact that it has to be removed with care and carried back to camp provides a precedent and a framework for the sharing of all the rest of the meat, which is called *manako eta Hadzabe*, people's meat. This meat, always much greater in quantity than *Epeme* meat, does belong initially to the hunter. He has applied his labour and skill to make his hunting equipment and then to hunt and kill the animal. This in Hadza ideology entitles him to ownership.[6] Most Hadza hunting is carried out individually by a lone hunter who has made his own hunting equipment and ownership of a kill is usually unambiguous. There are procedures for establishing who is the owner when this is not the case.

The notion of single ownership of a kill is very widespread in hunter-gatherer societies, both those with immediate-return systems and those with delayed-return systems (Dowling 1968; Barnard and Woodburn 1988: 25–7). It is this fact that makes the use of the term 'donor' appropriate in this discussion even though in many cases the donor has little influence over who gets the meat.[7] The distinction between donor and recipient is usually clearly defined even when, as among the Hadza, the donor of a kill is also the recipient and consumer of some of the meat of the same kill.

The people's meat is widely distributed among all the men, women and children of the camp unit – maybe twenty-five to thirty people. There are several stages of sharing. The meat is first shared at the kill site among the men, women and children who have gone out to carry the meat. Back at camp it is then shared again with those who remained behind. When it has been cooked, the cooked meat is shared again among those who are present.[8] As soon as one set of people in the camp finish their meat, gentle pressures are brought to bear on those who have any left to share again. Storing meat for later private consumption is unacceptable. Rates of consumption are extraordinary as people apparently seek to maximize their shares by eating more (and more rapidly) than others. But at the same time people behave politely to each other and these occasions are festive rather than competitive. Everybody, however undeserving or unpopular, should, and almost always will, get their share. But usually they do have to *claim* it. The sick, the senile and those with mental problems limiting their capacity to claim would not be denied a share, but people do not always seek them out to ensure that they get their proper entitlement. The Hadza with the strongest claim of all to shares of meat and of other foods are pregnant women. To deny a pregnant woman any food in the camp which she asks for is completely unacceptable and is believed to endanger her pregnancy.[9]

At the time of year when most large animals are killed, Hadza camp size is strongly influenced by the size of the animals being killed. People aggregate around successful hunters until the number is too great for people to get what they consider to be an adequate share of each kill. At this point successful hunters may try to break away and to set up camp elsewhere with a smaller number of people (Woodburn 1972: 199).

In comparison with large animals, small animals are less widely shared. None of their meat is *Epeme* meat. An animal the size of a hare or a fox will often be cooked and eaten in the bush by the hunter. Only if he gets a second one will he be likely to bring it back to camp and to share it.

Vegetable foods – wild roots and fruits – are gathered by the women, who eat their fill at the place where they gather them. They bring what is left back to camp and share it there. But the sharing is less rigorous and less stressed culturally than meat-sharing.

Personally owned objects – such as metal-headed arrows, knives, stone smoking pipes, bead necklaces, shirts and trousers – are constantly asked for. People who have more than they manifestly need are put under relentless pressure to share. It is rare for anyone to be able to retain more than one shirt or more than one knife for long. These objects are also gambled for. Men spend as much time gambling as they do obtaining food.[10] It is a game of chance and wins and losses usually roughly balance out. But many objects pass through a man's hands and he withdraws from the game those that he needs and re-stakes those that he does not need. Winnings are neutralized, depersonalized, by being passed through the game. Gambling is, in fact, the major way in which goods are circulated among the Hadza.[11] It is more pleasurable than sharing but operates similarly. Objects are distributed without binding people together. In receiving goods, a person takes on no obligations to the person from whom the goods originated.

A few personally owned objects are not normally transferred to other people. A man's bow is the most striking example. A man makes his own bow, carving it from the wood of the *mutateko* tree. His wife makes the bowstring from the nuchal ligament of one of the large game animals. He will use his bow until it wears out and will then throw it away. Arrows lacking poison or metal heads which are used for killing birds and small animals such as dik-dik, hares or hyrax are sometimes shared, but, like bows, are not eligible as stakes in the gambling game. The leather bag, in which men carry tobacco, arrow poison, spare arrow-heads and so on, is similarly excluded from the gambling game. The effect of these rules is significant. Sharing and gambling can, and often do, take away a man's poisoned arrows, and hence his capacity to kill large game. But he always retains his means to defend and to feed himself – his bow, his bird arrows and his leather bag.

It is worth noting that, for the Hadza, it is transferability which gives objects value. In spite of their indispensability, bows, bird arrows and leather bags are regarded as being almost worthless.[12]

The Hadza do not normally assert rights over land or fixed resources. People live in small nomadic camps which move from one site to another about every two or three weeks. They usually contain on average some twenty-five to thirty people, although their size and membership are constantly changing. People are free to live, hunt and gather anywhere they wish within Hadza country without restriction. But they do tend to limit their personal nomadic movements to particular areas of Hadza country large enough to offer good resources throughout the year, rather than ranging over the whole country. They identify themselves and are identified by others with these areas. Access to land and resources is obtained automatically by being born a Hadza. People do not inherit rights to any particular region. They tend to be associated with areas with which their parents were associated, but they have no greater rights to live in these areas than anyone else.

Inheritance is rather unimportant to the Hadza. Nobody depends on inherited property, and it is of little value. The principle of sharing applies here too. The Hadza say 'Everybody cries, everybody gets something.' A man's arrows, knife, axe and other possessions will be shared out among close kin and associates in the camp in which he dies. Kin may come from elsewhere to claim things, but there will not be anything left for them to share unless they come quickly.[13]

## The repudiation of accumulation, reciprocity and exchange

More can now be said about attitudes to property and about some of the principles underlying the association between people and things in this society. Great stress is laid on sharing as a moral principle. People say that sharing is important and contrast their own virtuous willingness to share with the individualistic wickedness of outsiders who will not share properly with them.[14] Linked with the notion that sharing is virtuous is the notion that accumulation is deeply objectionable and unacceptable. To accumulate is to deny other people the shares to which they are entitled. Just as accumulation of material goods is unacceptable, so too is accumulation of claims. One way in which the Hadza differentiate themselves from their neighbours is over the notion of indebtedness. 'We have no debt', they say. Only the general right to share is carried forward over time. Specific claims are not.

Exchanging with other Hadza is reprehensible. To barter, to trade or to sell to other Hadza is, even in the 1990s, really not acceptable, particularly in one's own camp. It does occur, but not very often. The problem for the Hadza seems not to lie simply in the notion that they should not profit from other Hadza. Even mutually beneficial bartering without thought of profit is very difficult. The central problem for the Hadza seems to be that reciprocation is objectionable. In their dealings with other Hadza, people should ask and be given what they ask for. People should give freely without expectation of return. People should share, not exchange.[15]

With non-Hadza outsiders, exchange is possible but very undeveloped and unsystematic. There are early records of silent trade (Obst 1912: 17–18; Reche 1914: 19; Woodburn 1988b: 9–10) and, at least since the beginning of the present century, Hadza have been trading with the neighbouring Isanzu and Iraqw farmers and Tatoga pastoralists. The Hadza seek locally made knife and axe blades, scrap metal for making arrowheads, metal pans, tobacco, hemp, cloth and clothing, beads. They give wild honey (used by their neighbours to make beer), animal hides and tail hairs, herbal medicines and some game meat (Woodburn 1988a: 51–2). But they prefer, as they see it, to share with their neighbours than to trade with them. Since they are few and their neighbours are very many, they trade on their exoticism and obtain most of their meagre requirements simply by asking for them. Their neighbours may, of course, define this behaviour not as requests to share but as begging.

If there is meat in camp and a tribesman whom they know from a neighbouring group visits them, he would usually be given a generous amount of meat to eat and to take away with him. But the Hadza greatly fear the witchcraft of their neighbours, especially of the Isanzu, which they believe causes many Hadza deaths. Most Hadza therefore seek to minimize their trade and other contacts with such dangerous people (Woodburn 1979; 1988a: 45–7).

The Hadza eat food that is hunted and gathered by themselves and other Hadza. No significant amount of food is obtained in trade or by working for outsiders. But for the past thirty years the government has been pressing them to settle, and government and aid agencies have periodically donated quantities of maize flour. Neither before nor during this period have the Hadza devoted any significant amount of their time to seeking goods to trade, except during rare seasons when honey is abundant. The situation is quite unlike that of some forest hunter-gatherers, who may obtain more than 50 per cent of their calories from traded cereals and other agricultural foods (see, for example, Hart and Hart 1986: 31). In return these forest groups must set aside much of their meat for their neighbours, and much of their time for working in the fields of their neighbours. In contrast, the Hadza do not set aside significant quantities of food or other objects for trade with outsiders, nor do they do significant amounts of work for them. Commodity trade is negligible and completely peripheral to people's interests. There is no question at all of sharing with fellow Hadza being eroded by the need for commodities to trade. In this respect the Hadza are unusual in comparison with some other hunter-gatherers with immediate-return systems who are much involved in commodity trade and whose community obligations to share seem to show signs of erosion by the desire to seek out and to set aside goods for trading (see, for example, Morris 1977; 1982).

As one might expect, people are more willing to subscribe to the moral principle that sharing is desirable than they are to practise fully effective sharing themselves. There are frequent efforts to avoid sharing or to minimize its effects. I have already stressed the speed with which people consume large amounts of meat. Once eaten it cannot be shared.

Those who are slow to eat their share have to give some of it away to those who have already consumed theirs. I have also stressed that most sharing is recipient-initiated rather than donor-initiated. People are expected to ask for the share to which they are entitled. If people can avoid requests to share, they will often do so. The most frequent way of doing this is by concealment of whatever it is that should be shared, and by telling lies or misleading other people about it. People who have a hidden stock of tobacco, which is one of the few things that can be readily concealed, frequently deny that they have any.

Individuals who win in the gambling game may gather together their winnings and set off to another camp. They are well aware that those who have lost their poisoned arrows and other possessions will be particularly persistent in their demands that the winner should gamble again, to give them a chance of winning back their lost possessions. They will also demand that he should share out his winnings. Some losers will follow him to the new camp, but the pressure on him there will be less and he may succeed in holding on to some of his winnings for a few days or, much more rarely, even for a few weeks.

Although in the ideology sharing is asserted as a universal moral principle, in practice, of course, it is limited by spatial and social distance. The camp boundary is significant here. Within a camp everyone, close kin, affines and those not closely related, will get a share of the meat of a large animal. Visitors from other camps will always get a share if meat is visible when they visit. But there is no obligation to notify people of neighbouring camps that meat is available and there is a tendency to suppress information about its availability until most of it has been consumed. In line with the principle that shares should, in general, be asked for, there is no systematic giving of meat (or, indeed, of anything else) to those living in other camps, except when they come as visitors. When people go as visitors to other camps, they do not normally take food or other things with them to give away.

### Hadza and !Kung sharing compared

The !Kung system for sharing meat has many resemblances to the Hadza one and should, I believe, be analysed in a similar way. Interestingly the !Kung also stress sharing in their most important religious activity, the trance dance. Men who go into trance expel illness, actual and potential, from the men, women and children of the community. A man pays no fees to the healers who teach him to become a healer, and when he is qualified he shares the yield of his ability to heal with everyone in his community without fee or expectation of reciprocation.

His ability to heal is believed to derive from *n/um*, a personally owned substance or force within him which is said to be warmed up and made available for curing with the help of other dancers and singers. He shares *n/um*, or the yield of *n/um*, in a way that is directly analogous to the sharing of a personally owned carcase of a game animal he has killed (Barnard and Woodburn 1988: 20; Lee 1984: 109–13).

However, the Hadza and the !Kung transfer their beads, clothing, poisoned arrows and other non-consumable personal possessions rather differently. The Hadza seek to transfer such possessions to each other in ways that do not create binding ties between individuals or between two groups. In contrast the !Kung seek to transfer such possessions by a system of gift-giving which they call *hxaro* and which is used to build relationships. Property is put to work explicitly to develop symmetrical ties of friendship between people.

The average person among the !Kung has sixteen *hxaro* partners with whom he or she exchanges personally owned objects such as beads, arrows, clothing or pots, but not food. All personally owned non-consumable items can enter the system. Gifts are given, often on request, and are then reciprocated after a delay of weeks or months.

A person's *hxaro* partners include most of his or her close kin – parents, children, siblings are all eligible as well as more distant kin. In general *hxaro* relationships are superimposed on kinship relationships. As in many other societies with immediate-return systems, kinship by itself implies little in the way of commitment (Woodburn 1979: 257–9). By giving property to each other as gestures of friendly intent, *hxaro* exchange partners build up selected kin relationships into more committed ones, some of which will be useful in providing access to groups and to the food resources of groups in areas other than one's own. Most personally owned possessions enter into *hxaro* but, according to Marshall (1976: 308), people do not come to depend on *hxaro* for access to the type of goods which are transmitted through it.

*Hxaro* has a number of distinctive characteristics that differentiate it from most systems of gift-giving described in the ethnographic literature and which, taken together, tend to identify it as a product of an immediate-return system. Little emphasis is placed on the goods themselves. People even ask for things they do not need in order to perpetuate the relationship. The goods given do not have to balance: little attention is given to parity of value. The amount given is likely to relate roughly to the amount available to the donor at the time. The exchange is non-competitive, and partners are not seeking to define their relative status on any basis other than an equal one. Men and women both take part in *hxaro*, and both have partners of both sexes.

The nature of the objects given is not defined by the sex of the donor or of the recipient; men can give or be given women's aprons, and women can give or be given men's arrows (Wiessner 1982: 71). A recipient of a *hxaro* gift often alters it, gives it a personal touch, before passing it on. But there seems to be no Maussian mystical notion that gifts embody the donor or that gifts are identified with people in ways that make reciprocation a necessity.

So here we have a system of exchange which, when superimposed upon a kinship system in which people are not, in general, linked to each other by binding relationships, creates bonds. Each individual develops bonds with many others of both sexes and such bonds are all of the same sort – simple, voluntary, non-competitive, symmetrical, contractual ties in which the giving of gifts opens the way for visiting and hospitality. Unlike exchanges in many other societies, they do not mark out or confirm the status of the participants: they do not, for example, establish that individual A is a male headman while individual B, with whom he transacts, is a subordinate male household head, or that individual Y is a mother's brother and that individual Z, with whom he transacts, is his sister's son. Nor, apparently, can they be used politically to gain influence or power or wealth. Everybody, male or female, young or old, has access to the system and participates in it. The objects used are made personally or obtained from other contractual partners or obtained from outsiders: they are specifically not obtained through non-*hxaro* ties with dependants – there are no dependants to provide them.

It is important that affines do not normally become *hxaro* partners (Wiessner 1982: 66). Affinity and *hxaro* (the major form of exchange) are seen as incompatible. People are said to feel that, if affines were to become *hxaro* partners, and if a dispute over *hxaro* broke out, there would be a danger of serious conflict between the kin of the husband and the kin of the wife (*ibid.*). *Hxaro* is given to affines but only indirectly. A man gives *hxaro* gifts to his wife, and she gives *hxaro* gifts to her kin. Each spouse maintains a separate *hxaro* network and passes on the spouse's gifts to his or her *hxaro* partners, including close kin, in whatever way seems appropriate. There are two other relevant factors. Firstly, giving gifts to affines would tend to convert what is essentially a means of establishing a personal tie into a tie of alliance between sets of people: it would become politically charged. Secondly, giving *hxaro* to affines would run the risk of equating people and things, of matching in some way the gift of a woman to gifts of things.[16]

The differences between the Hadza system for transferring personal possessions and the !Kung system are important. The Hadza radically restrict exchange and reciprocation. They reject them as unacceptable means for transferring personal possessions. The !Kung live in a more precarious environment where food failure does occur and where building relationships in which trust is developed opens the way for visiting other areas when times are hard in one's own area (Wiessner 1982: 77). They stress sharing of consumables – of meat and of the power to cure – and they use a tightly constrained form of exchange or reciprocation to build undifferentiated relationships which are reciprocal, egalitarian, voluntary and responsive to the material needs of the recipient rather than to the enhancement of the power, wealth or status of the donor. What is particularly important is that both the Hadza and the !Kung ring fence the marital relationship so that it is kept out of the exchange sphere. In both cases brideservice is provided by in-marrying husbands but the labour that they should provide is hunting labour. They should share the meat of the kills they make with their wife and her kin and all the members of her camp. They should not exchange with them. As we have seen, the !Kung actually prohibit *hxaro* with affines. Most important of all is the fact that in neither society are women exchanged in marriage directly or indirectly by groups of men.

### Why do the Hadza hunt?

There is one issue which some people find puzzling. Why do Hadza men hunt large animals – an extremely skilled task – if they get so little material benefit from it? You might think that the answer is prestige, that the status of successful hunters is in various ways enhanced. Well, is it? The answer is, not by much. The hunter's success is marked by the acknowledgement of his ownership of the carcase. But the Hadza believe that, to be successful at hunting, the hunter has to be modest and play down his success. Ostentation damages hunting. It enables the animals to escape. This is particularly the case when an animal has been wounded, but has not yet died. The name of the species of animal cannot then be mentioned. It is referred to by a special term (e.g. *bami !ingiribiteya*, the one with bells, for an eland). The hunter who has wounded an animal comes back to camp. He sits down quietly and most often says nothing. He will usually have the recovered detachable shaft of the arrow he has used. This will be held with his other arrows but will be reversed. This is for the Hadza a clear indication that he has wounded an animal. After an hour or two, to give the poison time to work, other men go out with the hunter to track the wounded animal. If it is obtained, there must be no heightened emotion, no congratulation of the hunter. To do so would, the Hadza believe, endanger the fat on the carcase. Fat is much more highly valued than lean meat and the animal has to be treated with respect if the fat is to be safeguarded. The fat is only secure once the animal has been properly dismembered.

Good hunters are not marked out or given any particular respect or deference. I know of only one exception. The killer of a lion – lions are food, as well, of course, as being dangerous to people armed only with bows and arrows – is decorated with beads for a few days. Some other societies with immediate-return systems go out of their way to deflate any potential self-importance on the part of the hunter. Richard Lee (1969; 1982: 54) describes how the !Kung systematically tease hunters, complaining about the inadequacy of the animal they have provided. Successful !Kung hunters may stop hunting for a while lest people feel that they have become too proud.

If the rewards for hunting are not great, if hunters have to go through what they may well regard as the unfairness of being dispossessed of most of the meat and being given little public recognition for their skills, why do they bother? The answer seems to me to be straightforward. A high proportion of the most successful Hadza hunters are rather solitary people, not much interested in social rewards. Their reward lies directly in the satisfaction of accomplishing a highly skilled and difficult task. It is a real challenge to succeed at hunting and gives those who are successful a sense of achievement. There are endless parallels in our own society – solitary fishermen or mountaineers, for example.

A successful Hadza hunter may have more chance of entering into a marriage with a woman who is seen as desirable and of maintaining his marriage than an unsuccessful hunter. But the solitary disposition of many hunters tends to conflict with success in marriage and I do not consider that enhancement of marital prospects is the central factor in motivating Hadza hunters to hunt. The direct personal satisfaction and sense of achievement derived from successful hunting matter more.

### Production and disengagement from property

The obligation to share, and the constant, remorseless pressures put on people to meet this obligation, do depress production. The evidence suggests that people would hunt more if they could derive more personal benefit from the yield of hunting. People would also, I believe, be more energetic in trade and in craft manufacture if they could more readily retain the yield of their labour.

What is unique about immediate-return hunter-gatherer systems is that the lack of accumulation and investment and the depression of production can readily be accommodated without in any way threatening people's health and welfare. As nutritional research in which I participated in the 1960s clearly demonstrated, the nutritional status of the Hadza was exceptionally good by East African standards. It remains good in the 1990s. Access to adequate nutrition is not a problem, even if people are producing much less than they could.[17]

Where storage is important for people's health and welfare – as it is in some other hunter-gatherer societies with delayed-return systems – or where crops are grown or domestic animals are kept, such thorough-going sharing and denial of indebtedness would be inoperable. The Hadza ring fence a man's bow, bird arrows and leather bag, largely keeping them out of the sharing sphere. Other societies usually limit sharing much more. They restrict it in two main ways. Firstly, they confine it to the household and a rather narrow circle of kin. Secondly, the nature of the sharing itself is constrained and made to work more in the interests of the donor. Instead of demand sharing from the potential recipient, we find donor-controlled sharing and a stress upon generosity.

I have suggested in an earlier paper (Woodburn 1982a: 445) that in immediate-return systems people are disengaged from property, from the potentiality in property for creating dependency. Disengagement is the right word. The Hadza are keenly aware of the possibility of the property rights that they reject, of the ever-present danger that indi-viduals or groups may succeed in usurping such rights. People have direct access to the resources they need for adequate nutrition unme-diated by ties of dependence on parents or other people of a senior generation.[18] They do not have formal obligations to specific kin. Relations with kinsmen are relatively undifferentiated and are character-ized by mutuality, often affectionate mutuality, but not by dependence or commitment. More generally people are systematically deprived of opportunities for differentiating themselves from others and for making others dependent on them by accumulating property.

At the start of this chapter I suggested that hunter-gatherer sharing in immediate-return systems is best seen as a political phenomenon. What it does is to limit profoundly the possible development of inequalities of power, wealth and status (see Woodburn 1982a). Like the rest of us, Hadza men and women are highly conscious of the dangers of depen-dence and subordination and do their best to avoid them. Unlike the rest of us, they have an economy which permits the realization of a much greater degree of freedom from dependence and subordination than is possible almost anywhere else.

Let me return to the title of this chapter. Sharing here is, as we have seen, not a form of exchange. We must correct our models. Some societies operate with both ideologies and practices which repudiate reciprocation. It makes no sense to construct analyses of human social life which are based implicitly or explicitly on the notion of a universal necessity to reciprocate. Of course in day-to-day interaction Hadza do at times reciprocate. They show affection to those who show affection to them. They help those who help them. They are friendly to those who are friendly to them. But in their use of food and of other property, the expected behaviour is non-reciprocal sharing.

Marshall Sahlins, in his classic and highly perceptive account of what he calls the sociology of primitive exchange, makes a binary distinction between reciprocity and redistribution (Sahlins 1972: 188–9). The distinction is not always clear and is not always made in a way that I find satisfactory. In general he seems to see hunter-gatherer meat-sharing as a form of reciprocity. However, in terms of this binary distinction, sharing of the type that I have described in this chapter is, I believe, much better classed as a form of redistribution than as a form of reciprocity.[19] The individual hunter has no choice about whether he shares the animal he kills. It has to be redistributed. Elsewhere (Woodburn 1982a: 441–2) I have described Hadza meat-sharing as analogous in certain respects to taxation in our own societies. People are in both cases obliged to give up a portion of the yield of their labour. In both cases donation does not define future entitlement. Most welfare benefits in our societies are not linked to prior or to subsequent payment of tax. We, quite rightly, do not think of the redistributive aspects of our taxation systems as being a form of generalized reciprocity or exchange. In spite of the huge differences in scale, and the fact that Hadza meat-sharing is not linked with centralized authority or a money economy and takes place within a small community, all of whose members know each other and many of whom are closely related to each other, it is time that we recognized that they too redistribute.[20] Their transactions are defined more by political pressures than by personal choices.

John Price (1975) favours a tripartite categorization of modes of distribution as sharing, reciprocity and redistribution. Sharing is, he suggests, found in all societies and is the 'allocation of economic goods and services without calculating returns within an intimate social group' (*ibid.:* 4). Reciprocity is 'a rationalistic, egalitarian exchange pattern' (*ibid.:* 5). Redistribution is 'a public system of unequal centralized allocation' characteristic of chiefdoms and state systems. But, he points out, redistribution 'draws some of its ideals and patterning from sharing'. 'Sharing is capable of infinite expansion as an ideal and it can have some integrative influence wherever it is held. However, its character changes so much as it is used in the design of well integrated society-wide systems that it is better to say that in the "public" sector sharing is transformed into a redistributive system' (*ibid.:* 7). It seems to me sensible to accept and to develop for analytic purposes Price's tripartite categorization in preference to Sahlins' over simple binary categories. But we should also recognize that the prototypical sharing of the societies with the simplest forms of human social organization and the redistributive systems of societies with the most complex forms of human social organization have more in common than Price recognizes. Those who provide goods for such sharing or for such redistribution do so, often unenthusiastically, because they have to do so. They are dispossessed of part of what is seen as theirs. They derive little personal advantage from such transactions. Those who receive the benefits regard them as entitlements which do not have to be earned or even acknowledged.

# 3    Property as a way of knowing on Evenki lands in Arctic Siberia

*David G. Anderson*

In the former Soviet Union, the prescribed relationship between people and the land was captured in the paired slogans 'All Land Belongs to the People!' and its younger cousin 'All Land Belongs to the State!' Axiomatic and deceptively simple, these slogans neatly summarized the regulations of a hierarchical bureaucracy which strove to channel the activities of its varied citizens scattered over its immense territory towards centrally authorized goals. As is now well known, these slogans tell only part of the story of property and appropriation in this large Eurasian state. Common anthropological analyses of appropriative action in the former Soviet Union have focused upon 'informal' arrangements, 'black' activities, or *de facto* regulations. According to these analyses, the slogans should be considered mere decorations draped over the silent agreements occurring backstage. However, I shall argue that informal appropriative arrangements were not necessarily murky and by implication subversive acts. The subtlety of state proprietorship was reflected in the complex character of the people, institutions and ecology bound together. In a society where state institutions regulated nearly all instances of contact between people and the land, one can discover as many different types of relationships between people and territory as there are categories of the person and styles of state regulation.

A nuanced understanding of how the formal regulations of the Soviet state worked alongside and often assumed local appropriative arrangements is important in understanding contemporary resistance to privatization. As the structure of the Soviet state continues to crumble, producers who resist privatization are not articulating an ideological conviction against property, but are instead revealing the robustness of social relationships which are now being threatened by a narrow ideal of exclusive property. To demonstrate this point, I will explore the connection between knowledge and 'modes of appropriation' (Ingold 1986) in one state farm in a relatively remote rural district in Arctic Siberia. I will suggest that, for sixty years, appropriative action in this region was based on different yet complementary ways of knowing land – glossed here as 'property'. In short, local ideas of appropriation have been governed by complex ways of relating to the tundra within what might be described as a sentient ecology. The relationship between state managers and land here (and in many other state socialist settings) is best described as an exercise of intelligence-gathering. The intersection of two ways of attending to land created what to the Western eye is a somewhat ambiguous tenure system, but it ensured that every member of the community was entitled to participate in production. Although recent attempts to rationalize and individuate land tenure were nurtured within the old state socialist regime, at the present juncture they represent a radical transformation of social relationships. Thus, it is not surprising that they are experienced by local people as a form of theft.

### Land privatization in Taimyr

The Taimyr (Dolgano-Nenets) Autonomous District encompasses the largest continental polar peninsula in the world – the Taimyr peninsula – situated where the mighty Yenisei River opens to embrace the Arctic Ocean. Although the climate of this district is temperamental, the land offers both native people and industrial corporations many riches. The six native groups of the area (Dolgans, Evenkis, Nenetses, Enneches, Ngos, Sakhas) have for centuries exploited the rich resources of forest and tundra along the flat escarpments of the Pultoran plateau and the marshy expanses which stretch north to the sea. The sharp ravines of the mountains, which shelter fur-bearing animals and migrating wild deer, also hold some of the richest stores of strategic heavy metals. Although remote from central Russia in the imagination of most Muscovites, the Taimyr lies at the heart of political debates over the fate of the mining city of Noril'sk, its 300,000 residents and a nickel-smelting operation which is the largest of its kind in the world. Although in this chapter I shall be concentrating on the appropriative relationships in a rural territory of Taimyr, it would be incorrect to assume that this place lives in pristine isolation from the industrial crises common to the whole post-Soviet space. The political links between Noril'sk and its satellite rural communities are so complex as to make rural and urban sites part of a continuous social space (Anderson 1996b). Similarly, the arguments developed through this case are relevant to the crisis in social production throughout Inner Asia and Eastern Europe.

A map of the Taimyr Autonomous District appears as a mosaic of bounded spaces which fracture into progressively smaller territories. None of these are (yet) 'private' in the strict sense of the word. However, within each space the connection between people and the land becomes tighter and more circumscribed. Although autonomous districts are jurisdictionally weaker than regular Russian provinces, in the sense that they are subordinate to a distant provincial city, they are unique in that they have their own parliaments, ministries of education and distributive agencies. Taimyr is further broken down into two rural counties and the extensive metropolitan council of the city of Dudinka. Within the Dudinka city council there are four state farms. The state farm Khantaiskii, which will be the subject of this chapter, is just under two million hectares in territory. This extensive territory is then further broken into smaller territories, which have become associated with particular families and particular individuals. Groups of authorized labourers known as 'brigades' (*brigady*) are often given the exclusive right to exploit hazily bounded regions within the farm. Brigade tenure intersects and overlaps with the tenure of state hunters, who are assigned specific 'points' (*tochki*) as their exclusive territory. Finally, within brigade territory or hunting points, producers exercise varying possessive relationships with the animals that they encounter within their authorized spaces. Although, since 1970, there have been various movements within the Soviet and Russian states to assign specific spaces to individuals in a manner that emulates private property, in practice many social and legal obligations make 'private' appropriation conditional upon the wider social and political context (see also chapter 8). As a general principle, each local producer carries an obligation to behave properly toward both the animals that he or she may encounter and to the administrative level immediately above them, which attempts to survey their activities. It is my argument and that of many native observers, that the land reforms initiated in 1990 are aimed at severing these mutual obligations to such a degree that it is entirely justifiable to raise the alarm of a 'Great Transformation' in Polanyi's bitter sense of the term.

The nested model of concentric circles of social obligation described above may seem an isolated anachronism in the contemporary era of aggressive privatization. One of the interesting qualities of Taimyr is the difficulty (or reticence) with which agents can stake claims to land independent of the wider social context. At the start of 1997, despite desperate encouragement from various federal ministries of the Russian state, the vast majority of state lands reserved for hunting and herding in Taimyr remained under the control of state farms. The state farms have become somewhat liminal legal entities. Since 1992 all directives from the District Department of Agriculture had ceased (along with all interest-free subsidies), yet the structure and authority of each of the

seven state farms of Taimyr remained intact. The unbroken coloured
blocks of state farm territories on the land-use map hanging on the
wall of the office of the District Land-Use Administrator of Taimyr
were marred only by a sprinkling of pin-pricked islands of private
land-leasing. Within this vast expanse of state lands only a handful
of entrepreneurs and extended families had established private farming enterprises (*fermerskie khoziaistva*) or clan enterprises (*rodovie
khoziaistva*).

Although resistance to privatization is not uncommon in Russia, even
in the Siberian context the durability of collectivized land tenure in
Taimyr is striking. For example, by the summer of 1993 the vast
majority of the former state farms in the neighbouring Evenki Autonomous District had been broken up into 'clan communities' (*rodovye
obshchiny*) (Popkov 1994). It is tempting to attribute this lack of change
in Taimyr to a certain parochialism. Indeed, Russian newcomers like to
joke about Taimyr being 'a nature preserve for communists'. However,
collectivized land tenure has a certain quality which allows multiple
modes of appropriation to coexist (Humphrey 1983; Hann 1993a).
Such coexistence makes this type of territorial formation remarkably
stable. This is not to say that exclusive types of land tenure are
impossible to construct – indeed there is no shortage of proposals to that
end – but there is considerable evidence to indicate that allocating
bounded territories to specific individuals or corporations in this region
of Siberia would be socially disruptive if not explosive. The attempts of
Muscovite administrators to instil an idea of property in land 'as a thing'
interfere radically with the way that the environment is perceived and
acted upon. Thus the present political stalemate regarding land privatization in Taimyr is not so much a product of apathy or a parochial lack
of imagination as a troubled peace resulting from an unsteady constella-
tion of diverging forces.

My research has focused upon land use and social identity within one
state farm. Named after the deep and still waters of Lake Khantaiskoe,
the Khantaiskii state farm was the home of 600 Evenkis, Dolgans and an
assortment of 'newcomers' ranging from Ukrainians to Azerbaidjanis.
According to the ledger books, the most important productive activity of
the farm is fishing. However, for Evenkis or Dolgans the hunting of wild
deer is one of the most well-loved pursuits of the region. This farm is
unique among the state farms on the right bank of the Yenisei in that it is
the only native territory where domestic reindeer herding is still possible.
In the majority of native communities in western and central Taimyr the
herds of domesticated draft reindeer, which have for centuries carried
people across the land, have been starved due to the acid rain produced

by the Noril'sk smelting complex, or have lost animals to the exploding population of wild deer chaotically migrating around the devastated spaces of the tundra. Although my research has taken place during a period of intense political and economic change, I have observed many continuities in the heavily centralized land allocation system, which has managed to encapsulate a wide variety of 'modes of appropriation'. For the sake of contrast I will begin with Evenki modes, before comparing them to general state socialist and more recent practices of monopolistic intelligence-gathering.

### Knowing the land

Evenki ideas concerning the proper relationship between people and land cannot be considered to be a pristine view of property, uncontaminated by sixty years of state interference. The industrialized mode of reindeer husbandry common to Taimyr, with its large unruly herds, high-walled accounting corrals and helicopter supply-lines bears little resemblance to the practice of caring for domesticated reindeer at the turn of the century. However, the experience of the Number One Reindeer Brigade at Khantaiskoe is a logical place to begin, since both professional herdsmen who work on the land and those who manage the paperwork in Taimyr's settlements argue that the Evenki *pastukhi* (herdsmen) are the ones who 'know the land well' (*khorosho znaiut zemliu*). Through the silent implication of this repeated phrase, all Evenki, Dolgan and even Russian informants insisted that those who worked in the reindeer brigades had the most experience to share on this topic.

The Number One Reindeer Brigade has always been composed entirely of family members – a type of labour organization which in the late 1980s and 1990s was thought to be the most 'progressive' (Humphrey 1989). The brigadier – Nikolai Savel'vich Utukogir – was one of the most experienced herdsmen in the community. His maternal grandfather – Mikhail Elogir – was the first large reindeer owner to surrender his herd in 1923 in order to create the collective farm 'Red Hunter', the forerunner of the contemporary state farm. Like his grandfather and his father, Nikolai Savel'vich was a member of the Communist Party. His cousins were herdsmen or brigadiers in the other three reindeer brigades in the state farm. The staff of the Number One Reindeer Brigade was composed of Nikolai Savel'vich's wife (Liuba Fedorovna), their four sons (Vitia, Andrei, Kostia, Volodia), and one nephew (Vova). Although, in a formal sense, a brigade of reindeer herdsmen within a state farm could be arbitrarily dissolved or restructured by an order from the director of the

state farm, this brigade had a strong and confident sense of its own
tradition and identity. Its members saw themselves as 'the most-Evenki
brigade' – a self-appellation which referred to the fact that all members
chose to register with the state as Evenkis, and that their particular skill as
herders was the best repository of Evenki traditions within the farm.
Thus, each member of the brigade would often point out that their
reindeer were the fattest and the healthiest, that only they were capable of
exploiting the pastures most distant from the state farm offices (some 300
km to the south), and that only they could still 'ride like Evenkis' on the
backs of their reindeer (rather than harnessing them to sleds winter and
summer). It was made clear to me during the eight months that I spent
with the Number One Reindeer Brigade that to become a herdsman had
as much to do with coming to 'know the land as an Evenki' as it had to do
with seeking the permission of the authorities within the farm.

From the outset of my apprenticeship, I was continually baffled by
what seemed to be a very loose relationship between people and the
resources around them. This ranged from an apparently random
criterion for selecting trees for firewood or places to gather snow or
water, to an extreme confusion when trying to catch reindeer each day
for harness. For the first months I displayed what must have seemed like
an obsessive concern with which tree to cut down or which reindeer to
chase. Whenever I asked 'Which tree should be cut?' or 'Where is it
better to fetch water?', the answer was 'Don't you know wood yet?' or
'It's better not to then.' Although I soon became used to these non-
sequiturs as part of everyday life (and finally learned not to ask), upon
reflection it now seems that the question of the relationship of the
*pastukh* to the land is best understood through the category of
'knowing'. Knowing (*znat'* (Rus.) 'to know'; *hade-mi* (Ev.) 'knowing') is
a concept which is not codified but is demonstrated in performance. If
the English word 'competence' were not so far from the actual vernacular terms, it might be the best translation of this idea. Another
appropriate synonym might be *sobrazitel'nost'* (Rus.: awareness or sharp-
ness): a quality which I was told was most needed in a herdsman.
Rarely, elders might talk of the old man who 'could fly like a ptarmigan'
or the old woman who 'knew thunder'. These examples of the *hamanil*
(Ev.: shamans; knowing ones) are both distant in time and in relevance
to everyday life on the brigade. However, the concept of knowing
persists both in the stories of people being able to rescue themselves
from impossible circumstances created by poor weather, poor luck or
bad drink and in the day-to-day obsession with performing tasks upon
the land 'properly'. Knowing the land properly for these 'most-Evenki'
herdsmen is what legitimated their right to take wood, water and

animals from the land, whilst at the same time explaining their capacity to do so.

I only experienced 'knowing' a very few times during my apprenticeship. One of my proudest achievements was during a 200-km journey by reindeer sled when, after stepping off my sled for a second time to untangle the leads from under the reindeers' feet, I stood up decisively to snap the reins against the lead reindeer's harness. This brought all three reindeer abruptly to attention and set them off at a great clip on to the trail, allowing me to sit calmly on the sled as it whisked accurately behind my knees (and did not trip me up, as was usually the case). At this rare triumphant display our brigadier sucked his breath slightly and with a smile said that 'he knows driving' (*on znaet ekhat'*). It was only after this incident that I was allowed to stray from the main trail on my own and was allocated small tasks to do with reindeer by myself.

A competent performance of one's knowledge earns a person respect and establishes one's status. It also entitles one to enter into a relationship with the land as an independent person. This idea parallels the idea of 'rights' (in this case 'rights to land') that are granted to 'individuals' in our society when they become 'mature adults'. I do not think that any of these three terms is appropriate to classify the type of relationship to land that I saw in Khantaiskii. None of the Russian equivalents for these words were ever used by my Evenki teachers when speaking of the land or of one's performative competence in using its resources. Moreover, each of these terms implies a relationship of power, sovereignty and licence between people which can be elaborated in both liberal-democratic and Marxist theories of society, but not in vernacular ideas which address a rather wider social field. Relationships of power, sovereignty and licence here are not exclusively relationships between people, but between people and tundra. Thus property is understood not only to be a jural, political and economic relationship in human society but also a 'proper' relationship between humans and other entities, which constantly monitor and adjust themselves to human agency.

The entitlement to enter into a relationship with land goes beyond demonstrated technical competence to include a sense that particular objects and tasks are suitable for specific persons. Personalized appropriation and consumption are commonly seen in terms of matching commodities to a person's taste. The harvesting of resources from the land in Taimyr is also highly selective but in the more fundamental sense of being related to a person's skills, her biography or his dreams. What appeared at first to me to be an inconsistent preference for certain places, certain types of wood, or a team of reindeer, was governed by an element of predestination. For example, in the selection of wood for burning or for carving, a number of technical factors have to be weighed such as location, dryness and quality. However, beyond these criteria different people see certain types of wood as perfect matches for their skills. For example, when cutting wood for carving, suitable logs are not evaluated through the terms 'good' or 'bad' but with personal prefixes. Typically, when I suggested trees for carving I would be told 'that's not a runner', or 'that's Vova's [*Vovanyi*] not mine'. In short, as the months of my apprenticeship went on, the immediate environs encircling each home camp appeared not as arbitrary zones of supply but as complex sites of specific trees, hollows and expanses which were more or less suited both to the people I lived with and to my own modest skills.

Leaving the mundane realm of my direct experience – the realm of wood and water – the point of a personalized entitlement becomes clearer. The hunt of the wild deer, as narrated by my companions, is a fine example of the very intimate intersection of destiny and awareness in the 'taking' of resources from the land. These stories supply a catalogue of techniques, but also a poetic image of young men taking reindeer trained with their own hands up into the windswept escarpments to hunt those deer's wild cousins. In condensing these stories I wish to show how the harvesting of a wild deer is only conceivable if a person holds not only appropriate technical skills, but also a proper relationship to the land and the animals upon it. Thus when older Evenkis speak about having 'their places' to hunt wild deer, this surprisingly possessive phrase signifies both a legal and a moral entitlement to take resources from the land.[1]

As with harvesting wood, technical skills are necessary in the successful hunt of the wild deer. In addition to marksmanship, great stamina is needed to travel for up to twenty hours without food or water, while keeping a firm hold on the reins of one's harness reindeer. Furthermore, the hunters typically travel with only an axe, a rifle and a knife, emphasizing a solid competence in survival skills in an environment where the weather can change suddenly and tragically. As an illustration of this hardiness, I heard one gripping story of the rescue of a hunter who, after seeking shelter under his sled from a gale-force blizzard, found himself encased in a sarcophagus of hardened, drifted snow. While survival skills are necessary, the hunter must also have a basic understanding of the habits of the wild deer and the places where they may be found. There are certain clues which may help in this regard. Crows are thought to fly over the camp in the direction of wild deer, indicating their location 'since they want to eat too' (cf. Shirokogoroff 1933: 44; Vasilevich 1969: 188, 218). Such hints are combined with an extensive knowledge of the micro-climates that offer shallow snow, year-round water sources, or salt-licks for the wild deer.

The possession of survival skills and an awareness of the landscape does not sufficiently capture the central role of 'knowing' in legitimate Evenki appropriation. While knowing the land's places is one of the key factors in hunting, a proper interpersonal relationship with animals is also crucial. The wild deer are reputed to have a heightened if not a supernatural sensitivity to people (cf. Vasilevich 1969: 220). They, like the bears, can hear the boastful words of a hunter and be forewarned of a hunt. During a hunt, those who remain in the camp do not speculate on its success or prepare for a feast. A hunter should not even sharpen his knife before heading out. The ethnographers of Evenkis postulate that respect for the deer's perception necessitates the use of a parallel language, which avoids naming the creature by its proper name (Suslov 1927; Shirokogoroff 1933: 81, 90). The *pastukhi* in Number One Reindeer Brigade speak of wild deer as 'the wild ones' in both Russian and Evenki (*dikie, baiur*). The heightened perception of deer extends to their senses of smell and sound (Kwon 1993: 71). The *dikie* can smell a hunter from a long distance —necessitating the choice of a damp, blizzardy day for a successful approach. Before setting out, the hunter will remove all metal fasteners from his reindeer sled so that the only audible sound is the staccato clicking of hooves on snow. The deer's perception also pierces the hunter's physical presence to examine his character. A 'greedy' man (*zhadnyi*) may find the small groups of wild deer very skittish and liable to bolt at the smallest sound. This idea is globally illustrated in comments on another's misfortunes that 'the land does not take him' (*zemlia ego ne vozmet*) or more ominously 'you don't find bad people on the tundra'. The perceptive man, and the good man, will foresee a successful hunt by dreaming of a woman (sometimes offering a gift) during the nights preceding the hunt (cf. Vasilevich 1969: 232).

Context: A drunken evening in Vitia's *balok* following the unexpected visit of the Russians from the nearby meteorological station.
Vova: Let me tell you this . . . listen . . . I know it's not modest – but if it is a true story modesty does not figure – right? . . . That time up on the *tengkal* it was that night – I saw it from a dream. I knew that it would be that day. We went up between the mountains. Just coming over the rise they were just standing there. Two wild ones [*dikie*]. I knew they were for me [*dlia menia*]. I shot my gun. BAM!! They both fell one by one.

The use of a possessive construction in this passage is quite common in Evenki hunting narratives. Appropriation here is signalled in an imperative mood – as if this opportunity was so suitable as to be predestined. The sense of suitability is reinforced in other stories through the maxim 'it is a sin [*grekh*, *odie* (Ev.)] not to take'.

It is tempting to focus upon this possessive aspect of suitability as an example of primal acquisitiveness – but this would be taking the moment of the hunt out of its context of obligations and proper treatment of the harvested prey. There are limits on the harvesting of animals, even if they are not codified in the explicit manner that wildlife management agencies prefer. Vova, the master of our caravan, liked to speak of the 'law of the tundra' (*zakon tundry*) whereby the hunter never took so many animals that lone animals were left by themselves ('things should be in pairs'). Taking is also regulated by certain responsibilities. This is best illustrated by the respect shown for the meat taken from the land. The taking of wild meat was always acknowledged through 'feeding the fire' (*kormit'*) or through making a gift directly to the land (*podarok zemle*). The bone marrow from the wild deer's femurs was often fed to the home fire, who occasionally speaks as an authoritative witness to the hunter's future.[2] At the site of a specific kill, especially if it is known that there is a *shaitan*-rock or *shaitan*-idol nearby, some shells, coins or buttons will be left on the ground or thrown out on to the land.

The images of the 'giving land' or of 'animals giving themselves' are commonly quoted to identify a special moral economy of circumpolar societies and of hunting societies generally.[3] Colin Scott (1989) captures this idea as a 'root metaphor of reciprocity' which he argues is common to many hunting societies and is at odds with industrialized ways of knowing the land. However, Khantaiskie Evenkis describe the hunting of animals as 'taking' and not as 'animals giving themselves'. Although reciprocity with the land was an important detail for the hunter-herders of Number One Reindeer Brigade, the possessive aspects of their stories were mediated more commonly by the emphasis on 'knowing as taking' than by the idiom of gifting. This difference suggests a way for anthropologists to identify a concept of appropriation which is rich in themes of reciprocity without being politically naive (cf. Woodburn's discussion of the politics of 'demand sharing' in the preceding chapter).

Although informants do not distinguish different types of 'taking', it may be useful to explore two contexts in which it is invoked in order to illustrate the broad usage of the term. The first is the 'taking' of knowledge. Among the many things that the old man Sergei Sergeevich mercilessly taught me was the childish refrain 'when they give – take it; when they beat you – run' (*kogda daiut – vozmi; kogda b'iut – begi*). For a long time it struck me as odd that this refrain was sung by him as I groaned in exasperation while my sled was completely unpacked and retied before me (since it was 'all wrong') – until I realized that in fact I was not being beaten but being given something. If I asked to be taught to harness a reindeer I would be presented with a lightning-fast performance of the task without any explanation. More than once the eldest son, Vitia, would mutter that at my age he just had to be shown something once for him to know it.

Another context of 'taking' is the taking of opportunities that the land offers. This can occur when the animal signalled in a dream confronts the hunter out on the land. It may occur when a large and coveted fish, such as a salmon (*kumzhe*), is caught.[4] Opportunity might be evoked in contexts often thought to be controlled closely by people. I was loudly derided when my lasso fell short of capturing a pernicious bull who ran in a very accurate and predictable fashion between me and a bluff of trees ('How can you not take him – he was coming to you!'). When the director of the collective farm opened the farm warehouse, the brigadier exhorted everyone to take everything they could get. I find the idea of knowing an appropriate opportunity nicely illustrated in the intense interest that hunters find in card games like *tysiacha* or *duraki* when highly valued trump cards are triumphantly played (and the events of play are remembered and reworked to prove that someone 'did not play right' or 'did not take the right card'). In all of these contexts – contexts which might often be seen to be controlled by 'chance' – the *pastukhi* of Number One Reindeer Brigade read a sense of opportunity that is realizable only by the person who knows when and how 'to take'.

These two contexts of taking represent not only moralistic stories of how one should behave. They also stress the interaction of the land's providence with the hunter's whole memory of technique and skill, which he took from others around him. The overlap of biography, awareness and a generous landscape accounts for the drama of the hunt, as in the following exchange:

Context: During a blizzard in February, I was asked to read out an account of the hunt of the wild deer from my fieldnotes.
D. A.: Today the tasks of the camp were set aside in favour of a hunt of deer. In the morning Vitia said that we would catch special reindeer. I asked Vova what he meant by special reindeer. I was told that you need special 'alpine reindeer' with short legs in order to go up high [laughter – this turns out not to be true]. We spent several hours chasing very strong *khory* [male reindeer] and tying them to harness. There were four reindeer on each sled but Vova had only cows.
Kolya: No, no, there's too many words there [*boltaesh*]. It's not like that. You should write something like this: 'You sit and drink your tea. You eat a piece of bannock. [Long pause.] You have no thoughts of the trail ahead. Drink some more tea. There's no rushing. [Pause.] You sit and drink slowly. Then you stand up. You put your knife on and look out through the door. Get up without

rushing and ... and then you go out.' See? That's all you need to say.
Vova: You should write that down. That's very good.

Although Evenki accounts of hunts are not nearly as wordy as my renditions, these stories – especially when they employ possessive constructions – can be best understood as claims of entitlement. Entitlement is understood here as being a more subtle and personalized relationship to land than that which is generally codified as a 'right of common access' or a 'right not to be excluded' let alone an 'individual or privately exercised right of use' (Macpherson 1978). This complex notion of a personalized entitlement can be approached through a reinvigorated concept of 'property', 'value' or of 'distribution', along the lines suggested by Hann in his introduction to this volume. However, to grasp the subtlety of the idea, the anthropocentric language of rights and relationships must be refashioned to work within a sentient ecology where wild deer and the land itself watch and judge the activities of the hunter. The significant social world of the *pastukh* is not the distant and regimented institution of the state but a perhaps stricter social community of kinsmen and animals. By placing animals and trees into a social context I am not implying that for the Evenki hunter they are the same as human persons. However, the competent hunter is aware of the fact that while he tries to know both the animals and the land, the animals and the land also come to know the hunter. If the language of rights stands for a set relationship between an individual and a narrowly conceived human institution of property, the aspect of entitlement in a sentient ecology refers to set understandings in the reciprocal action between human persons and other non-human persons.[5] The emphasis here upon a reciprocal way of knowing – and upon the role of knowledge in legitimate relationships of 'property' – has the dual advantage of allowing us not only better access to the ideas of Evenkis but also a novel path for exploring the meaning of other types of appropriative action in very different agricultural or industrial contexts.

### Gathering intelligence

Knowing how to use the land and how to maintain a proper relationship with the sentient persons that one may encounter are necessary skills for gaining an entitlement to land for a *pastukh*, but this does not encompass the entire spectrum of social appropriation within the state farm. Although its legal status has been uncertain in recent years, the herdsmen of the Number One Reindeer Brigade are still considered to be authorized employees of this quasi-state enterprise. As such, they are obliged to coordinate their actions and movements with those of other producers of food and fur and of statistical accounts. The officials within the state farm still present proprietary claims on the produce and the productive activity of herdsmen and other employees. Their claims are enforced through a different way of knowing: that of intelligence-gathering.

The history of intelligence-gathering on the extensive lands of the Lower Yenisei Evenki predates the consolidation of collective farms. In 1928, the Moscow-based Committee of Mutual Assistance to the Peoples of the Northern Frontier passed a resolution calling for the formation of discrete and bounded territories upon which the native peoples of Siberia could be contacted, serviced and enlisted in the elaboration of an industrial division of labour (Skachko 1930: 22–3). The need for such boundaries and executive attention arose out of a strangely prescient crisis in Siberian development. The early Bolshevik slogan 'All Land Belongs to the People!' had inspired an aggressive land-grab by Russian peasants and urban opportunists who saw themselves to be more deserving 'people' than the backward 'proto-people' they were displacing (Skachko 1930: 15–17; Berezovskii 1930: 74, 77). In addition to 'protecting' the native peoples of Siberia – people who were held to possess a precious yet rough-cut communalism – the campaign for territorial formation led to the establishment of the first surveillance posts upon the tundras, which were used to gauge and guide the development of native people. In the Lower Yenisei Valley, Territorial Formation Officers were sent on research expeditions between 1928 and 1934 to study the habitual patterns of land and water use of mobile Evenki, Nenets, Enneche, Sakha and Ngo households. The primary goal of their research was to identify the physical and habitual channels of economic and political power by locating the stationary nodal points where mobile hunters and herders would return in order to trade, fish or to encounter friends and relatives. The maps of economic gravitation produced by these early fieldworkers resemble a spider's web, where a trading post or Tsarist tribute warehouse lies at the centre of long, straight rays which reach out to grasp the most isolated pasture. On the basis of these studies, sites were chosen for the first state trading posts, collective farm offices, party or trade-union cells, boarding schools, nursing stations and cultural clubs. There is a striking contrast between the intelligence gathered to draw these maps and the relational ideal of 'knowing the land'. In place of the proper, personalized relationship of a person to the land and its animals, gaining intelligence of the forces of economic gravitation within arbitrary territories focused upon locating the sites from which the engagement between people and the land could be most easily counted and managed. Although the process of 'collectivization' in the late 1930s is often cited as the decisive divide separating traditional and industrial modes of production in the former Soviet Union, the practice of territorial formation in the late 1920s seems to have left the most lasting marks on local ideas of economy and of property. If 'knowing the land' respects the moral demands of a sentient ecology, intelligence-gathering respects only the political ecology of production quotas and five-year plans.

The distinctive flavour of social power created by intelligence-gathering has been much analysed in the literature. An early analysis termed it a 'command economy' (Rostow 1960). Later, dissident Hungarian philosophers Feher *et al.* (1983) captured this social form with the cumbersome but evocative phrase 'dictatorship over needs'. The term 'economy of shortage' was devised by János Kornai and adapted for anthropological use by Katherine Verdery (1991). All three of these concepts invoke symbolic or 'superstructural' attributes to contribute to the explanation of the puzzling rules of motion of a state socialist economy. The analysis of immaterial things is often the key element for understanding actually observed appropriation. Perhaps property and power under state socialism are more eloquently captured by a term which describes what administrators and producers actually do: gather accounts and undertake surveillance. Although commands, forced distribution and unplanned shortages might signal to a Western observer that these economies are different from a capitalist market economy, most actors in socialist and post-socialist economies tend to talk about appropriation using a rhetoric of 'connections' or of 'mafias'. As Verdery describes in chapter 8, it is the people who 'know' how to sell things and how to move things (and most importantly how to work with paper) who are making profits from the transition. Gathering intelligence is a powerful appropriative act.

A remarkable structural feature of intelligence-gathering as a mode of appropriation is its relative independence from the state socialist economy which engendered it. Although the new economy of the Russian Federation is supposed to be emulating some kind of 'free' market principle, this field of social interaction, where buyers and sellers encounter one another, is pitted with obstacles of distance, poor communication and a lack not only of commercial credit, but often of paper money as well. The post-socialist market of the Russian Federation is being built upon vastly uneven terrain, where those individuals who know how to move goods and how to find buyers enjoy a monopoly over trade not unlike the 'command' position enjoyed by their state socialist forebears (Anderson 1994). Some of the most knowledgeable gate-keepers to the marketplace are those who gained their experience as intelligence-gatherers – like the director of the state farm at Lake Khantaiskoe. During my research, many producers were no longer legally obliged to sell their goods through the state farm. However, the ever resourceful director was able to use his influence among the bush-plane pilots, the administrators of the Noril'sk nickel plant and the Department of Agriculture to continue to control the terms of trade. Valuable fur, ranging from the Taimyr Arctic fox to the coveted Yenisei sable, kept flowing through the warehouses of the state farm due to the director's monopoly on fuel, spare parts and even humanitarian assistance.[6] Although, in a formal sense, this director should have been able to control the fur hunt and its trade through his position at the head of an impoverished but still intact state farm, his most important possession was not his legal title but his dual intelligence – of goods circulating outside the territories of the farm, and of the goods that could be surrendered within the farm's arbitrary but very real boundaries.

Within the state farm there are more blatant forms of property in land which, having evolved within the state ethic of intelligence-gathering, can now be seen as the foundation of a new form of exclusive tenure. Collective forms of economic activity were already somewhat archaic in late Soviet times. From the beginning of the 1970s, when many dispersed collective farms were consolidated into specialized complexes known as state farms, agricultural ministries all over the Soviet Union began to experiment with forms of 'socialist' individual land tenure. When the Khantaiskii state farm was established in 1969, it was immediately restructured to support a number of exclusive employment positions such as 'state fisherman' or 'state trapper'. These well-paid and well-supplied professions were often distributed upon the basis of nationality, since the highly technologized tasks of the fishermen were thought to demand a higher level of education and civilization than locals could offer (Anderson 1996a). Russians or Ukrainians who were hired as state fishermen or state trappers would be licensed to use a fixed production point within the territory of the farm. This centre of individual economic action was literally called a 'point' (*tochka*). It was designed to function like a model of the state farm inscribed within the activity of a single authorized producer – a modelling which was no doubt thought to make surveillance more efficient but seems instead to have nurtured an individual and exclusive form of intelligence-gathering.

A typical *tochka* was a numbered location on the map of the state farm territory which contained a large log or plywood cabin with a two-way radio station (tuned to the single authorized frequency), a large collection of equipment ranging from outboard motors to snowmachines and electrical generators, and an outhouse with a Russian sauna. Employees with permission to reside on a *tochka* were authorized to harvest all fish and fur from one territory between their residential point and a formally fixed boundary. Crossing this boundary was thought to be both unethical and potentially dangerous, since it could enrage the holder of the neighbouring *tochka*. In exchange for these exclusive rights, the *tochka*-holder was obliged to 'surrender' a certain quantity of the fur or fish caught to the state farm. In exchange for this 'tribute', the state farm in Soviet times supplied transport, clothes, ammunition, fuel and a not unreasonable pay-cheque. Perhaps most importantly, the holder of one of these exclusive locations was granted the lucrative luxury of solitude. Although the *tochka* concept was designed as a regulatory tool to facilitate the gathering of intelligence about the numbers of animals harvested from the land and to prevent any individual from harvesting animals without entering into a contract with the state, in practice it was based on mutual trust and culpability. On a two million hectare farm buffeted by gale-force winds for most of the winter, large oversights in enforcement allowed individuals to harvest furs and to trade them informally for goods or for cash without much difficulty. Thus when seen from the point of view of the producer, the *tochka*, with its scrap-lumber walls and log steam bath was a 'black hole' within which one could both enjoy autonomy and profit from the state's lack of capacity to police its territories (Shmelev and Popov 1990). However, 'the state' was represented locally by a very human director who was also concerned about managing his accounts and surveillance system. The outcome was that the state trapper and the director would usually 'give each other their due' (*ia tebe – ty mne*). The director could not afford to lose a good hunter by being too strict with his regulatory powers, so a hunter or fisherman could generally trade informally within reasonable limits beyond his quota to the state. The fact that, even after the collapse of subsidized payrolls, the director of the state farm continued to receive applications for the position of state hunter, illustrates the lucrative promise of exclusive access to state farm territories.

### Post-Soviet privatization

Thus the territory of the state farm encompasses the possessive performances of seasoned hunters and herders, the intelligence-gathering of state farm administrators, and the more exclusive forms of land occupation practised by *tochka* hunters. In the Soviet period these different modes of engaging people with land coexisted, with only *tochka* tenure threatening to upset the social compact. The agricultural forms of 1990 set the jural stage for a struggle between these ways of knowing the land – a struggle which now seems to be a zero-sum game. Since 1990 both Evenki reindeer herders and Russian newcomers have met the challenge of the privatization reforms by seeking ways to escape the surveillance of state farm administrators through establishing more exclusive forms of relationship to the land. Local Evenkis, be they herdsmen or state hunters, wished to maintain the territory of 'their farm' in one unfrac- tured but nationally homogeneous whole. Russian newcomers have unsuccessfully petitioned for private tenure of their particular *tochki*. Some Evenkis and Dolgans who were not born within the territory of this state farm toyed with the idea of group tenure of 'open term leases of land' (*perevod zemlii na bessrochnoe pol'zovanie*). No one advocated open and unbounded use of all tundra lands. Whether the future was envisaged through exclusive individual tenure or through nationally homogenous common territories, the common point of departure for all claimants was some form of fidelity to a bounded, authorized space. This was in essence the idea that the Soviet state had tried so ardently to cultivate since the initial territorial formation campaigns of 1929. However, the aim of the would-be reformers was to displace the state intelligence-gatherers, either as individual frontiersmen or kin-based collectivities.

Although the herders of the Number One Reindeer Brigade were most distinctive for their flexible yet strict ideal of attaining an entitle- ment to land through a proper possessive performance, both young and old members experimented with the rhetoric of exclusive tenure. When confronted with the knowledge that one newcomer family had laid claim to a small portion of land around a lake traditionally associated with the brigade, the experienced brigadier of the Number One Reindeer Brigade did not conceal his anger:

The talk about privatization is just greed. Already I heard on the radio that those Ukrainians were shooting down on [Lake] Delamakit. Shooting on the tundra! . . . But it's wrong too that [this family] is asking for land. This is our land. I have travelled all over this land. If they try to take it from us I will fight for it.

The rhetorical resistance to attempts by this particular household to gain private lands can perhaps be dismissed in terms of jealousy. However, I interpret statements of this type as a different kind of rhetoric which points to a growing consciousness of the benefits of belonging to a consolidated territory. This statement implies a claim of 'aboriginal right': the right to a territory deriving not from a personalized entitlement but from a life invested in a certain place.[7] This 'right' is not necessarily subject to a proper possessive performance before sentient animals or kinsmen but is framed instead as a sense of civic belonging (Anderson 1996a). This sentiment of 'our' land or 'our' state farm is one that is framed by the collectivized boundaries of this unstable state institution and dissipates beyond its boundaries. Finally, there are also practical and technical considerations which necessitate the defence of an integrated territory – although none of these aspects were spelled out explicitly to me. In the case of the proposed privatization of the lake shore, the ire of the brigadier was no doubt raised by the memory that he had taken his herds across that land in the past and would presumably want to do so again. Access rights over allocated territories were easily negotiated within a state farm which, despite its administrative distortions, nevertheless represented a common community of interest. Such access agreements would be more difficult to arrange with freehold farmers who would be jealous of their territories.

Newcomer *tochka* hunters tended to lobby for more classically exclusive allotments where one individual would be the 'master' (*khoziain*) of a discrete bounded territory, with no formal obligations to any other authority. To this end, a group of nine newcomers incorporated a 'Union of Hunters' in 1992, which produced a ringing Manifesto calling for absolute private property of their production points (see appendix). In the words of one of the instigators of the union:

Everything you see here – this cabin, this stove – all of this I have built with my own hands with materials that I have had to find or bring here. The farm helped a little, not much. Mostly I have good friends who helped. Sometimes a helicopter flies by and leaves me some fuel. I sometimes keep a [fur] skin around to give to them. Why shouldn't I own this land? For instance the other day a helicopter just landed on the hill outside of my cabin. They didn't ask me. They were just sitting there. If this was my property I could just pick up my gun and shoot at them!

While the aggressiveness of the attachment that this newcomer hunter feels for 'his' land is hopefully rhetorical, his most concrete goal is summarized in point four of the manifesto. A conspiratorial silence should shroud the activities of private tenure-holders, in order that they may help each other avoid the intelligence-gathering activities of the state middlemen who for the time being still have a claim on their lands.

Although these various proposals for exclusive tenure suggest a new form of appropriation, as of 1997 they have only been weakly implemented. In particular, petitions from the Union of Hunters have been twice rejected by the state farm authorities and the land-use administrators in the city of Dudinka. These functionaries are skilled in the old school of state administration and as such may have a deep aversion to private tenure. However, their caution may be based in other factors. A flexible form of common land tenure conditionally called a 'state farm' still allows multiple points of access to land for many different types of person. More pragmatically, most political actors in Taimyr are aware of the amount of land which has been rendered unusable by heavy-metal pollution from Noril'sk. This issue raises the odd prospect that a two million hectare farm may not have enough land for extensively oriented Evenki herders and newcomer fishermen and trappers. Finally, the upper echelons of the civil service in Dudinka, which is notable for drawing its cadres from the ranks of Nenetses and Dolgans, may be cautious about releasing land 'to the people', as happened in the early days of the revolution. The free anarchy of appropriation by Russian peasants and frontiersmen led to violent rebellions all over Siberia and especially in Taimyr.[8] The 'ambiguous' policy of allowing multiple rights of access to land in Siberia can thus be seen not as an anachronistic feature of a chaotic command economy, but as a creative attempt to harmonize different and potentially conflictual models of social practice.

## Conclusion

Anthropological analyses of the concept of property have tended to focus upon the question of whether or not recent Western models of exclusive appropriation enjoy universal validity. As the contributions to this volume illustrate, in order to understand property in a cross-cultural context (or even within the Western tradition itself) one must locate this social relation within broader networks of power. This case study of multiple modes of appropriation within a rapidly changing social context supports a broad interpretation of 'property' but it also calls for a nuanced study of different categories of the person and of how appropriation is effected. Evenki notions of appropriation suggest that in order to understand the legitimate entitlement of a person to land, one must consider how that person attends to the landscape. A proper Evenki entitlement reflects not only a lifetime of contact with a territory but a proper way of knowing all the sentient persons on that landscape. This relational idea encourages anthropologists to move beyond an anthropocentric notion of 'property relations *between humans*', and to consider property in an ecological frame which recognizes the agency of other than human persons. In this light, the slogan 'All Land Belongs to the People!' loses some of its powerful simplicity.

'Knowing the land' as an Evenki may at first seem to be the antithesis to exclusive ways of apprehending land as 'a thing'. In this chapter I have tried to show how the radically exclusive rhetoric characteristic of current privatization initiatives in Russia is consonant with ways of knowing land generally. Claims to exclusive tenure can be shown to have arisen with the state socialist period, specifically through *tochka* and brigade styles of tenure in the 1970s, but also more generally through the distinctive state socialist approach to 'intelligence-gathering' devised by bureaucrats in the 1920s. Rather than suggesting a monolithic 'command economy' or an 'economy of shortage', a state built on intelligence-gathering suggests that power can be won through the capacity to monitor and define those persons who have an entitlement to appropriate. Knowing how to sell things through one's connections, it turns out, is no less valuable in the post-Soviet period. In many respects, appropriation through knowing represents an important continuity across the divide of 1990. There is, however, one significant difference. The innovation of Soviet statecraft was an institutional model which allowed different 'ways of knowing land' to coexist through multiplex (or 'ambiguous') rights of access which left every human person (and other sentient beings) entitled to a stake in society. The post-Soviet land reforms, stressing exclusive tenure, have had the effect of entitling only those who know how to reach the marketplace. The defensive reactions of Evenkis to these new operators are demands for ownership of exclusive spaces, which are presently bounded against their reach by Chinese walls. Although it is difficult to foresee what the future will hold, as of 1995 these exclusive claims to territory were not articulated in the language of individual freehold property but instead in an equally aggressive language of nationalism ('All Land to Evenkis!'). It is an open question as to whether, under the severe pressure of forced privatization, the security of a nationally stratified sense of belonging will give way to an individualist citizenship regime.

   Understanding property as a way of knowing not only allows us to understand how the clamour for private spaces in the former Soviet Union arose out of a seemingly stable hegemony, it can also help anthropologists to specify notions of property which are both inclusive and politically astute. The language of 'sharing' and 'reciprocity' in hunting contexts has often been used in the literature as a foil for making utopian critiques of Western property relations. However, open access to 'take' from the land need not be seen as an act of enlightened altruism when that act of appropriation is understood locally as an enskilled entitlement. As with recent conversational analyses of the Australian Aborigine concept of the 'dreamtime' (Povinelli 1993), 'knowing as taking' should be seen as a shrewd and politically astute way of managing a complex environment. Although this Evenki case study lends itself to a rather pessimistic conclusion, people who share 'the common' need not always have to face the dire choice between disappearing as a people or emulating the language of exclusive access. The rhetorics of knowing and dreaming overlap at some times with surveillance in a privatized state economy but at other times with the disciplines of animal behaviour and urban planning. An invigorated concept of property can help anthropologists along the paths of exploring these hopeful connections.

### Appendix

*Manifesto of the Union of Hunters of Khantaiskoe Ozero (1992)*

Those individuals who want to preserve their humanity (*chelovecheskoe dostoinstvo*) and to be masters on their trapline (*uchastok*) have entered into the Union of Hunters with full responsibility for their actions according to their good sense (*zdorovaia smysl'*) and these laws:

1. Live and work as if you will be here forever. The economic success of our work is directly related to an ecologically exploited trapline.
2. Having been asked for help ... help out! Each of us could wind up on a hard spot.
3. Ownership is inviolable (*neprikasnovenna*). The first task is to remain within the trapline and the natural resources spread out within its boundaries.
4. Be able to keep a secret. You may speak with whomever you choose, but do not compromise the interests of the members of the Union of Hunters.
5. The programme of privatization of traplines is the necessary foundation for the preservation of the interests of the members of the Union of Hunters. Private property in land is the path to freedom!

# 4      Property and social relations in Melanesian anthropology

*James G. Carrier*

Chris Hann is correct when he says that property is not an issue that excites a great deal of anthropological interest. Certainly this is the case in the anthropology of Melanesia, my concern in this chapter. While the published work on the region deals with a range of topics, property has never loomed very large. The area of interest that seems to be closest is land tenure. Frequently, however, that takes the notion of property in land for granted, and concerns itself instead with kinship and the practicalities of social relations (e.g. Crocombe 1971; Lawrence 1955, 1984: ch. 3).

The topic that most anthropologists outside the region associate with Melanesia is probably exchange. This was, after all, the focus of Malinowski's *Argonauts of the Western Pacific* (1922). Exchange is also the most plausible claimant to the status of premier topic within Melanesian anthropology itself. Perhaps spurred by Marshall Sahlins' (1963) paper laying out the big-man system, a form of leadership based on exchange, the 1970s and 1980s saw an impressive number of works on the topic. While this wave of interest had many sources, it was triggered partly by a growing awareness that the lineage model that had been imported from African ethnography could not explain the structure of the societies of the Highlands of Papua New Guinea, a region that became open to anthropologists only in the 1950s (Barnes 1962). Increasingly, anthropologists came to conclude that exchange was important (see A. and J. Carrier 1991: 8–22). While ethnographers initially linked exchange to group formation, as a substitute for the discredited concept of patrilineal descent, they soon began to see it as being of great importance for understanding Melanesian societies more generally. Indeed, it became so central to anthropological interpretations of the region that one commentator in the middle of the 1980s could say that 'exchange itself is the central dynamic' of Melanesia, apparently without feeling the need to argue the point (Whitehead 1986: 80).

This flourishing of interest was concerned with the way that exchange was implicated in the formation of social groups. It therefore had little direct bearing on the notion of property. However, since around 1980, studies of exchange have shifted their orientation to a different question: the way that exchange is implicated in social identity and relationships. This is most prominent in the writings of Marilyn Strathern, whose *The Gender of the Gift* (1988) is probably the most widely cited work in the Melanesian anthropology of this period.

While the focus remained exchange, the change in orientation brought the topic closer to conceptions of property. Anthropologists increasingly investigated the ways that objects or things (in the extended sense) are associated with different people in different settings. After all, when people exchange, they pass objects back and forth and the owner-ship of the objects changes by the act of exchange. In addressing the ways that people identify and relate themselves to one another through the giving and taking of things, the literature on exchange necessarily includes, even if only obliquely, information on Melanesian notions of property.

My purpose in this chapter is to explore some of the things that the exchange literature can tell us about notions of property in Melanesia. I do not, however, intend this chapter to be a survey of the pertinent anthropological literature. It is too vast. Instead, I mean to draw out and illustrate one of the central conceptions of relationships between people and things. Briefly put, that conception is that Melanesian societies are characterized by an *inclusive* notion of property, wherein an object is embedded in and reflects durable relationships between those people implicated in its past. This attribute is taken to distinguish Melanesia from the modern West, where property is taken to be *exclusive*, under the sole control of and associated only with the person who happens to own it at the moment. However, it is important to bear in mind that this theme of inclusive property does not emerge spontaneously from a naive contemplation of societies in Melanesia. Rather, it is motivated by the intellectual assumptions and interests that shape ethnographic per-ception and production. Consequently, I will address those assumptions and interests to show how they are manifest in the ethnographies that they inform. Ultimately this entails considering the ways that people think of property in the West.

### Gift and property

The reorientation of the Melanesian literature on exchange drew on many sources. However, the easiest point of entry, particularly for those interested in property, is Marcel Mauss's *The Gift*, an explicit point of reference for much of that literature. At the most general level, Mauss was concerned with the ways in which people understand and organize their relationships to things, especially as these are manifest in their relationships with each other.

In *The Gift* Mauss described three different types of societies, which he arrayed in terms of a continuum that is developmental and even evolutionary: archaic societies, societies of the gift, societies of the commodity. His description of societies of the gift draws on material from Melanesia and it attracted attention from anthropologists of the region. Gift societies are dominated by groups that are constituted by kin. In them, kinship defines people and their relations to and obligations towards each other. Just as people are defined in terms of their relationships with others, so are things, with the result that people and objects are, in important ways, inseparable. This link between people and things is apparent in Mauss's discussion of the 'spirit of the gift', the Maori *hau*, probably the best-known and most debated part of *The Gift* (Parry 1986: 462–6; Sahlins 1974: ch. 4). In this famous passage Mauss (1990: 11) relates the words of Tamati Ranaipiri, a Maori, as reported by the ethnographer Elsdon Best. To paraphrase what Ranaipiri said: if a person gives me an important item that I then pass on to another person, and if that other person then repays me with a different item, I need to return that different item to the first person, because it contains the spirit or essence of what the first person gave me. If I fail to do so, 'serious harm might come to me, even death'.

This passage points to a fact that is central to anthropological interpretations of the way that Melanesians think of property. Objects are not considered abstractly, as neutral things; neither are they defined solely by the power that their current possessor has over them, in the manner of exclusive conceptions of property. Instead, the previous possessor has a claim on the object and its fruits even after it leaves his or her possession, a claim that, if denied, can even result in death. In other words, here objects are invested with a durable relationship with those who possessed them in the past.

In the case of important items, this relationship can be contained in the histories associated with the objects in question. As a result of this history, the item is not just a fungible thing, an anonymous member of a class of like objects. Instead, it is unique. One type of important item in Melanesia is the valuables that are transacted in the *kula* exchange in what is now Milne Bay Province in Papua New Guinea. As Mauss (1990: 24) says of these valuables, they 'are not unimportant things, mere pieces of money. Each one has its name, a personality, a history, and even a tale attached to it.' The *kula* valuable is, then, like an heirloom, an object that bears the identity of those people and events that were part of its past. This identity can be so strong that the person who possesses the object possesses its past as well. This, says Annette Weiner, occurs with a particularly valuable type of Maori heirloom, the *taonga*. These carry not just the identity of the people and groups in their past, but their power as well, so that to gain one is to gain that power and identity. To acquire another's *taonga* 'is to acquire another's rank, name, and history' (Weiner 1992: 64).

*Taonga* and important *kula* valuables are, by their definition, extra-ordinary objects. However, the principle that applies to them applies to lesser objects as well, albeit to a lesser degree. The ordinary *kula* valuable of modest age has an ordinary history, but a history none the less, so that it carries the identity of the ordinary *kula* traders who possessed it. For more mundane items, this social identity is weaker still, but as Mauss says, when such items are given from one person to another, they 'are never completely detached from those carrying out the exchange. The mutual ties and alliance they establish are compara-tively indissoluble' (1990: 33).

As my sketch of the basic Maussian model of the society of the gift indicates, when he constructed a model of a type of exchange, Mauss also constructed a model of the relationship between people and objects, which is to say a construction of a kind of property.[1] Things are not construed solely as neutral, alienable chattels under the control of the person who happens to have them at the moment, in the manner of exclusive conceptions of property. Rather, they are inalienable, 'part of the self, somehow attached, assimilated to or set apart for the self' (Beaglehole 1931: 134). Furthermore, and because of this inalienability, they tend to remain attached to the people in their past, and especially those from whom one receives them. Here, then, the object is construed as bearing and being a part of one's relationships with others, in the manner of inclusive conceptions of property.

It is important not to idealize this Maussian construction of societies of the gift by seeing such societies solely in terms of the logic of their beliefs and values. To say that an object bears the identity of those in its past, and most notably those from whom a person receives it, is to say that the object is inalienably linked with that person. However, that link does not exist in itself. Rather, it is maintained only because people remember it and act in ways that reaffirm it. In the kind of society Mauss describes, there is no institution that guarantees memory and enforces inalienability in the way that the modern state registers and enforces types of ownership. Consequently, the link between a person and an object can be denied, and those who are persistent and powerful are likely to be able to make such a denial stick. Those who wish to maintain their links with objects of any value need to have the power to do so.

Equally, in such societies the social identities and relationships that objects embody are not valued simply for their cultural preeminence or intrinsic merit. Even those who are temperamentally uninterested in such things are obliged to attend to them, if only because they are important materially. In these sorts of societies, social rights and access to people and to resources are governed by social relationships, especially kinship and gift relations. As Mauss says, in the gift 'all kinds of institutions are given expression at one and the same time – religious, judicial, and moral, likewise economic' (1990: 3). C. A. Gregory (1982) makes the same point in a different way when he describes how, in gift societies, control of material resources comes through the control of people.

The place of this Maussian, inclusive conception of property in anthropological understandings of Melanesia is well illustrated by Marilyn Strathern, particularly in her discussion (1988: 148–65) of Lisette Josephides' *The Production of Inequality* (1985).[2] Josephides analysed exchange and gender relations among the Kewa, a society in the Highlands of Papua New Guinea. Put most simply, she argued that women's labour was crucial for rearing the pigs that were a central part of Kewa ceremonial exchange. However, she said, when these pigs were given in exchange, it was these women's husbands who decided how the pigs should be given and who received the credit and prestige of the giving. Unlike Western societies, then, where alienation occurs in the process of production, among the Kewa it occurs in the process of exchange, for it is there that women are dispossessed of the products of their labour.

Strathern rejected Josephides' analysis, arguing in effect that Josephides was using an exclusive rather than an inclusive conception of property, a Western rather than a Melanesian notion of the identity of objects. Hence, for Strathern, Josephides' analysis was culturally inappropriate. Strathern argued instead that Melanesians see things as they see people, as 'the plural and composite site of the relationships that produced them' (1988: 13). The pig in question, then, does not belong in any unitary and restrictive sense to the woman who reared it or to the man who gave it away. Instead, it 'exists as a specific combination of other identities' (1988: 159), which include the identities of those involved in its rearing. Because of this complex, inclusive identity, the pig is inseparable from the woman, so that it cannot be alienated from her when the man gives it in exchange. This reconsideration of Kewa production and exchange is itself open to criticism.[3]

However, it does illustrate nicely the distinctiveness of the conception of property that is common in Melanesian ethnography. Following Mauss, the object is seen to bear the identities of those involved in its past, which includes those from whom one received it.

I have said that anthropologists have commonly accepted Mauss's notion of societies of the gift as a basic representation of Melanesian social life, and I have shown how this contains a model of property that stresses its inclusive nature. While the Maussian approach has become dominant in the regional ethnography, the model of property within it has remained implicit. Anthropological interest has focused on exchange and its links with social identity and relationships. Property as an analytical issue in its own right has not attracted much attention.

## Ponam property

I want now to illustrate the way that property is considered inclusively in one Melanesian society. I stress that my purpose is only illustration, to provide empirical examples of the rather abstract conceptual scheme that I have laid out, and through these examples to indicate some of the limitations of the Maussian approach as it has been used in regional ethnography. The society is Ponam, the people of a small island of the same name that lies off the north-central coast of Manus Island, in Manus Province, Papua New Guinea (for basic Ponam ethnography see A. and J. Carrier 1991; J. and A. Carrier 1989).

At the time of fieldwork, roughly 1979–85, there were about 500 Ponams, of whom about 300 were resident on the island, while the remaining 200 were migrant workers or their dependants, living in other parts of Papua New Guinea.[4] As this high rate of migration suggests, Ponams were closely involved with the national economy and were heavily reliant upon it for their survival. Islanders were fortunate because migrants typically had desirable jobs that paid well, so that they were able to send substantial amounts of money home. Previously, Ponams had survived by fishing and trading within the Manus regional economy. Islanders had control over extensive areas of reef and sea, but apart from some limited subsistence production they seem never to have paid much attention to agriculture. Because the island is a sand cay, its soil had been poor even before much of it was covered with crushed coral concrete to make an air base during the Second World War.

Ponam social organization was complex enough to satisfy the most exacting ethnographer. The 500 villagers were divided into fourteen named, land-owning patrilineal descent groups, called *kamals* (*kamal* = male), themselves divided into constituent lineages and sub-lineages.

Further, each islander belonged to one of nine matrilineal totemic groups, or *kowuns*. These groups were important for regulating women's fertility and for life-crisis rituals. Avoidance of group totemic plants and animals was important for members' general health and well-being. Finally, each islander was a member of a number of cognatic stocks or *ken sis* (*ken* = base; *si* = one), descended from every ancestor who had children. These were activated primarily during ceremonial exchange, a frequent occurrence, though they were also important in recruiting assistance for any project larger than a household could undertake on its own. Of these three types of island social units, the patrilineal *kamals* were the most important for the ownership and transmission of land, my concern here.[5]

Other than areas set aside for the village church, school, cemetery and streets, Ponams used land in only two important ways. One was as a site to build dwellings, almost all of which were in a dense cluster that covered only a small part of the island. The bulk of the rest of their land was used for subsistence agriculture. Land owners planted coconut palms and gathered the resulting nuts or cultivated small patches of pumpkins. Such land was also important as a source of firewood.

Ponams said that originally their island was settled by people from the Manus mainland. In most cases islanders no longer knew the names of these settlers, where they came from in Manus or how they were related to living Ponams, nor did they really care. What islanders did care about were those ancestors considered to be the first owners of the different parts of the island. These were the men who were remembered as being responsible for the first clearing of the land and the first building of houses on it. (Women did not feature much in their tales.) These men were the ancestors who had fundamental rights in that land, to plant and build on it, to manage it and to exclude others from it, and who passed those rights on to their children. It is worth noting that the notion of right, of jural authority, was extremely important to Ponams and they frequently used the English word or its Pidgin equivalent ('rait') in their debates about who could and should be where and doing what.[6]

At various points in the past, men who owned land built men's houses for themselves and their sons and the patrilines descended from them, patrilines that were the *ke kol* (*ke* = base or origin, *kol* = place) of a particular piece of land. However, even though *kamals* were land-owning groups, they did not manage their land centrally or redistribute it to members in each generation. Instead, land passed from a father to his sons or, in the absence of sons, to his nearest male agnates. His daughters had the incontestable right to use his land so long as they remained unmarried. Once they married, each had the incontestable right to use her husband's land. The right to land could be disposed of permanently only if it were given in compensation, typically to allies who had suffered losses in pre-colonial fighting. Such transfers seem to have been rare.

However, usufruct rights, the right to use land belonging to another, could be given temporarily, and frequently were. 'Temporarily' meant until such time as the giver or his heirs revoked the gift. However, revocation was difficult, especially after a few decades had passed. Consequently, such gifts tended to be permanent in effect, though Ponams were careful to distinguish between the alienation of land in compensation and the revocable gift of use rights. The gift of such rights was heritable following the same rules as the inheritance of the unqualified right to land. Further, rights received as a revocable gift could themselves be given revocably to someone else. (This situation resembled what Macfarlane says in chapter 5 on user rights in medieval Japanese and English land tenure: see p. 119). The result, particularly in the populated area of the island, was that people were commonly using land that did not fully belong to them, and the re-granting of use rights meant that three or four granting groups could stand between those identified as the original, fundamental owners of a piece of land and those who were currently using it.

Consequently, many of those who occupied land did so, and saw themselves as doing so, only because of two sorts of social relationships that were embedded in the land itself. The first of these was the link between the original land owner and the person to whom he had granted use rights. Such grants commonly occurred in two situations. One, which effectively ceased after the imposition of colonial control in the early part of the twentieth century, was between a land owner and refugees whom he had taken in. In this case the grant solidified a relation of patronage with the recipient. The second situation, though never very common, did not disappear after colonization. Here a land owner whose daughter had married a man with relatively little land, and especially without adequate land for a house site, would grant the right to use land to the daughter, and this right would pass to her children. The second set of relationships embedded in the land linked living Ponams to these original donors and recipients of the grant of use rights. Most grants were several decades old, so that the original parties were dead. The present occupant could claim continued use of the land only through descent from the ancestral recipient.

The consequence of this granting and re-granting was that most people were not living on land that was wholly their own, land of which

they were the residual owners or *ke kol*. Rather, they were living on land
to which use rights had been granted at some time in the past. Thus, in
the early 1980s there were fifty-eight households headed by married
men or single women. In only sixteen cases, less than a third, was the
household head patrilineally descended from the person who had owned
the land three generations previously. Of course, there is no reason to
think that all of those ancestral owners were themselves residual owners.
Of the nineteen households headed by widows, in only seven was the
widow's deceased husband descended patrilineally from the ancestral
owner (J. and A. Carrier 1989: 51).

For Ponams, then, land was neither a neutral commodity nor something that was linked only with its owner. Rather, when Ponams walked
across their village they were walking across a map of social relations
that linked them to those who occupied the land and that linked the
occupiers to those who were the original owners. As might be expected,
these social relations were more visible at some times than at others. In
the normal daily round, islanders did not pay much overt attention to
the social identities and relations embedded in the place where they
were walking. Likewise, in the normal daily round, islanders did not say
much about the place on which they had planted their palms or built
their houses. However, this relative silence is not a mark of indifference.
Instead, it marks the way that their knowledge of property and its social
aspects was taken for granted.

This knowledge came to the fore on ceremonial occasions, when
people's social identities and relations were being celebrated in one way
or another. One such occasion was in the activities of intra-village
ceremonial exchange, which was invariably organized and executed by
kin groups. When, as a part of such an exchange, a group of villagers
carried a collection of gifts to the intended recipients, they did not
casually walk through the village. Rather, they were careful to walk only
where they had an undeniable right to walk. There were two such
places. One was the main streets of the village, three of which ran east to
west and three of which ran north to south. These, together with a few
other pieces of land, were public, effectively free to anyone at all times.
The other place where these villagers could go with impunity was on
those lesser paths that crossed the land of people to whom they stood in
the appropriate social relationship. The villagers carrying a brideprice
payment from the groom's relatives to the bride's would avoid the path
that went across the land of those who were much more closely related
to the bride's family than to the groom's, as they would avoid paths that
went across the land of those with whom they were in dispute or to
whom they were only distantly related. Equally, they might very well

intentionally take a path that went across land that their ancestors granted in usufruct to another, as a public statement and reminder of their relation to the land and its current occupants.

Because *kamals*, patrilineal descent groups, were the main institution associated with land, attention to property in land was pronounced in *kamal* activities. Most notable was the building of a new *kamal* men's house. The building and associated festivities were crucial for establishing the legitimate, autonomous existence of the descent group, for establishing that they really were a *kamal* and not merely a disaffected, dependent rump of another *kamal*. As a common part of the festivities that celebrated the completion of a new men's house, a piece of cloth was thrown on to the thatch of the roof. This was public recognition that the men's house was built on land that had been loaned, rather than belonging to the *kamal* itself. The cloth was collected by a representative of the heirs of the man who had loaned the land in the first place, a collection that reaffirmed the loan. This ceremony was a common feature of men's-house building because historical changes in the placement of these houses meant that almost none built after the Second World War were on the *kamal*'s own land.

Although land shows most clearly the way that Ponams located objects in a web of social relations, the same theme is visible in the collection and distribution of gifts in ceremonial exchange. The average Ponam was engaged in such an exchange about one day out of four. While these ceremonies were important expressions of Ponam self-conception and cultural values, they had a material importance as well. Erik Schwimmer (1973: 49) pointed this out in his study of the Orokaiva, of mainland New Guinea:

Westerners often criticise Melanesians for being too grasping and mean in gift exchange. Absurd though this criticism may seem, it arises from a real cultural difference: Westerners depend on institutions other than gift exchange for the acquisition of desired scarce resources. Hence the institution of exchanging Christmas presents need serve no other end but the fostering of social exchange relations. For the Melanesians gift exchange must serve economic as well as social ends.

For Ponams, much of the wealth that migrants remitted to the island was sent back as contributions for these ceremonial exchanges.

The items in an exchange were collected and distributed in a complex pattern of accumulation and dispersal. I will illustrate this pattern with only one example, the sort of distribution made by the leader of the group receiving the gift. Logically it is possible to make such a distribution in many different ways. One could, for instance, place all of the items of the gift in a heap, take each item in turn from the heap, announce who is to get it, and hand it over. Ponams, however, used a more complex system. For all but a type of distribution associated with mortuary ceremonies, the distributor would lay out the items in a series of piles, arrayed in front of the dwelling or men's house selected for the site of the distribution.[7] The distributor or a public speaker would then walk through the display and announce the name of the recipient of each pile. While this may, at first glance, seem to differ little from merely picking up one item after another and announcing the recipient, in fact there was a significant difference. The piles of items were given to those who were the prime figures in the distributor's kindred, and they were laid out in the form of a kinship diagram. Moreover, most of these prime figures were long dead, and their share of the distribution went to their living cognatic descendants (see A. and J. Carrier 1991: ch. 6). Thus, the method of distribution stressed that people received items only because of their kin relationship to the person making the distribution, who had items to distribute only because of his or her kin relationship to the person making the gift in the first place.

I have described Ponam systems of land tenure and ceremonial exchange to illustrate the ways that objects such as land and items distributed in exchange are enmeshed in and embody a set of social relationships. My intention has been only to flesh out with ethnographic examples the basic Maussian model that I described. In my illustrations I have, moreover, reproduced a key element of the way that the Maussian model is used: I have stressed what might be thought of as the jural and structural nature of Ponam property. The flurry of recent research on exchange in Melanesia that utilizes this Maussian approach attends primarily to the basic principles or cultural understandings that are said to underlie the relationship between people and things. While these principles and understandings certainly are important, the result is rather bloodless. Simply because social identities and relationships are important in shaping people's relationships with valued resources, one would expect, and Ponams themselves certainly expected, that there would be disputes about those social identities and relationships, that there would be disputes about who is linked to whom and what, and in which ways. The all-encompassing Maussian approach turns out to leave little room for such dispute.

Consider again Strathern's re-analysis of Josephides' description of the Kewa. If the pig bore the identity of the woman who reared it, then perhaps it could not, strictly speaking, be alienated from her, or from her husband or from their conjugal relationship. Further, as Strathern notes in this volume (p. 221), the woman's claim is recognized (and apparently extinguished) by the payment to the woman of a portion of pig, a process analogous to the wage given to factory workers that extinguishes the workers' claim on what is produced. However, the relatively frequent disputes between Kewa husbands and wives over the disposition of the pig suggests that wives frequently do not see things this way and are alienated from their pigs. This indicates that attention to basic cultural understandings about relationships among people and things needs to be complemented by attention to patterns of practical social outcomes. It is in these outcomes that factors more mundane than inalienability or the spirit of the gift make their mark, and so help qualify what we know of those understandings. Such outcomes have attracted less attention than the cultural understandings they seem to qualify and complicate.[8]

Certainly Ponams had an articulate awareness of the distinction between the structure of their system and the processes of its practical application and manipulation.[9] This distinction is clearest in disputes about land, which were very common. In fact any inheritance of land, granting of usufruct rights in land or repossession of granted land was almost certain to lead to a dispute. Typically disputes were at first euphemistic. Claims alleging the theft of coconuts, for example, were covert claims about who had rights to the land on which the palm tree stood. At this early stage the disputants simply quarrelled, using gossip and other techniques to try to mobilize public support. Relatively few disputes went beyond this informal stage to court proceedings, which meant the Village Court, an entity authorized by national statute to hear minor disputes and apply customary law. Because Village Courts could not hear cases about land, the province of the national Land Mediators and Land Courts, the disputes that went this far still used claims of theft as a way of disputing ownership of land without seeming to do so. Few cases went beyond the Village Court.

Disputes were sufficiently common for Ponams to recognize a set of practical factors that complemented their formal rules of gift, grant and inheritance in shaping land ownership. Their concern with rights, if you will, was complemented by an articulate awareness of wrongs. These factors can be codified. First, while sons have an inalienable right to a share of their father's land, they can be disinherited by a strong brother, paternal uncle or agnatic first cousin. Second, a land owner can face overwhelming social pressure to make or refrain from making a grant of use rights. Third, the land of someone who dies without heirs may go to the strongest near relative rather than the nearest patrilineal relative. Fourth, a strong group may be able to claim that it is the residual owner of a piece of land not actually its own. Fifth, the more distantly one is linked to a person who holds land in usufruct, the stronger one has to be to claim rightful inheritance of residual ownership of the land or to repossess it.

These practical rules speak of strength rather than formal justice. Ponams did not think that the formal rules were only for show, and that these practical rules were the real ones. Rather, they saw both as real. The formal rules were what proper people followed and what they could be criticized harshly for violating. However, islanders recognized that people are not always proper, that they are guided by self-interest as well as rules, and that power as well as justice affects actions and outcomes. The power that was important in these disputes was of three kinds. The first kind of power, and the most legitimate, was knowledge – the ability to produce good speakers who were reputable elders with a detailed knowledge of patriline genealogy and land history. Those who could not produce this sort of knowledge stood little chance of defeating those who could, if only because they would be reluctant to take cases to the level of formal dispute. The second source of power was the strength of numbers and persistence. Ponams did not regard any dispute settlement or court ruling as really final, and losing parties could re-open disputes whenever they chose. Thus, a numerous, wealthy and persistent patriline could keep up a steady stream of disputes and ultimately wear down weaker opposition. The third kind of power was intimidation. This ranged from the semi-legitimate and overt (such as ostracism, which could be very effective when used by a large group against a small one) to the highly illegitimate and covert (especially sorcery).

## Constructing Melanesia

I have devoted attention to land disputes on Ponam because they show the way that anthropological understandings of property principles, and of cultural understandings more generally, need to be complemented by anthropological attention to property practices, and to social practices more generally. These raise questions about the ubiquity of inclusive notions of property, about just what it means to say that villagers like Ponams can be understood adequately using the Maussian model. Certainly islanders understood orderly and proper land succession, as they understood orderly and proper distribution of gifts, in terms of principles that identified the objects with the previous owner or with the distributor and with the kin relationships between that person and the recipient. My point is, however, that they understood practical succession and distribution as reflecting other things as well – as reflecting forces that were shaped by economic, social or political interests that did not march easily with the principles of the Maussian model. To say that

Ponams recognized these other forces is necessarily to say that they understood property in more than one way.

These other understandings had a place in older Melanesian ethnography, particularly (and perhaps ironically) the work on exchange and group formation that preceded the shift to a more Maussian orientation (e.g. Finney 1973; Sahlins 1963; A. Strathern 1971). However, these understandings seem to have slipped from view in the 1980s, in the exhilaration of pursuing the more systemic, structural, cultural logic of the Maussian approach. This approach has been given a powerful statement recently in *Of Relations and the Dead* (Barraud *et al.* 1994). In their comparative study of exchange in four societies, the authors reiterate their concern to take a Maussian view of society, which means focusing resolutely on the structural logic of the whole of a society's system of exchanges in order to 'bring to light the values at work' (1994: 108). While they are right to argue against the utility and desirability of extreme individualist approaches (1994: 104–5), their extreme holism leads them into the sort of difficulties that I have described in this chapter. In particular, they fail to consider ways in which the idealized structure of exchange and meaning that they elicit from the field can or cannot be said to exist independently of the contingencies, strategies and circumstances that induce individuals to act in one way or another, just the sort of factors that Ponam Islanders recognized in their discussions of how the inheritance of land works in practice rather than in theory.

Certainly the more inclusive, Maussian conceptions of property did not seem to apply much to Melanesians when they were dealing with the urban, capitalist economy. The Ponam women living in Port Moresby who bought from indigenous vendors at the local food markets did not seem to see the objects they transacted as durably linked to the seller, any more than islanders who cashed a cheque thought the bank teller had a moral claim on the money that changed hands. One could, of course, argue that these are alien introductions that do not reflect the inherent logic of Ponam life, or Melanesian life more generally. But such an argument ignores the fact that Ponams, like others in Melanesia, routinely and conventionally transacted in ways that do not look terribly Maussian, as they thought about the objects that they acquired in ways that do not look terribly Maussian (see Gell 1992).[10]

An example from Manus free trade will illustrate not just the existence of such transactions, but also how differing conceptions of property were made manifest in concrete circumstances. Manus villagers had long engaged in free trade, by which I mean transactions that took place outside of the regulating structures of village markets and trade partner-

ships. Free traders were simply villagers with a large quantity of something that they wanted to sell. They would transport their wares to a
place where they thought there would be people who wanted to buy.
During the early 1980s, the typical free traders who came to Ponam
were villagers from mainland Manus carrying betel nut or bundles of
dried sago, the staple starch.

In December 1980, one young man came to Ponam with 170 bundles
of sago that he had purchased from his village church group. Sago was in
demand on the islands of the north coast of Manus, and he loaded them
on to a hired motor canoe and went to Ponam. He said that he planned
to sell as much as possible there before moving on to other islands
further east. This young man came to Ponam simply because he knew
that people there were likely to want to buy sago, and not because he
wanted to trade with kin or trade partners. He landed on a public beach,
whereas a trade partner would have landed close to the house of his
Ponam counterpart. He displayed his sago bundles on the open ground
just above the beach in front of his canoe, each bundle with a price
clearly written on it. He sold to anyone who wanted to buy, and did not
appear to give special discounts to anyone. During the afternoon and
night he spent on Ponam he sold all of the sago. To do so, however, he
lowered his prices twice, partly because Ponams complained that the
sago was too expensive, and partly, he said, because he felt sorry for
Ponams, who, as fishing people on an island with poor soil, had no food.

What does this event tell us about Ponam conceptions of property?
First, the mere existence of free trade indicates that these villagers
engaged in transactions that did not conform to the Maussian model,
but instead resembled the sorts of impersonal buying and selling, the
transacting of fungible equivalents, that occurred in the urban, capitalist
economy. While many islanders knew this young man, they did not
transact with him as a relative in a relationship of mutual obligation and
identity. Second, this event shows how the understanding of transactions
and objects can be a source of disagreement and conflict, with one party
claiming and the other denying that the object transacted is inclusive
property, embedded in and expressive of a social relationship.[11] The free
trader said that his initial prices were fair, but that he lowered them out
of pity for hungry Ponams. He was asserting, then, that his lower prices
meant that he was trading in light of a social bond between himself and
Ponams, in which he gave and they benefited. Ponams, however, dis-
agreed. They said that his initial prices were too high, that they were not
suited to a neutral exchange of equivalents. Ponams were correct to a
degree, as his initial prices were high compared to the common price of
sago in the market between Ponams and their mainland market

partners, though they were not high in comparison to the price prevailing in the cash market at Lorengau, the provincial capital, four hours away by motor canoe. Ponams saw no need to be overly generous with this man, no kinsman of theirs, and bought little of his sago. It was only after he lowered his prices twice that islanders thought that they were getting a fair price in a transaction that bound neither party to the other.

I do not mean by this example to argue that islanders routinely engaged in totally impersonal trade of anonymous objects. In fact, in the pre-colonial period free trade required kin relationships, for only they could provide the safety that free traders needed if they were to travel and trade away from home. However, free trade existed then, as it existed at the time of fieldwork, and it was distinguished from most other forms of transaction precisely because it amounted to the exchange of equivalents between people with no durable links to each other or to the objects that they transacted. Here, unlike ceremonial exchange and trade partnerships (though not unlike market trade), the thing that the purchaser bought had no significant social identity. At least in relation to the seller, it was the buyer's exclusive property, rather than inclusive.

The argument I have put forward in this section brings me back to a point I made near the beginning of this chapter, that the Maussian theme of inclusive property in Melanesia does not emerge from the naive anthropological contemplation of societies in the region. Rather, it reflects the assumptions of the anthropologists doing the contemplating. One cluster of assumptions concerns me particularly – those that stem from an apparent desire to treat Melanesian societies as exhibiting a common essence, one that is defined in its opposition to a conception of modern Western societies that is equally essentialist. My concern reflects what I see as anthropological Occidentalism, a concept that draws on Edward Said's (1978) arguments about Orientalism. I have discussed this in detail elsewhere (1995b), so here I will sketch the argument only briefly.

A key element in Said's *Orientalism* is that Oriental Studies scholars tended to construe the Middle East as a uniform and timeless region that was both radically separated from and radically different from the West. The Orient became something like a mirror image of the Occident as those scholars understood it. While Said took pains to argue that the resulting construction of the Middle East is incorrect, he did not attend to the accuracy of scholars' constructions of the West, the Occidentalisms that exist in dialectical relationship to their Orientalisms. In my view something similar has happened for Melanesia, and I have looked particularly at the image of the West that ethnographers of Melanesia invoke. These twinned anthropological Orientalisms and Occidentalisms are particularly apparent in the Maussian rendering of exchange in Melanesia, and so are pertinent to my arguments in this chapter.

It is important to remember that the Maussian society of the gift is not a neutral description based on ethnographic evidence. Rather, Mauss developed and presented it as part of a scheme that was intended to lay out key differences between the modern West and societies in other times and places. Mauss was hardly the only social scientist to undertake this project, which seems to have been almost ubiquitous in the early periods of sociology and anthropology. Likewise, those studying Melanesia are not the only modern anthropologists to make use of such a tactic. It is also notable among, for example, South Asianists, including those who have influenced Marilyn Strathern (e.g. Marriott and Inden 1977 and especially Dumont 1970, 1977; on this aspect of Dumont's work see, e.g., Fuller 1989; Macfarlane 1992/93; Spencer 1995). But this oppositional stance produces the same kinds of distortions that so exercised Said.

Thus, ethnographers in Melanesia have been reluctant to investigate the sorts of transactions that I have described in this chapter that do not fit the Maussian model. Consequently, they find it hard to consider the implications of those transactions for their rendering of Melanesian understandings of the relationship among people and things. For example, the authors of *Of Relations and the Dead* say that 'exchanges are all activities in the course of which something is seen to circulate' (Barraud *et al.* 1994: 5, emphasis omitted), yet the two descriptions of Melanesian societies mention no activities that seem other than strictly traditional and alien. Likewise, when Marilyn Strathern wrote an article about marriage exchanges for *Annual Review of Anthropology*, she said her task was 'understanding the role of exchanges in items other than persons when these items are part of or move in conjunction with transactions (such as marriage) conceptualised as exchanges of persons' (Strathern 1984a: 42). However, she made no mention of money, a key item of exchange in much of the region, and so could not consider the ways that Melanesians might understand money, the ways it is transacted and the relationships in which it is acquired.

This Orientalist construction of Melanesia takes the form it does partly because the region is understood in terms of its distinction from an Occidentalist understanding of Western societies, one that reduces them to impersonal commodity transactions and a wholly exclusive view of property. This is not the place to review the voluminous work that indicates that transactions in the West are not so uniform as this essentialist rendering indicates (see Carrier 1995b: 88–94), though it is pertinent to note that little of this work has been produced by anthropologists. Suffice it to say that when anthropologists concerned with exchange in Melanesia created models of the region, their models were shaped by understandings of the West that 'ignore exchanges and productive activities concerned with non-commodities' (Davis 1973b: 166). Thus, the basic Maussian distinction between gift and commodity systems can be seen, without too much exaggeration, as a surrogate for an essentialist simplification of the distinction between the modern West and Melanesia. Although it makes scholarly work more elegant, it distorts the rendering of each area.

## Conclusions

While anthropologists may seriously exaggerate the ubiquity of certain sorts of transaction and certain social identities of objects in Melanesia, they have produced a substantial body of descriptions and analyses that bear clearly, if indirectly, on concepts of property. As I illustrated with my discussion of land and exchange in Ponam society, the Maussian model provides a good summary of the way that many Melanesians think about objects and social relations in many situations. Likewise, the Occidentalist rendering of the West that is part of the Maussian model points accurately enough to the ways that many Westerners transact and think about objects in many situations. And even if the model does lead to an oversimplified view, it has had the virtue of encouraging scholars to investigate a set of issues and processes that are important for the understanding of property. As these comments indicate, I am not arguing that the distinction between gifts and commodities should be abandoned, as Arjun Appadurai (1986) suggests. Rather, I think it should be applied with greater sensitivity.

In particular, I think that the main shortcoming of the Maussian Melanesianists lies in their assumption that 'gift' and 'commodity' apply to entire societies and even regions despite Chris Gregory's point (1980, 1982) that those studying the region need to attend to both gifts and commodities. When the idea that Melanesia is a gift system is taken for granted in the influential anthropological literature, it tends to become self-sustaining. It comes to define what is authentically Melanesian, what is worthy of anthropological attention, and so indirectly defines what is inauthentic and not worth consideration. The result is something that André Béteille (1990: 490) identified in Indian studies – a 'shift from the fieldview to the bookview of society, culminating in the assignment of a privileged position to traditional structure over contemporary reality'. Put bluntly, the Ponam reality of free traders, trade stores, wage labour, bank accounts and all the rest gets swamped by the traditional structure of the Maussian society of the gift.

More sensible, I think, is a disavowal of the essentialism that has accompanied the Maussian model in Melanesian anthropology. Certainly most people in Melanesia are more likely to transact and think about objects in gift terms more often than are most people in the West. However, this observable difference in degree should not become the scholarly assertion of a difference in kind and quality. Melanesians have commodities and exclusive property just as surely as Westerners have gifts and inclusive property, a point made recently in slightly different terms by John Davis (1996). We ought, then, to be cautious about investigating the logic of Melanesian gift systems, just as we ought to be cautious about investigating the logic of Western commodity systems. We ought to be cautious until we spend more time investigating a prior question, one that is raised by Maurice Bloch and Jonathan Parry (1989) in their discussion of different transactional orders. That question is: when and under what circumstances do people in a given society transact objects in a web of social relations and think about objects in inclusive terms, and when do they transact objects impersonally and think about objects in exclusive terms? While such an approach doubtless has its disadvantages, it has the prime advantage of making scholars more open to the diverse forms of property that exist in the societies they study.

# 5    The mystery of property: inheritance and industrialization in England and Japan

*Alan Macfarlane*

'Well! Some people talk of morality, and some of religion, but give me a little snug property' (Edgeworth, cited in Goody 1962: 284).

## The mystery

In one way or another most of the great social theorists have seen the development of individualized property relations as the central and decisive factor in the rise of modern civilization and, in particular, capitalism. The link was apparent to Locke at the end of the seventeenth century (1956: 43, 48, 63). Private property was a natural right and the sole purpose of the state was its protection. The security of property was likewise seen as the basis of liberty and wealth by the eighteenth-century political economists (Millar 1812: 114–15; Kames 1796, I: 91; Smith 1976: 415). Nineteenth-century theorists continued to stress the central importance of property distinctions. De Tocqueville (1956: 184) noted that wealth and private property seemed to be connected in England. Maine thought that 'we are indebted to the peculiarly absolute English form of ownership for such an achievement as the cultivation of the soil of North America' (1875: 126). Tönnies believed that the opposition between private and communal property was the essence of the distinction between *gemeinschaft* and *gesellschaft* (1955: 75, 60). But it was, of course, Karl Marx who most famously emphasized the connections. In his earlier philosophical notebooks he outlined how the history of the growth of landed property mirrored the growth of capitalism (1973: 107, 252; 1964: 27). Then in a central passage in *Capital* he argued that 'The legal view . . . that the landowner can do with the land what every owner of commodities can do with his commodities . . . this view . . . arises . . . in the modern world only with the development of capitalist production.' 'Modern' private property is seen as an essential feature of 'capitalist production'. Marx argues that capitalism institutes modern, freehold property, thus 'transforming' feudal landed property, clan property, small peasant property (1974: 3, 616–17). It is his work above all which has led writers such as Mann to talk of 'that single universalistic, diffuse set of property power relations we know as capitalism' (in Baechler *et al.* 1988: 18).

These views of the nature and importance of private property have continued in the twentieth century. Anderson (1974: 424–9) sees the development of private property as central to the origins of modern capitalism. Jones stresses, as Locke, Kames and others did, the necessity for security of private property for economic growth. He suggests that: 'Economic development in its European form required above all freedom from arbitrary political acts concerning private property' (1981: 85; cf. 93, 165 for the contrast).

It thus seems clear that the development of secure private property has had immense consequences. But how and why did it emerge? It is here that the mystery lies, for as yet there has been no satisfactory explanation for this puzzling phenomenon.

For those who speculated most deeply on the subject from the middle of the eighteenth century the puzzle could be solved by some version of a *necessary* development or evolutionary *tendency*. For eighteenth-century thinkers, the sense of private property was both innate and justified. It was a seed present in all primitive societies which would finally grow into what had emerged in favoured parts of north-western Europe. Kames believed that 'Among the senses inherent in men, the sense of property is eminent' (1976, I: 86). Locke had written that the origins of property rights was in labour: 'As much land as a man tills, plants, improves, cultivates and can use the product of, so much is his property' (1956: 17). Adam Smith echoed this: 'The property which every man has in his own labour, as it is the original foundation of all other property, so it is the most sacred and inviolable' (1976: 136). The writers of the second half of the nineteenth century inherited this concept of the inevitable and natural evolution towards private property. Maine originally developed his famous ideas of the movement from communal to individual property in *Ancient Law* (1890: 244 ff.). He gave this flesh in his later works. Yet, despite all his wide-ranging speculation, he was not able to provide a solution to the mystery. He sensed that the growth of new views of property was somehow linked in the West to the developments after the fall of the Roman Empire, and in particular the development of feudalism, a system which 'had somehow been introduced into the Western world by the barbarous conquerors of Roman imperial territories' (Maine 1901: 149). Morgan likewise accepted an evolutionary view, arguing that the concept of private property was absent in the simplest societies: 'commencing at zero in savagery, the passion for the possession of property, has now become dominant over the human mind in civilized races' (1877: vii). It was Marx who most powerfully expressed the sequence. His evolutionary views of a movement from 'tribal' (communal) through 'ancient' (communal and state), to 'feudal' (or estate) to capitalist private property, with some odd exceptions such as the 'oriental' (Asiatic) and 'slavonic' are scattered throughout his voluminous writings. The important point is that for Marx there is no real *puzzle* insofar as we know that this movement, which gradually made the unit holding property both smaller and more individual, both happened and *had* to happen. Even Weber, with all his realization of the peculiarities of the West, does not help us much in understanding how private property emerged beyond suggesting that 'money is the father of private property' (1961: 179) and that new property relations were somehow linked to the rise of cities in the West.

While such an approach allows the mind to rest from the task of explaining the emergence of private property, there has been increasing awareness of anomalies in the paradigm. One of these was recognized by both Marx and Weber. If there was this natural tendency, why had most of the world's population managed to avoid it, namely all those who lived outside the charmed circle of north-western Europe and America? As information increased, it became apparent that the natural progression had *not* happened in most of Africa, Asia, the Pacific, Eastern Europe and elsewhere. This could not be satisfactorily brushed aside with talk of the 'stationary' Asiatic mode of production.

A second difficulty was the discovery by historians and anthropologists that the simple sequence along a continuum from 'communal to individualist' property, most notably suggested by Morgan, was mistaken, or at best a half-truth. Of course, as many anthropologists have documented, concepts of highly individualized, absolute, property tend to be absent in many tribal societies. Indeed, as Gluckman wrote, in such societies in relation to ownership of land 'it is too simple to talk of them as marked by either communism or individualism' (1965b: 41). Some of the evidence for the complex situation in 'simpler' societies was summarized by Lowie. He reported, for example, that in the Torres Straits, 'Every rock and waterhole had its owner, the only common piece of common land being the village street' (1929: 216), and went on to add that a parent 'may deprive any of his children from a share in his estate' (*ibid.:* 232). Lowie effectively attacked the idea of 'primitive communism', though he admitted that collective ownership was indeed common (*ibid.:* 196 ff.). Later Forde emphasized what every anthropologist now knows: that private property is to be found in the very simplest hunter-gatherer groups (1946: 15, 29; cf. Woodburn, chapter 2). A similar undermining of a straight evolutionary path had been effected by Maitland. He showed that private rather than family ownership was characteristic of Anglo-Saxon England, which maintained 'the most absolute individualism' (Maitland 1921: 340, 346–7, 353).

The most interesting and wide-ranging recent theories put forward to explain the development of private property have been those of Jack Goody. Among the theories he considers are the following. He first draws attention (1977: 19) to the connection already noted by Morgan between individual property rights and a particular kinship terminology (Eskimo), which isolates the nuclear family. Secondly, Goody suggests that there may be a technological factor: the presence of the plough. He suggests, noting an overlap with an earlier theory of Vinogradoff, that the development of ploughing seemed to encourage private land owner-ship as land rather than labour became the scarce resource (1977: 6, 20, 33). A related argument put forward by Goody concerns the importance of population density. He notes an absence of individual rights in land where population is light, as in sub-Saharan Africa, and the reverse in Europe (1971: 29). More recently, Goody has added two further arguments. The first concerns the role of the Christian church, which protected individuals against the pressures of their family from the eighth or ninth centuries, and hence encouraged the idea of individual ownership of property (Goody 1983). Finally, there is a set of arguments concerning the effects of writing. For instance, Goody suggests that 'literacy permits or encourages' among other things the accumulation of landed property. More specifically, he argues that 'Writing was used to record personal loans . . . but in no area was it of greater importance than in registering title to land' (1986: 19, 79).

All these points seem to provide necessary but hardly sufficient or determining causes. They may explain why private property did *not* develop in oral, lightly populated, hoe-cultivating societies, but when faced with the vast variations of property arrangements in Europe and Asia, the argument has to become more complex. Some of the difficul-ties of finding any correlation between population density and the forms of property, for instance, were pointed out long ago by Sorokin (1928: 395–6), and it is not difficult to add to his counter-instances. Many parts of India or China, for example, had very dense populations, use of the plough and a stratum of *literati*, yet they were not notable for their development of individualized property. All they lacked was cognatic kinship, but it is difficult to see how this can be the *cause* of the difference, particularly if we even half accept Leach's famous suggestion (1961: 305) that 'kinship structure is just a way of talking about property relations'. How are we to proceed further? The classical theories are unsatisfactory and the major twentieth-century theories, as synthesized by Goody, are clearly only a beginning. Let us start by looking at what Marx and others considered to be the earliest and classic case of the development of private property and its association with capitalism, namely England.

## The case of England

England is an extreme case, though there are some striking similarities with Holland. I have already dealt with the subject at length elsewhere (Macfarlane 1978, 1987: chs. 7, 8). I have argued that the widespread view that a revolutionary change in property relations took place in the sixteenth to eighteenth centuries, for the first time creating modern private property, is far too simple. The medieval situation was long ago outlined by Maine, who suggested (1901) that the basic move to private ownership occurred in the later twelfth and thirteenth centuries. The central change was from concepts of divisible to indivisible property. By the application of the principle of primogeniture not only to the nobility but to ordinary people, 'a wholly new conception of landed property had arisen' (1901: 344). He even suggested an ingenious theory to account for the change, which incorporates political pressures, cattle raising and growing population pressure and hence an increase in the value of land (1901: 346 ff.). What Maine saw very clearly was that the growth of the conception of a particularly strong property in land was intimately associated with feudalism. What feudalism did was to substitute contract for status, in other words it placed artificial and political relations rather than blood relations at the centre of the social structure. Maine believed that the 'link between Lord and Vassal produced by Commendation is of quite a different kind from that produced by Consanguinity'. Without the destruction of the smaller kinship groupings, 'we should never have had the conception of land as an exchangeable commodity' (1875: 86–7). Marx picked up this hint when he wrote that 'feudal landed property is already essentially land which has been disposed of, alienated from men' (1963: 133).

Maine's insights were given precision and documentary support by Maitland. He showed that at every level by the thirteenth century, while recognizing the distinction between seisin/possession and property/best right (Pollock and Maitland 1923, I: 146; II: 29 ff.), strong property rights were very widespread. Ordinary tenants, holding by customary tenures, also had strong rights. 'We can produce no text of English law which says that the leave of the lord is necessary to an alienation by the tenant' (1908: 29). Thus there was freedom of alienation at the lower levels of society by the thirteenth century. Even those who were supposedly 'unfree', the serfs, could hold property and dispose of it almost as they wished. 'In relation to men in general, the serf may have land and goods, property and possession and all appropriate remedies' (1923, I: 419). Hence it is not surprising to find that the 'plea rolls of Richard's reign and John's are covered with assizes of novel disseisin, many of which are brought by very humble persons and deal with minute parcels of land' (1923, II: 48).

In terms of *freehold* land, by the thirteenth century, English law was grasping Bracton's maxim '*nemo est heres viventis*' (no one is the heir of a living man). As Maitland summarized the situation:

Free alienation without the heir's consent will come in the wake of primogeniture. These two characteristics which distinguish our English law from her nearest kin, the French customs, are closely connected . . . Abroad, as a general rule, the right of the expectant heir gradually assumed the shape of the *restrait lignager*. A landowner must not alienate his land without the consent of his expectant heirs unless it be a case of necessity, and even in a case of necessity the heirs must have an opportunity of purchasing' (1923, II: 309, 313).

Thus children had no birthright from the thirteenth century onwards, they could be left penniless. Strictly speaking it is not even a matter of 'disinheritance'; a living man has no heirs, he has complete seisin of property. As Bracton put it, 'the heir acquires nothing from the gift made to his ancestor because he was not enfeoffed with the donee' (1968: 66). In effect he has no rights while his father lives, they are not co-owners in any sense.

In my earlier work this was as far as I was able to go. All I could show was that a peculiar individualistic form of land tenure was present in England by the early thirteenth century and that this is linked to England's later development into industrial capitalism. While this may help to explain why it was, as Wittfogel observed, that 'there emerged out of the womb of feudal society one of the strongest forms of private property known to mankind' (1957: 84; cf. 417), it only deepens the mystery and pushes it further back in time. We are still left with problems of both origins and causes.

It would be possible to pursue several further lines of argument. The first concerns the question of whether Maine was right to think that there was a revolution in the late twelfth century. Was this a complete transformation, or was it one of a series of changes which had started to occur much earlier? There has for a long time been a belief that there was something odd about the concepts of property of some of the Germanic peoples who settled in parts of Europe after the collapse of the Roman empire. This was a point made by Montesquieu in the mid-eighteenth century when he wrote that 'In perusing the admirable treatise of Tacitus *On the Manners of the Germans* we find it is from that nation the English have borrowed their idea of political government. This beautiful system was invented first in the woods' (1949, I: 161). As Montesquieu went on to observe, the Germanic system as described by Tacitus was one of absolute individual property. There was no 'group' which owned the land, and hence no idea that the family and the resources were inextricably linked. In his description of the Salic law he stresses that it 'had not in view a preference of one sex to the other, much less had it regard to the perpetuity of a family, a name, or the transmission of land. These things did not enter into the heads of the Germans' (1949, I: 283). This point was taken up by Marx, who noted the basic difference between the Germanic mode of production and the Asiatic (1964: 75). Likewise Weber noted (1961: 25) some of the tendencies towards private property, primogeniture and the exclusion of younger sons in old Germanic laws. It is thus not surprising that Maitland found no evidence of family property or communal property in late Anglo-Saxon England. Property was in the hands of the individual (1923, II: 247; cf. 1921: 340, 346, 353).

The problem can now be restated as follows. If much of north-western Europe was colonized by peoples who had a rather unusual property system and if this combined with the insecure conditions of conquest to create a form of feudal civilization which laid the foundations for the later emergence of full-blown individual property, why, by the late seventeenth century, was England so very different from most of the rest of Europe? When did the trajectories of England and the continent diverge, and how great were the differences?

In Macfarlane (1978) I give evidence to suggest that both English and foreign observers had noticed a wide divergence of property law and social structure back to about the fifteenth century. The major differences lie in the area of primogeniture, freedom of disposition and the expropriation of 'peasants', that is the severing of the land from the family, which is often thought to have occurred in the late fifteenth and sixteenth centuries. Yet the greatest of legal and social historians, Maitland and Bloch, see the basic differences as present earlier, going back to at least the thirteenth century. Under the heading, 'A great and sudden change', Maitland notes that 'our law about the year 1200 performed very swiftly an operation that elsewhere was but slowly accomplished. Abroad, as a general rule, the right of the expectant heir gradually assumed the shape of the *restrait lignager*. A landowner must not alienate his land without the consent of his expectant heirs' (1923, II: 313). England took another line and allowed free alienation. This was linked to a difference which Bloch had noted going back even earlier, namely that 'In the England of the Norman kings there were no peasant allods' (1962: 248). In other words, all land was ultimately held from the crown. The allodial system was later the basis of peasantry. As Bloch realized, from the second half of the twelfth century the agrarian structures of England and France were different (1967: 58–62). It was this difference which led all over Europe to the institution of small landed peasant family properties, in contrast to the case of England.

Thus by the end of the twelfth or early thirteenth century there were already signs that something unusual was happening on parts of this island. But there were many other parts of Europe which probably still resembled England. What then seems to have happened is perhaps best described as an *absence*. Something did *not* happen in England which happened over the whole of the rest of Europe. Elsewhere a tide turned and brought all the varying property laws into a uniform and different system. This was the 'reception' or re-introduction of Roman law, which basically suppressed what was remaining of the more individualistic Germanic customary systems.

As the legal historian Baker writes, 'Within Europe . . . England was and has remained to this day an island in law' (1971: 28; cf. 11 ff.). It preserved through the fact of its island position an unusual legal system. The importance of this in conserving and extending the concepts of individual property is only apparent if we look briefly at the major differences between Roman law and common law concepts of property. Maine wrote that:

Nothing can be more singularly unlike than the legal aspect of allodial land, or, as the Romans would have called it, land held in *dominium*, and the legal aspect of feudal land. In passing from one to the other, you find yourself among a new order of legal ideas . . . no subversion of an accepted legal notion can be more striking than that of the Roman (which is the developed allodial) view of land as essentially divisible by the feudal conception of land as essentially impartible (1901: 342–3).

He sees what he terms 'this great revolution of legal ideas' (*ibid.*: 345), as allowing a far more flexible and ultimately capitalist view of property to emerge.

The difference has been well summarized by Stein and Shand. They note for example, that the Roman law tradition 'reflected in the Codes of France, Germany, Switzerland, Italy, and even the Soviet Union', tends to identify ownership with the thing owned, and to limit its definition of things to movable or immovable property, as opposed to more abstract rights. The common law, on the other hand, has developed from the tenures of medieval feudalism and has been more ready to analyse ownership in terms of bundles of rights, obligations and interpersonal relationships arising from the control and enjoyment of property (1974: 216). The common law system is a far more flexible system and the one needed for capitalist endeavours. They note that 'the resulting flexibility has enabled the common law to accept more easily than civil [Roman] law systems such abstract rights as copyrights, patents, shares, and options as forms of property' (*ibid.*: 217). The absence of private property rights in traditional Roman law is shown, for example, in the fact that 'adult descendants unless formally emancipated from the power of the *paterfamilias*, could own no property in his lifetime' (*ibid.*: 116).

## English concepts of property

This discussion takes us into the heart of a question which I have hitherto left on one side, namely what *is* property? All I want to stress here is the well-known anthropological point that property is ultimately a relationship between people in relation to 'things'. As Gluckman put it with regard to tribal society, 'Property law for tribal society defines not so much rights of persons over things, as obligations owed between persons in respect of things' (1965b: 46). This definition of 'property' follows that famously outlined by Maine: 'The rights of property are, in the eyes of the jurist, a bundle of powers capable of being mentally contemplated apart from one another and capable of being separately enjoyed' (1876: 158). Distinctions may be drawn between hereditary and acquired possessions, movable and immovable property, and so on (1890: 281, 283). But behind these stands the much deeper difference which sees property as a *relation* between persons and things, as in feudal and capitalist relations, and those systems which see property in the thing itself, a form of *fetishism* in Marx's terms.

This contrast has been explored by Maurice Bloch (1975), who found among the Merina a concept of property as a 'relationship between people and things', in contrast with the neighbouring Zafimaniry, who saw it as 'nothing other than part of the many rules which regulate interpersonal relations'. Bloch works with a binary distinction. He suggests that modern societies, like the Merina, misrepresent property as a relation between a person and a thing, whereas, as Gluckman, Goody and other anthropologists have stressed, 'the notion of property as a relationship between a person and a thing is a contradiction in terms'. In contrast, Marx and Engels realized 'that property is represented by ideology as a relationship between people and things but is in material terms a social relationship' (1974: 204–5). In fact, of course, property is a three-way matter: that is, a relationship between people in relation to a 'thing'.

Part of this difference can be seen in a preliminary way if we contrast Roman and common law concepts of property. Roman lawyers saw *the thing* as property and it could be divided almost *ad infinitum*. Thus a piece of land could be divided and sub-divided among heirs again and again. Feudal lawyers on the other hand saw the *thing* as indivisible, but the rights in it, that is the relationships between people, the bundle of social ties between people and resources, were almost infinitely expandable. The difference is partly caught in Maine's observation that 'there is no symptom that a Roman lawyer could conceive what we call a series of estates – that is, a number of owners entitled to enjoy the same piece of land in succession, and capable of being contemplated together' (1901: 343). Once one has this idea of *relations* in a thing, it becomes easier to treat these interests as temporary and relocatable. The thing *itself* is not altered, but people merely buy and sell rights in it. As Marc Bloch described it, 'Medieval law in contrast with Roman and modern notions of landed property conceived the soil as being subject to a great number of real rights differing among themselves and superimposed. Each of them had the value of a possession protected by custom (*saisine*, seisin, *Gewehr*) and none was clothed with that absolute character which the word property carries with it' (1935: 206). What happened was that this peculiar system was stripped of some of its overtones and *became* that private property whose essence, as Marx notes, was the right to sell and alienate (1974: 101).

Thus feudal lawyers had a very flexible and realistic view of property. Yet, by a strange process, the more flexible the system became, the more it began to appear that *the thing* was the property. Property relations became 'mystified', as Marx, Maine and others later reminded us. Ultimately, under capitalism as under feudalism, property is a power relationship. As Marx noted, 'property signifies a relation of the working (producing) subject . . . to the conditions of his production' (1964: 95). That relation was one of people to each other in relation to a 'thing', and it is necessarily a political relation. This is the heart of the mystery of the growth of private property. The Goody arguments took us some way, suggesting some of the background features which would *condition* this power relationship. The problem is that these conditions applied over much of Western Europe from the fifth to the nineteenth century, and yet property systems varied enormously. At a gross level it may be true that all of Western Europe had a property system different from that found in the rest of the world. But at a deeper level the difference between the capitalist system that emerged only in particular parts of

Europe, and in particular in England, needs explanation. The explanation must be found not in technology, kinship or Christianity *per se*, but in these in combination with a particular and unusual set of power relations.

The essence of the feudal property system in England lay in the particular relations between the crown and the people, in other words in the tenurial structure. The central fact is that the property of subjects is most secure and developed when the ruler is strong but not too strong. Let us consider the extreme cases. In a situation of total fragmentation, that dissolution of the state which is how Bloch (1962: 214, 443) describes French feudalism, the leaders are unable to prevent the workers of the land from appropriating *dominium* – allodial rights. This is what happened over much of Europe between the eighth and the thirteenth century. The centre was weak and families built up the basis of family rights to inalienable peasant holdings. England avoided this extreme situation. But then, as the power of the state grew towards absolutist governments, the reverse difficulty arose. The 'reception' of Roman law went hand in hand with absolutism to undermine the security of the property of the citizen. As Davis summarizing Pizzorno puts it, Roman law is designed to protect the power and property of the state against the citizens, while English common law is the reverse (1977: 102).

Wittfogel recognized the central point that 'in addition to being a legal and social institution, property is a political phenomenon' (1957: 228). It was all a matter of the balance of power. 'Strong property develops in a societal order which is so balanced that the holders of property can dispose over "their" objects with a maximum of freedom. Weak property develops in a societal order that is not so balanced' (*ibid.*). Speaking of the contrast between Western, feudal-type societies which he calls 'stratified', and the absolutist societies which he equates with 'hydraulic' agriculture, Wittfogel comments that 'In a number of stratified civilizations the representatives of private property and enterprise were sufficiently strong to check the power of the state. Under hydraulic conditions the state restricted the development of private property through fiscal, judicial, legal and political measures' (1957: 78). He then asks, 'Why were the feudal lords of Europe able to buttress their landed property to such an extraordinary degree? Because, as indicated above, in the fragmented society of Medieval Europe the national and territorial rulers lacked the means to prevent it' (*ibid.*: 83).

We may understand this better if we remember de Tocqueville's recognition of the need to keep a balance between too strong or too weak a state (1968: 98). What is needed is a state that is strong enough to guarantee order and to protect property, and not to give in to the pressure to relinquish too much power either to the great lords or the peasant families. The 'dissolution of the state' is not a good basis for modern private property which is ultimately underpinned, as Locke and his successors recognized, by powerful, if largely invisible, state power. This is evidenced in that 'due administration of justice', peace and easy taxes which Adam Smith thought were the basic prerequisites for the wealth of nations (cited in Stewart 1854, V: 68).

On the other hand, if the state becomes too powerful, as it tends to do over time as its revenues build up and it makes heavier and heavier demands on its citizens in the name of 'protecting' them against internal and external enemies, then property is again threatened, this time by predation from the state. This is what happened increasingly over much of Europe from the twelfth century until it reached its climax in the age of absolutism. But it did not happen in Holland and England. According to Landes (1972: 16), the necessary platform for economic growth included 'the growing assurance of security in one's property . . . the ruler abandoned, voluntarily or involuntarily, the right or practice of arbitrary or indefinite disposition of the wealth of his subjects'. He goes on to argue (*ibid.*: 17) that 'Europeans learned to deal with one another in matters of property on the basis of agreement rather than of force; and of contract between nominal equals rather than of personal bonds between superior and inferior'. All this did not happen in much of Europe until the nineteenth century – but had done so in England from the medieval period. It fits very well with Milsom's description of Maitland's vision of medieval property law: 'The world into which Maitland's real actions fit is essentially a flat world, inhabited by equal neighbours' (Milsom 1968, I: xlvii).

This helps to explain the puzzle which Weber tried to solve concerning the disappearance of 'peasants' in fifteenth-century England. He suggested a fruitful line of thought. 'Thanks to its insular position England was not dependent on a great national army' (1961: 129). This led, he believed, to a peculiar social structure since it was not necessary to protect the peasants as a potential fighting force. Hence they could be evicted and a new commercial agriculture and social structure could develop. But the argument can equally well be reversed. Because there was far less of an imminent threat of invasion, the coercive pressures which the king could put on his people were diminished. It is perhaps here, above all, that the answer lies, and it is worth elaborating a little on the effects of islandhood and the absence of the threat of war on the political relations of rulers and people, and hence on property.

The connection between liberty and the absence of the threat of

invasion was made in the eighteenth century by the Scottish philosopher, Millar. He placed the turning point as 1603, the unification of the
crowns of England and Scotland: 'By the union of the crowns of
England and Scotland, an entire stop was put to the inroads and
hostilities between the two countries; which, at the same time, from the
insular situation, were little exposed to the attacks of any foreign
potentate.' This meant that the crown had 'few opportunities of acting
as the general of the national forces' and was hence far less powerful in
relation to the people. There was no need to keep a large mercenary
army. Hence taxation could be lighter, and could be withheld by the
commons without immediate danger of invasion: 'the secure and peace-
able state of their dominions afforded no plausible pretence for the
imposition of such taxes as would have been requisite for keeping on
foot a great body of mercenary troops'. As a result of all this, Millar
believed, there arose a radical difference between constitutional monarchy in Britain, and absolutist governments on the Continent (1812,
III: 120–4).

This theme has been pursued by more recent historians. The only
substantial explanation given by Anderson for what he considers to be a
very short absolutist experiment in England is the absence of a standing
army (1974: 135–9). Truth may be the first casualty of war; the balance
of power upon which a constitutional monarchy rests is the second. If
there is a constant state of 'Warre', in Hobbes's sense, then people are
forced to accept 'protection' at the cost of their liberty. The sea barrier
round Britain was a necessary, if not sufficient, background feature to
the development of constitutional monarchy based on the security of
private property, freed from the predatory demands of a ruler above
the law.

If this is correct, then we have the following model. Some of the
necessary conditions for the development of modern private property
are those to which Goody drew attention, namely a productive agriculture where land has a high value, a bilateral (cognatic) kinship system,
and a monastic religion which encouraged people to bequeath their
wealth away from their families. To this we may add the development of
a market economy. All these were present across much of Western
Europe by about the tenth century. What made England increasingly
different from its continental neighbours was a peculiar politico-legal
system based on a curious form of 'centralized feudalism' (see Macfarlane 1987: ch. 8), an island of common law, and a powerful, but not
absolutist, state where the crown was ultimately beneath and not above
the law. There is one principal reason which explains both why England
was not subjected to Roman law and did not gravitate to absolutism and

the extinction of the balance between centre and periphery out of which private property grew. This was the sheer accident of islandhood.

How can we test the hypothesis? Do we know of any other large, relatively densely populated island lying off a sophisticated continent which might have gone through a not dissimilar development?

## The case of Japan

When Peter Thunberg visited Japan at the end of the eighteenth century, he found a country where 'Upon the whole, both the supreme government, and the civil magistrates, make the welfare of the state, the preservation of order, and the protection of the persons and property of the subject, an object of greater moment and attention in this country than in most others' (1796, IV: 11). It was a description which John Locke could well have written of England. How had this situation emerged?

Marc Bloch some time ago pointed out the curious similarity between European and Japanese feudalism, suggesting that the latter was of the same order as that in England (1962: 382, 446–7, 452). This was a view which has been shared in many respects by a number of other observers (e.g. Maitland 1911, III: 303). The insight was developed by Norman Jacobs in his comparison of Japan, China and Europe. The central feature was, as Maine had argued earlier, the development of primogeniture. 'In China, the mandatory institutional pattern for the inheritance of all strategic (i.e. landed) property was equal division between all the legitimate heirs; normally the sons . . . In Japan (as in western Europe), in contrast, strategic property is inherited by a single person: normally the eldest male' (Jacobs 1958: 149). This grand change had occurred in England at the end of the twelfth century, and it was roughly a century later that it occurred in Japan. It was based on the same idea – that a military leader needed to link himself to his followers. The best way to do this was to give them lands which were considered indivisible, but in which there were a multiplicity of overlapping rights. That *bundle* which Maine had described, combined with primogeniture, is exactly what we seem to find in medieval Japan. 'In Japan (as in western Europe) the conceptual rights and privileges of ownership and transfer developed concomitantly with the practical demands of the development of true feudalism, so that a new concept of private property holding and descent was created, namely primogeniture' (Jacobs 1958: 153).

The complex bundle of rights in a single indivisible unit is likewise well described by Jacobs: 'The inheritance system in the proto-manorial period of Japanese history denoted an inheritance of rights to landed property (*shiki*) but not necessarily of ownership. There was a complex overlapping of many types of rights to any one piece of property . . . Property rights could be inherited by any number of heirs' (1958: 150–1). The complex of rights has been described more recently as follows, 'Each type of *shiki* carried specific administrative authority or economic benefits . . . *Shiki* differed from modern landownership rights in being property rights to a part of the agricultural enterprise . . . an individual could concurrently hold different *shiki* to a single or several *shoen*' (Ryavec 1983: 377). This sounds similar to one element of early feudalism in England, likewise just before primogeniture became wide-spread. The same pressures seem to have led to the transition. 'There was interest in consolidating holdings, resulting from constant sub-infeudation . . . to divide property among all heirs was to invite political and economic disaster' (Jacobs 1958: 151). The *shoen* or manorial estates thus bore a strong resemblance to English manors.

This was a system with old roots. In the eleventh century, as the centralized Chinese-style system broke down, the situation was caught in the *Genji*. In describing the world of the Shining Prince, Morris notes that the society was 'ruled by an aristocracy with strong traditions of private ownership' (Morris 1969: 88). There were 'manors' and a complex system of rights in them. For instance 'The comparatively favourable position that upper-class women enjoyed in the Heian period was partly due to their privilege of inheriting or being given rights in manors, which provided them with an independence they lacked in later ages' (*ibid.*: 92). This multiple ownership has that same feel as in England. 'It was a complex system, in which no one enjoyed complete ownership of the land, and in which an individual could hold different rights in different capacities on the same manor or on widely separated manors' (*ibid.*: 90). As in England, it was a world which strangely combined a law based on oral customs with an enormous use of those literate instruments to protect contracts to which Goody drew our attention. 'The importance of the pen in this culture of the sword was truly remarkable. Oral arguments played only a small part in judicial procedure . . . Pleadings were submitted in writing, while agreements as to property and service were regularly drawn up in the form of charters, deeds and bonds' (Sansom 1962: 284).

The recent publication of the *Cambridge History of Japan*, summarizing a great deal of the recent research on medieval and early modern political and economic life in Japan, allows us to pursue these themes a little further. As in England, proprietary rights were centralized. Under Hide-yoshi, 'At the highest level, all proprietary rights became securely lodged in the hands of the national hegemon . . . This use of the concept of land held in trust for the overlord became the basis for the new centralization of power' (1991: 103). Although holding land of the shogun, the lords at the next level also had strong rights. Lordship, as in England, gave immense *de facto* power. Thus under Nobunaga, Hideyoshi's immediate predecessor, 'complete proprietorships' were developed. We are told that this 'meant that within their domains, the *daimyo*, as proprietary lords, held the right to assign fiefs, command military forces, and exercise police and judicial authority' (*ibid.*: 101). The effect of this, and the fact that it was not something newly introduced in the later sixteenth century, is shown in the fact that 'local landholders possessed legally protected entitlements to their lands, including the right to buy, sell, and bequeath their holdings. Landownership was transferable . . . In the Tokai region, small-scale private land-holders . . . could buy and sell land, expand agricultural production, and open markets' (*ibid.*: 479). What Nobunaga and his successors did was to simplify and strengthen this preexisting system.

Several authorities in volume III of the *Cambridge History* indicate a similar multi-layered feudal model of ownership to that of England. The 'organization of proprietary rights or tenurial hierarchy in the *shoen* system was complex and multi-layered' (1990: 261; cf. 264, 100). Within this system, those at the bottom technically had user rights, but, in fact, as in England, their practical power was much greater. In the early modern period the small tenants were 'given certain rights to the use of land. In a technical sense, these might be called . . . "user rights", although in actual practice they amounted to a close equivalent to what we would style ownership rights' (1991: 124). Likewise 'In the early medieval period, peasants did not hold land as private property in the true sense of the word.' The proprietor formally registered the title in the land registry and because this land was the basis for certain rents, 'peasants were forbidden to buy and sell it without permission' (1990: 329). The same description could be applied to a customary tenant on an English manor, who had to come to the lord's court to transfer his land; in practice, however, he had considerable rights in the holding. Likewise, in Japan it is noted that 'the peasants' rights to cultivate *myo* were protected, and the fields could be passed on to their descendants as heritable *myoden*' (*ibid.*: 122).

Potentially such land could be sold off. For instance, in villages near the cities of Nara and Kyoto, 'the sale of the peasants' right to possess arable land began early. This included selling land outright, using it as collateral for a loan, and, in many cases, becoming a tenant on the land as a result of debt default' (*ibid.*: 329). Land became increasingly viewed as a valuable commodity and not merely as a family entitlement. Hence,

'In the mid to late medieval period in central Japan and other nearby economically advanced areas there was a great change in the perceived value of land' (*ibid.*).

The complex web of multi-layered tenures, thought to be unique to England with its peculiar land law, also seems to be found, though with some variations, in Japan. Through a paradox which applies to both cases, the fact that all land was in theory held in a firm contractual and mutual relationship between superior and inferior made it relatively easy, in practice, to alienate the land. Ultimately, in both societies, political and then economic forces had displaced the family as the determinant of what happened to land. In most civilizations, including China, India and countries under Roman law, the first call on land is the next generation, the blood line. In these two islands the controlling interest was the lord. Such a lord could be paid off with cash, leaving the current holder free to do what he or she wished with the land in his or her lifetime, and to dispose of it by will at death. The differences between the *de jure* and *de facto* are noted by Bellah for the Tokugawa period. 'The institution of property was rather well developed. Land was inalienable in theory but by means of universal legal subterfuges this provision was a dead letter and land was in fact often bought and sold' (1957: 32).

The unusual nature of the situation in Japan becomes apparent when we compare it with China. The point is noted by Wittfogel who wrote that 'the Japanese peasants cultivated their land individually and under conditions which resembled tenancy rather than serfdom' (1957: 295). Thus 'the decentralized and property-based society of the Japanese Middle Ages resembled much more closely the feudal order of the remote European world than the hydraulic patterns of nearby China' (*ibid.*: 199). The Japanese did not, he writes, 'adopt their system of private landownership from their continental neighbours' (*ibid.*: 295). Indeed he stresses the 'persistence with which China's bureaucratic patterns of power, property and class were kept out of Japanese society' (*ibid.*: 415).

Both England and Japan had moved to the very unusual system of primogeniture early on. But what if the eldest-born male was unsuitable or quarrelled with his parents? In the English case, except in certain periods with the very richest families through entails, it was easy enough to disinherit the heir through sale or a will. There was no security even for the first born. The situation in Japan was different because it was much more important that the *ie*, or 'family estate'/'house', should continue. The Japanese were faced with a contradiction. They needed to maintain an institutional structure which appeared to be based on family farms, yet to do this using blood ties leaves one open to the inefficient and random dealings of demography and genes. They solved the problem in an unusual way, by combining *gemeinschaft* and *gesellschaft* to create 'artificial kinship'. This they did through the system of adoption.

In those societies where there is very frequent and widespread adoption, the custom is to adopt close relatives as a 'strategy of heirship', particularly brothers' sons (cf. Goody 1977: ch. 6). In Japan, however, one could, and often did, adopt anyone, including non-kin. Chamberlain described the effects of this: 'It is strange, but true, that you may often go into a Japanese family and find half-a-dozen persons calling each other parent and child, brother and sister, uncle and nephew and yet being really either no blood-relations at all, or else relations in quite different degrees from those conventionally assumed' (1971: 17). The subversion of the blood family which this caused, and the turning of the family into an artificial corporation, is well summarized by Ratzell. In Japan 'this custom, which in course of time became extraordinarily widespread, had a destructive effect of the family. This, on adoption becoming customary, sank to a corporation; and, with the admission of fresh strangers, the reputation of natural kindred grew to be an abuse' (1898, III: 497). Rein noted in the later nineteenth century 'the further right of expelling members of the family and introducing strangers into it'. He continued that 'In this way the Japanese family lost much of its natural character, and assumed the aspect of a corporation' (1884: 422). The same point was made more recently by Robert Smith: 'The frequent adoption of successors shows clearly that the Japanese household is essentially an enterprise group, not a descent organization, and that passing over a son in favour of an adopted successor for the headship among merchants, craftsmen, and artists is a manifestation of a universalistic element in the definition of the role of the household head' (1983: 89–90).

The important fact was that the apparent 'descent group', the lineage or *ie*, was not based on birth (blood) but on choice (contract). As Smith puts it, 'The widespread practice of a bewildering variety of forms of adoption involves yet another principle. People do not generally unite to form groups, not even households, but are instead recruited into them.' The major considerations, according to Smith, are 'the highly pragmatic ones of competence and availability' (*ibid.*: 90).

We can thus see why there was a structural similarity between England and Japan. Both had broken the nexus between family and land. The property relation was disembedded, to use Polanyi's metaphor. England is the extreme case. Japan is somewhat more hybrid. This was partly the result of its relations to China and perhaps the necessities of wet rice cultivation or, as Wittfogel would say, hydraulic society. Wittfogel himself gave a characterization of this mixed situation as follows: 'traditional Japan was more than Western feudalism with wet feet. While the Far Eastern island society gave birth to a property-based and genuinely feudal order, its many and cherished elements of Chinese policy and thought show that, in a submarginal way, it was related to the institutional patterns of the hydraulic world' (1957: 200). Japan, in fact, stood poised between the two extremes. Looked at in one way its stem-family system of *ie* was extremely powerful and it seems a perfect example of the attempt of all real peasantries to 'keep the name on the land'. Yet the families were truncated – only one son – and often the whole 'family' was artificial and more like a business than an institution based on blood. This odd situation may not only be explained by the needs to keep estates intact and well run by family labour, but also by developments after about 1600.

It is a curious fact that if one had looked at English and Japanese property relations and land in general in about 1400 they would have seemed very alike (see Macfarlane 1995). The deeper separation of Japan, partly geographical and partly self-imposed, allowed the Tokugawa rulers to institute a form of government which was in some respects very authoritarian. It had not moved towards absolutism, but it moved in an opposite direction from the increasingly balanced rule which obtained in England. The Tokugawa attempted to bring order and discipline to the country, to keep people in their place both socially and ritually. The property system therefore looks much more like a familistic peasant system than that of England. There appeared to be little private property in land. An individual did not own the estate, the estate owned him. As one writer put it 'The farm family consists of the fields, wealth, and heirlooms handed down from ancestors. This property does not belong to us, the living members of the family. We must not imagine it does even in our dreams. It belongs to the ancestors who founded the house; we are only entrusted with its care and must pass it on to our descendants' (quoted in Smith 1988: 205). This was the system that was dismantled in the 1860s at the Meiji Restoration. Sansom wrote: 'The provision of the new civil code by which a house-member could own, succeed to or bequeath property as an individual was a complete reversal of tradition, since before 1868 no house-member could exercise separate, personal property rights. Whatever he possessed, he possessed not as owner but by permission of the head of the house' (1950: 474). We can thus only understand the Japanese situation if we bear in mind two apparently contradictory tendencies:

the enduring presence of an apparently fixed family estate, small corporations into which people were born or recruited, combined with very considerable movement and artificiality.

We thus end up with a theory which suggests that the only way to understand property relations is to combine a series of dynamic parameters over long periods. There is no *innate tendency* in any direction, as some nineteenth-century theorists had thought. Rather the nature of that political relationship which is property will fluctuate over time as an aspect of the power and nature of the state. This is a lesson which nobody who has watched the rise and fall of communism in the twentieth century should need to be reminded of.

Nothing, therefore, was inevitable. Yet we can still see roughly what happened. It could be argued that modernity (capitalism), was very much the result of private (non-family) property, which was first and longest developed in England, which had never had 'peasant' or allodial property. Why did the 'normal tendency' towards peasantry not occur? This problem can better be understood if we look at the case of Japan, where there was a similar absence of a proper peasantry, although at a superficial glance the *ie* looks like a peasant holding. What unites Japan and England but separates them from their neighbours? It would seem to be the realm of law and politics, where on both islands there developed a peculiar form of 'centralized feudalism' and social structure. What allows this to survive and blossom, when elsewhere de Tocqueville's tendency first towards destructive fragmentation, and later towards too much political centralization and absolutism tends to occur? The answer seems to be the absence of protracted internal warfare and of the threat and actuality of outside invasions. Marc Bloch long ago suggested the 'extraordinary immunity' from outside invasions in which Western Europeans 'have shared the privilege with scarcely any people but the Japanese', which 'was one of the fundamental factors of European civilization, in the deepest sense, in the exact sense of the word' (1962: 56). England, like Japan, was the extreme case of this 'privilege' and it had, as Bloch implied, very deep consequences for political relations. The absence of invasion and the threat of invasion changes the relations of threat and power between rulers and ruled, so that a dynamic balance can be achieved and maintained between tenants and lords and, later, between subjects and rulers. There was nothing inevitable about this process; but it did happen – twice.

# 6   An unsettled frontier: property, blood and US federal policy

*Paula L. Wagoner*

For immigrant Europeans who first landed on the shores of what was to be called America, the west became a metaphor for wilderness, vacant land ready for the plough guided by a steady industrious hand and a perpetual promise of opportunity for everyone who was willing to work. Evidence of its abundance could be seen in the products of trappers' labour and heard from explorers who brought home fabulous tales of beauty and bounty on the western frontier. The land was already inhabited by Indians.[1] However, it was assumed that they would accept European religions and lifeways once they were enlightened through contact with the 'superior' European and, later, American cultures, and that the more persistent infidels could be eliminated if necessary.

In this chapter I trace the history of property relations in a rural South Dakota county, where personal and group identities have been shaped through federal policies that categorized residents by land tenure and race. These complex property relations are best understood in conjunction with longstanding social categories expressed in racial terms. 'Fullblood', 'mixedblood' and 'white' classifications divide the county along ambiguous racial lines. In times of social crisis, disputes more properly situated in issues of taxation, land ownership and shifting federal Indian policy affecting Indian tribal land are often expressed in racial terms.

## Contemporary Bennett County

Bennett County is an expanse of rolling prairie comprising approximately 1,173 square miles that supports a population of 3,206, of whom 1,151 reside in Martin, the county seat and only organized town. Residents boast about the 'breathing room' here, but the economy is weak. This rural area is kept afloat by family-operated farms, cattle ranches, federal aid to farmers and ranchers, general assistance and Indian programmes. Recent budgetary constraints at the federal level have heightened tensions between neighbours vying for limited resources. In addition, environmental, cultural and demographic factors divide South Dakota into 'East River' and 'West River' regions along the 100th meridian. East of the Missouri River lie rich farm lands and larger urban centres with a more cosmopolitan population. In comparison, West River people are marginalized. Their farms and ranches include large acreages but are limited in production capacity by land characteristics and climate. The growing state tourism industry attempting to capitalize on the 'Wild West' character of the area does not yet yield substantial income. Towns are further apart and, consequently, highway construction and road maintenance are prime concerns of smaller population centres which need to transport their goods to distant processing centres. Recently the governor of South Dakota reminded the mayor of Martin, who had been arguing for the allocation of more state highway funds for this county, about 'the golden rule': 'Those who've got the gold *rule*!', which just about sums up the county's underprivileged economic position in state politics.[2]

There are few trees indigenous to this area; most were planted to serve as shelterbelts to protect homes from ferocious winds that freely race across the northern Great Plains, once known as the Great American Desert. Due to its proximity to the sand hills on its southern border, Bennett County land is marginal for growing wheat. It is also marginal for raising cattle. An adequate living can be made from the land only if farmers and ranchers own enough acreage to compensate for its poor quality. It is not unusual for southern winds to blow sand into cultivated land one day and northern winds to blow good farming soil over grazing pasture lands the next.[3] Despite its inadequacies, this land is remarkable because of its 'spiritual geography', its ability to inspire reverence and unshakeable fidelity among residents (Frazier 1989; Hasselstrom 1991; Norris 1993).

Just as winds have mixed sand and soil here, shifting federal policies have produced unique social, cultural and racial admixtures. Red and white dichotomies and static conceptualizations of historically based social relations are inadequate. Most Bennett County residents find the categories 'fullblood', 'mixedblood' and 'white' expedient conceptualizations that avoid the problematics of histories over which they have no control. They also provide space for redefinition of social identities partially based on legal relationship to land when racialized land policies open new fiscal opportunities.

The major contemporary problem in Bennett County – a shrinking tax base coupled with escalating demands for city and county services – is made more acute by multiple types of land tenure. The greater part of the land (534,903 acres of the county's 762,798 acres) is held in deeded taxable status.[4] This taxable land base, for the most part, finances the operation of vital county services, including schools, law enforcement, fire control and road maintenance. Second, there are 194,628 acres of non-taxable land currently held in trust for the Oglala Sioux Tribe or individual tribal members by the federal government, which provides certain allocated monies to defray educational costs for Indian children whose families do not pay county taxes and to provide fire-fighting services on Indian land. Third, there is the LaCreek wildlife and wetland refuge, consisting of 16,400 acres of non-taxable federal land. A large portion of the refuge was removed from the county tax base when it was taken from Indian allottees and non-Indian tax-payers by eminent domain in 1935. Later, the government bought out a large cattle ranch, removing this from the tax base. Federal monies amounting to approximately one-third of the actual tax value are paid to the county in compensation for loss of tax revenue. Finally, scattered throughout the county are state lands set aside as school sections. While the state pays no taxes on these lands, in some instances these parcels are vacant and leased as grazing land. In such cases, the lessee is required to pay county tax.

These complex arrangements effectively split the county into factions based upon whether or not an individual pays taxes on the land. In political discussions about the wildlife refuge, the split is often couched in terms of anti-federal government rhetoric. However, in conversations about taxes the division is generally expressed in terms of race, with allusions to the competency of tax-payers and the incompetency of Indians living on non-taxable allotments or tribal trust land. A few of the non-Indian residents place the responsibility for racial tension on the federal government, but most residents do not make this connection.

How did issues of land tenure, race, competency and incompetency become so inextricably entwined in Bennett County? To answer this question it is necessary to outline how land came to be seen as a commodity and how Indian blood quantum ratios came to be used as measures of legal identity. Juxtaposing Euro-cultural notions of proper relationships to land and kin with those of the Lakotas and exploring how they have changed in historical contexts, exposes the differences in how people classify the world and how the 'Other' is constructed and perceived.

### Two ways of knowing

The main conceptual differences in the significance of land between Lakotas and non-Indians were illustrated in Bad Wound's testimony during a meeting with government agents in 1883. He argued that 'we [Lakotas] cannot even talk about [property] values, for we are ignorant of them, but we know the Great Father [President of the United States] always consults our best welfare and we trust in him' (cited in Institute for the Development of Indian Law, n.d.: 130). Lakotas valued land for providing the plants and animals upon which their survival depended. Land was not viewed as real estate to be bought or sold, but rather 'represented existence, identity, and a place of belonging' (McDonnell 1991: 1). Lakotas perceived themselves to be related to all of nature, as integral parts of the cosmos. The often-heard Lakota phrase '*mitakuye oyas'iŋ*' is glossed as 'we are all related' or 'all my relations' and refers to their sense of kinship with all things, including land.

European attitudes to land are based on philosophies of conquering and taming nature, and more specifically in Lockean conceptions of land use and individual rights. John Locke posited that land could become one's own only through labour: it is labour that gives value to land. His *Of Civil Government* provided the justification for appropriating land occupied by indigenous groups and others who did not 'use' land:

A person has a right to possess a given object [land included] if and only if (1) he labours for it or else inherits it or has it given him by someone who has laboured for it, and (2) either (a) he uses it or (b) if he does not use it, his possession of it does not prevent anyone else who could and would use it from doing so. If either of these two conditions is satisfied, then, although someone may possess a given object, he has no right to do so, and thus he does not own it. But if it is not his property, then, it must seem, others have no obligation to respect it as such and indeed have a right to take it from him and use it themselves or else give it to someone else who will (cited in Hall 1991: 5).

Writing in seventeenth-century England, Locke acknowledged that Indians in the colonies used the land, but since their labour was not understood as such by European standards, Europeans perceived virgin land ready for the plough (McDonnell 1991: 126; Cronon 1983; Smith 1978). But the Plains, for the most part, were not suitable for cultivation, at least not before the introduction of modern irrigation systems. The arid West River country was best suited for hunting large grazing animals such as buffalo. Despite that fact, settlers from the east and hopeful newly arrived European immigrants familiar with the prevailing wisdom that 'rain follows the plough' came in droves to South Dakota. They sought, through honest labour, to bring abundant fertility to this portion of the Great American Desert. Lakotas were cast as part of a wilderness in need of taming by civilized Americans and European immigrants.[5]

Property relations in Bennett County also depended on differing cultural expressions of social relatedness. Kinship based in genetics meant nothing to Lakotas, whose social relations were determined by their place within their *tiyošpaye* (extended family). Adoptions were a common method of incorporating outsiders into the social system. As long as the adoptee fulfilled kinship obligations, he or she was considered a true family member and a Lakota. Today the criteria for being considered 'Indian' are based on blood quantum ratios, originally intended as a means to break up Indian communities. One-quarter Lakota blood quantum enables county residents to be eligible to vote and hold office on the Pine Ridge Reservation and in the county government, and to receive free services provided to tribal members. In Bennett County, 'identity' is the product of both ascribed status (especially membership in kin groups) and achieved status (particularly in land tenure). While mixedbloods play important roles in the history and politics of the county, as well as in tribal politics, they are viewed locally as marginal (Daniels 1970: 213). Fullbloods perceive them as 'white Indians', sell-outs and opportunistic traitors, while whites perceive them alternately as political allies or 'just Indians'. However, mixedbloods are well positioned to make strategic decisions (e.g., whether or not to return their land into trust status) based on political, economic or more personal factors. Recently there has been a trend among mixedbloods to return deeded land to tribal trust status, thereby further shrinking an already strained tax base. Although boundaries and legal designations of real property have shifted over time, personal and group identities based on historical relations to land have not kept pace with these often arbitrary legalities. Shifting federal Indian law is perceived locally as capricious and reckless. It underlies deep feelings of distrust among Lakotas, who fear the eventual termination of their unique rights as 'domestic dependent nations'.[6] At the same time, non-Indian residents are concerned that their land might one day revert to tribal control. An examination of some of the more pertinent federal laws relating specifically to land in Bennett County reveals that there is good reason for such fears of betrayal and loss.

### Property relations – blending land and blood

Dakota Territory was one small portion of the land acquired by the United States from France for three cents an acre in the 1803 Louisiana Purchase. It was explored by Lewis and Clark on the orders of President Thomas Jefferson in an expedition that began the following year, with the aim of improving relations with Indian tribes to secure the profitable continuation of the fur trade and locating a navigable river leading to the western coast. News from the expedition fuelled the ambitions of Americans desiring to move west, some seeking to settle on small farms, others hoping to build shining 'cities on the hill' further west, and still others seeking primarily to be free of governmental control. It was not until the 1840s that fully fledged western expansion brought settlers across the Plains. However, previous encounters with primarily French and Scotch-Irish trappers and traders had already led to intercultural trade and personal relationships between European men and Indian women.

At the conclusion of the American Civil War in 1865, the nation turned its attention to ending, once and for all, the Indian wars still being fought on the frontier. The defeat of General George Armstrong Custer at the Battle of the Little Bighorn in July 1876 caused an enraged eastern population to react strongly, but not in unison. Some preferred a military solution, while others argued that Indians should be settled on reservations where they could live unmolested by the intrusions of non-Indian traders, liquor salesmen and land speculators attempting to defraud them of their land. Since the expense of the Civil War had greatly diminished treasury funds and the cost of fighting Indian wars continued to escalate, those preferring reservations won out. The entire West River country and the eastern half of what was to become Wyoming was set aside as a reservation for the Sioux by the Fort Laramie Treaty of 1868 (15 Stat. 635). It was tucked far enough away from major population centres to render Lakotas invisible to those who were filled with entrepreneurial hopes of building another New York or Chicago on the prairie (Nelson 1996). Lakotas were to be 'directed' by Indian agents in proper farming skills and 'civilized' by exposure to the Bible, brought to them by Roman Catholic and Protestant missionaries. Such acculturative processes were but the prelude to the assimilative processes that followed.

Two provisions of the 1868 treaty underlie contemporary problems of land tenure and identity in Bennett County. First, individuals who were heads of families (including non-Indian men married to Indian women at the time of signing) could choose allotments of up to 360 acres if they wished to take up farming (Art. 6). This land would then be held in severalty as long as it continued to be cultivated. In essence, the treaty enabled non-Indian men well versed in Western understandings of land to become 'Indian' in terms of access to land, annuities, health and education benefits and future Indian programmes. Second, a problem of fractionated allotments resulted. The same Article provided that 'the United States may pass such laws on the subject of alienation and descent of property between the Indians and their descendants as may be thought proper'. Later 'proper' statutory actions concerning Indian lands and heirship contributed to a further diminution of Indian land, since land was often divided among hundreds of heirs. It was reported that one heir, for example, 'possessed equities in numerous allotments, up to the number of hundreds' (Collier, cited in Getches and Wilkinson 1986: 117). Since these equities were sometimes measured in inches, they could not be used for farming or ranching and they did not bring income to the heirs. To make matters worse, such parcels could be sold only with the agreement of all the heirs, a unanimity rarely achieved.[7]

Two conceptual formulations of the 'Indian problem' existed side by side in the late nineteenth century. Zealous reformers, most of whom lived on the east coast far from the frontier, and other 'friends of the Indian' sought to 'elevate and civilize savages' by teaching them 'useful' arts. In contrast, others advocated the forceful corralling of Indians on to reservations out of sight of the tide of western settlers and those who were simply passing through the territory to find their fortune in the gold mines further west. Either way, life was changing rapidly for Lakota people who, up until a few years before, had lived a socially integrated nomadic lifestyle. Some of the reformers' assimilative solutions, intended to help Indians, actually aggravated the 'Indian problem' because of the reformers' naivety and unexamined ethnocentric notions (Hoxie 1984). According to one historian, 'even the friends of the Indian who sought to have him safely isolated on reservations knew that American expansionism, technology and racial ideology would reduce the Indian to a pitiful remnant of a once proud and flourishing people. Inexorably, the force of Darwin's natural selection decimated the Indian tribes and reduced them to pauperage' (Blinderman 1978: 17). Value-laden judgements cloaked in the appearance of sympathetic concern lay beneath much of the reformers' rhetoric.

The General Allotment Act of 1887 (Dawes Act, 25 USC ss. 31 *et seq.*) is one of the policies that grew out of the assimilationist tradition, but there were dissenters. One senator decried an earlier attempt at allotting Indian land as a 'bill to despoil the Indians of their lands and to make them vagabonds on the face of the earth' (Otis 1973: 18). Displaying both understanding of cultural difference and prophetic insight into later events, he later argued that, 'if I stand alone in the Senate, I want to put upon the record my prophecy in this matter, that when 30 or 40 years shall have passed and these Indians shall have parted with their title, they will curse the hand that was raised professedly in their defense . . . and if the people who are clamouring for it understood Indian character, and Indian laws, and Indian morals, and Indian religion, they would not be here clamouring for this at all' (*ibid.:* 18). The initial purpose of allotting land to individual Indians may have been to protect Indians by reserving tracts of land for them, but by the end of the nineteenth century the policy became a tool to break up tribal land holdings and a device for assimilating Indians into the predominant culture (Getches and Wilkinson 1986: 111). President Theodore Roosevelt, himself an advocate of westward expansion and a speedy solution to the 'Indian problem', referred to the allotment policy as 'a mighty pulverizing engine' (*ibid.*) that would rapidly break down communal control of land and place it in the hands of individuals.

The chief provisions of the Act itself were (1) a grant of 160 acres to the head of each family, 80 acres to each single person over eighteen years old and to orphans under eighteen years old; (2) a fee patent issued to each allottee, but held in trust for twenty-five years, during which time the land could not be alienated or encumbered; (3) a stipulated time of four years for Indians to make their selections, after which agents of the Secretary of the Interior would select land for them; and (4) the conferral of citizenship upon allottees and any other Indians who severed tribal ties and adopted 'the habits of civilized life' (Getches and Wilkinson 1986: 112). The conferral of citizenship was an important provision of the Act. It applied to two classes of Indians – those who received allotments, and those unallotted who earlier had voluntarily taken up 'civilized ways'. However, the Burke Act of 1906 (34 Stat. 182) amended the Dawes Act regarding the first class of Indians. The Burke Act was intended to protect Indians from 'the vices of non-Indian society by keeping [them] under federal supervision as long as necessary' (McDonnell 1991: 88), except in cases when the allottee could be deemed competent. In those cases a fee patent (deed) would be issued. Here again, implementation of policy departed from expressed intent as the Act opened the way for agents to certify competency, despite the protests of Indians who did not wish to receive fee patents.

Early Lakota signatories of negotiated treaties and agreements did not understand that Western legal traditions allow for statutory amendments and even reversals of previous laws. In 1899, when agents of the federal government came to explain further planned diminution of Sioux land through the breaking up of the Great Sioux Reservation, Lakota spokesmen argued vehemently against such plans and criticized the results of earlier treaty provisions for Sioux tribes. The Act to Divide the Great Sioux Reservation (25 Stat. 888) served several purposes, but those most relevant to this study include the division and diminution of the reservation and 'protection' from further intrusions of non-Indians, who had streamed into the area in defiance of the treaty of 1868. This

Act also facilitated the implementation of the allotment process on the divided and greatly reduced Sioux reservations.

In the final analysis, as one opponent of the Dawes Act had prophesied: 'the primary effect of the Allotment Act was a precipitous decline in the total amount of Indian-held land, from 138 million acres in 1887 to 48 million in 1934. Of the 48 million acres that remained, some 20 million were desert or semi-desert . . . Allottees who received patents after 25 years found themselves subject to state property taxation, and many forced sales resulted from non-payment' (Canby 1988: 21).[8] Sioux legal scholars have argued that allotment policy 'redirected the thrust of the federal-Indian relationship to that of property management', with all the attendant bureaucratic structures to manage Indian resources (Deloria and Lytle 1984: 5). In addition to the increased presence of the federal government on reservations, allotment policy brought enormous pressures to bear upon Indian people to renounce their tribal ties and become US citizens.

Because individually owned land was a foreign concept to Lakotas, the imposition of the Dawes Act, combined with blood quantum rationales for severalty, set the tone for the anticipated rapid assimilation of Pine Ridge Lakotas. That legislation was 'the first comprehensive proposal to replace tribal consciousness with an understanding of the value of private property. The idea was not only to discourage native habits but to encourage Indians to accept the social and economic standards of white society' (McDonnell 1991: 1). Lakotas were going to have to deal with the realities of life in the late nineteenth century and learn to think of themselves in terms of property ownership, lineal descent and inheritance laws. Ella Deloria, an anthropologist and linguist trained by Franz Boas and herself a Dakota woman, sums it up elegantly:

And it came, and without their asking for it – a totally different way of life, far-reaching in its influence, awful in its power, insistent in its demands. It came like a flood that nothing could stay. All in a day, it seemed, it had roiled the peacefulness of the Dakotas' lives, confused their minds, and given them but one choice – to conform to it, or else! And this it could force them to do because, by its very presence, it was even then making their way no longer feasible (Deloria 1944: 76–7).

Over a decade before allotment of Indian land was formulated, laws relating to the opening of the west were passed by Congress. The Homestead Act of 1862 was intended to be a remedy for overcrowded cities and unemployment, which would improve labourers' wages in the city by encouraging some people to leave them. The Homestead Act provided 160 acres of land to anyone (US citizen or immigrant newcomer) who, for a small filing fee, would agree to live on the land for five years and make improvements. After six months, homesteaders were able to 'prove up' (make the specified improvements) and buy the land for $1.25 per acre. More affluent individuals opted to buy land outright as soon as possible in order to mortgage it and buy other parcels from less successful homesteaders. The law was intended to guarantee independence to hardworking farmers. Horace Greeley assessed it as 'one of the most beneficent and vital reforms ever attempted in any age or clime – a reform calculated to diminish sensibly the number of paupers and idlers and increase the proportion of working, independent, self-subsisting farmers in the land evermore' (White 1991b: 143). Other supporters believed it 'ensured a final realization of the old paired goals that had inspired the land system: a class of prosperous small farmers whose own prosperity fed the economic development of the nation' (*ibid.*). But the Act also served to enrich eastern speculators with ready cash and time to wait for homesteaders, who were not able to make a living in the harsh climate, to fail. According to Richard White, 'in the Homestead Act, Congress above all expected the American future to duplicate the American past. Congress embedded the ideal of a 160-acre farm in the Homestead Act. It was an ideal more suited to the East than the West and more appropriate for the American past than the American future.' By the time Bennett County was opened for non-Indian settlement in 1910 and, for that matter, when the Indians received their allotments, the government was aware that 160-acre plots were recipes for disaster in this part of the country. 'Without irrigation, a quarter-section farm in the middle of the Great Plains or the Utah desert was not a ticket to independence but to starvation' (White 1991b: 142–3).

The Homestead Act differed from the Dawes Act in that after the homesteads were paid for (which could be as soon as six months) the land fell into the possession of homesteaders who could then sell it to speculators for profit or mortgage it for funds to increase their holdings. Such provisions did not exist in the Dawes Act and the later Burke Act, except when an Indian person was deemed competent and had severed his tribal ties officially or had them severed by the practice of converting his land to deeded status. Lakotas had no opportunity to build large personal estates and, all too often, lost both their land and their identity.

## The secession of Bennett County

Bennett County was carved out of the Pine Ridge Indian Reservation in 1910 and formally organized two years later. It is bordered by the Pine

Ridge (*Oglala Lakota*) Reservation to the west and the north, the Rosebud Sioux (*Sicaŋǧu Lakota*) Reservation to the east, and the Nebraska state line to the south. It is a virtual jurisdictional island, and jurisdiction is complicated – and limited – because approximately one-third of the county remains 'Indian Country'.[9] Many Lakotas still consider all but the city of Martin, the county seat and its only formally organized town, to be reservation land (Wagoner 1997: 40–1).

From the outset, it was apparent that support for opening the county to general non-Indian homesteading would not be forthcoming from the fullbloods, who were in the majority in all reservation districts.[10] John R. Brennan, the superintending agent at Pine Ridge, expressed concern that the bill was premature, since only half of the slated 7,300 allotments had been completed and it would take at least two more years to complete. He observed that 'it is not clear why there is such a hurry to open [the eastern] part of the reservation unless it is entirely in the interest of some railroad or a few settlers along the north part of the reserve'.[11] He assessed that area to be 'better than any other portion of the reservation at the present time [because] the majority of the people living on the strip are mixed bloods and are fairly industrious and self supporting, are allotted and are in possession of their trust patents' (*ibid.*). Brennan concluded that, despite their industriousness, many were not ready for citizenship.

Against Brennan's better judgement, a meeting was held concerning the opening of the reservation to non-Indian settlement in 1909. His opening remarks included an ominous message about the importance of this meeting: '[It] will probably mean the beginning of the opening of a portion of your reservation to white settlers and the beginning of the breaking up of your tribal relations.'[12] Fullbloods evaded the question of opening any part of their reservation to non-Indians, demanding a reconsideration of what they considered to be extreme abuses of the Fort Laramie Treaty of 1868. They did not see how it would be possible for them to discuss relinquishing more land when the previous treaty had been so egregiously broken.

Unfortunately, another 'white man's law' (*Lone Wolf* v. *Hitchcock*: 187 US 533 (1903)) gave the federal government the right to abrogate treaties made with Indians unilaterally, as long as it was acting in 'the utmost good faith' as guardians of Indian people (Harring 1994: 147). The substance of *Lone Wolf* v. *Hitchcock* was that 'the Government was the guardian of the Indians; that guardians have the right to do that which is deemed best for their wards and that Congress has the power vested in it to open Indian reservations without obtaining the consent of the Indians thereto'.[13] A second council was held in Allen, which lay in the north-western corner of the Pass Creek district that was slated for opening.[14] Of the eighty Lakotas present, seven rose to articulate the fullblood position. According to minutes of the previous meeting in Pine Ridge, it had taken 'one hour and a quarter' to read the bill in council.[15] Many Lakota fullbloods were not literate, and even if they had been it would have been difficult to assess completely the legal complexities in a thoughtful manner after one reading. Horn Cloud's comments reflected the lack of real interaction between the fullbloods and others in the district, except when it was expedient for the mixedbloods and whites. He added that 'The white men living on the reservation and the mixed bloods never advise us in any way but now when this thing comes up they tell us it is good for us and it surprised us. If they showed us something like this [the proposed bill] before we would understand and would be willing to take their advice now.'[16] Themes of treaty violations and resentment of the government agents' impatience ran through each response. The agent finally closed this 1909 meeting by explaining certain provisions of the bill with the ominous message that 'no matter what the decision of the Oglala Council maybe [*sic*], there is a possibility of the land being thrown open anyhow'.[17] Bennett County was created in the following year by the South Dakota legislature, further diminishing reservation land by 1,173 square miles.[18]

It did not really matter whether or not the Lakotas agreed to the opening. *Lone Wolf* v. *Hitchcock* upheld the government's power to abrogate treaties, so the decision could be implemented in spite of Lakota protests. The federal government postured an earnest concern for their 'dependent wards', while at the same time driving a wedge between fullbloods and mixedbloods. Fullbloods continued to argue for rights guaranteed by the treaty of 1868 and the return of the Black Hills. Mixedbloods attempted conciliation that might increase their prestige and power with the government. The tension between resistance to and collusion with imposed federal policy caused a rift that persists today, both in Bennett County and on the Pine Ridge Reservation.

In their new role as a cultural elite, mixedbloods had one foot in each culture. They were able to proclaim their 'competency' by virtue of owning taxable land and thereby achieving the status of United States citizens. Many were also able to gain the support of some fullbloods through their connections to their *tiyošpaye*. Although they had severed their ties to the tribe, their *tiyošpaye* did not necessarily sever its ties to them and they were able to garner some measure of political power by drawing support from a diversity of groups in certain short-term situations. However, ultimately they were marginalized from both the whites and the fullbloods. Whites still perceived them as inferior because, while 'on the road to civilization', they were always far from arriving. Full-bloods increasingly perceived them as traitors, and in no way valued their 'achievements' as a new class of 'red whitemen'. They attempted to exclude mixedbloods when filing lawsuits against the federal government for the illegal taking of the Black Hills (see Lazarus 1991).

One such mixedblood was Henry Cottier who, in his eighties, proclaimed:

I am an Indian. I am glad and proud of it. All that I am and all that I have, I am and I have because I am an Indian. Perhaps the only time I ever wished I wasn't quite so much Indian – notice I said, 'Quite so much Indian' – was when my future father-in-law was giving my future wife hell because she wanted to marry me, and I had a few more drops of Indian blood in my veins than she had (Lewis, 1980: 199).

Cottier went on to offer a theory about his distant relative, Crazy Horse, a powerful symbol of Lakota identity because of his leading role at the Battle of the Little Bighorn and his unflagging resistance to settlement on reservations:

From what my parents told me of him, there is little doubt in my mind that he is part white, like my mother. He had light brown, almost blonde hair, and his eyes were not black like the Indians, but a curious kind of brown with lighter flecks. Neither was his skin of the same colour and texture as the skin of the other Indians (*ibid.*: 201).

Cottier, while proud of being 'Indian', cast one of the most prestigious leaders of the Lakotas as a mixedblood.

As a non-Indian married to a Lakota woman and adoptee into the tribe, Henry Cottier's father became eligible for an allotment under the terms of the 1868 treaty. Cottier himself understood Western concepts of private property, land allotment and the counting and categorizing of people by race, both by virtue of his job as allotment agent and, later, as taker of the 1910 census for the South Dakota Indian population. He was typical of mixedbloods who, though having only minimal education, were hired to work for the Indian Service. After Bennett County was opened in 1910, Cottier realized that unless it was formally organized before the non-Indian newcomers came to claim their land, power in the new county would pass entirely into non-Indian hands. Frustrated by the attempts of a few non-Indian men to hold up the official organiza-tion of the county until after incoming non-Indians had taken possession of their parcels of land, he took the initiative to collect the necessary signatures from residents in that county, and hand-delivered them to the governor.[19] He did this despite valid fullblood protests that not all Indians had received their allotments, and their fear that the best land would be given to non-Indian settlers. The local newspaper editor, a staunch supporter of independent county organization, reported that 'many of the mixedbloods are more progressive than a majority of white men in pioneer communities and are counted well-to-do men. It augers well for the new county if they must "take up the white man's burden" of a new form of government' (*Bennett County Booster*, 28 February 1912: 1). With all the talk of 'progressive' mixedbloods, fullbloods became further marginalized as residents continued to internalize the distinction between fullbloods and mixedbloods in terms of competency. Failing to mention that his own non-Indian father had married into the tribe and been one of the white men who was allotted land, Cottier levelled accusations against others in the same circumstance who were attempting to hold up county organization.

Cottier must have realized that an early organization of the county would assure him a position of power, since he had held responsible jobs in the white world and was able to gain the support of so many other mixedbloods. Once the county was settled by non-Indians, mixedbloods would become a further vulnerable minority. At the same time non-Indians needed mixedbloods to push for formal organization in order for them to stake their own claims to primacy and power before the new settlers arrived. Cottier's faction succeeded in pushing through the organization, and the first county elections were held on 9 April 1912.[20]

Thus land tenure has been a major factor in shaping social identity from the very inception of Bennett County. Early non-Indian settlers attempting to secede from the Pine Ridge Reservation argued that, by holding land in deeded (taxable) rather than allotted (non-taxable) status, mixedbloods would be able to free themselves from the 'tyranny' of fullbloods, who controlled reservation politics by privileging members of their own *tiyošpaye*. Mixedbloods were able to exercise 'real' power by holding county office. The only Indian people qualified to vote to secede from the reservation were mixedbloods and a few fullbloods who held their land in deeded status. Other Lakotas were not able to vote without relinquishing their relationship to the tribe and converting their land to taxable status. Fullbloods accused mixedbloods of selling out their Lakota birthright and tribal land base when they converted the status of their original allotments. Fullbloods, defined as people who held land in allotted status and received annuities, were considered by the federal government to be legally 'incompetent' to vote.

### Shifting federal land policies

Federal Indian policy has been rooted in proper relationships to land, and after the era of allotment hundreds of thousands of major and minor pieces of legislation, court decisions and dicta continued to affect both Indians and their non-Indian neighbours. Indians have experienced the frustrating cycle of losing and regaining tribal land bases: they reestablish tribal and personal identities at one moment, only to lose them again the next. Non-Indians have feared losing their own homesteads, established in good faith, by their forebears. No one can afford to become too comfortable in the relationship to land – everyone has cause to fear that it may belong to someone else tomorrow, depending on which way the wind blows in the nation's capital.

About thirty years after the allotment era, the implementation of Franklin D. Roosevelt's New Deal included the Indian Reorganization Act (IRA). This encouraged native arts and culture, but it also established tribal councils based on a US model of government and drove the wedge between fullbloods and fullbloods created by the Dawes Act even deeper.[21] Indian identity was assigned positive value, so mixedbloods claimed it despite having fought so hard to be considered 'competent' by severing tribal ties in the previous generation. One-quarter Lakota blood quantum and recognized historical ties to the Lakota gave Bennett County mixedbloods the right to vote, hold tribal office, receive free services provided to tribal members, and apply for contracts privileging tribal members. Many fullbloods resented these latecomers to 'Indian' identity. They were perceived as trying to capitalize on an identity they had forfeited years before, in order to stake their claim to cash settlements resulting from claims cases.[22]

In the 1950s, twenty years after the IRA era, termination policy sought to assimilate Indians forcefully by devising schemes to terminate their special relationship with the federal government. This included a one-off per capita cash payment of their interest in tribal trust monies. Incentives were also offered to persuade Indians to relocate to selected urban centres, which in due course became isolated ghettos of underprepared rural Indians. Two of the first reservations chosen for termination were the Klamaths of Oregon and the Menominees of Wisconsin. Both of these tribes controlled massive forest resources, needed for the post-war home-building boom, and both were doing well financially. After termination, tribal members were paid for the value of their property, but unscrupulous whites quickly acquired the Indians' money by raising prices and drawing them into doomed investments. While Lakotas were not terminated, fears of such a move were whipped up by local and national newspapers. Many Pine Ridge Lakotas did take advantage of relocation to urban centres, where they often experienced racism, unemployment and a deep sense of longing for the land and their families. The policy succeeded in keeping Indian people off balance and non-Indians hopeful of securing the Indian land base.

The late 1960s and 1970s brought an era of renewed pride and self-determination, fuelled by the successful African-American civil rights movement, and expressed in the American Indian Movement (AIM). In the 1990s, federal fiscal crises have forced yet another reevaluation of Indian affairs. States are clamouring for changes in gambling laws, to address the issue of non-taxation of Indian casino gaming profits. States are also winning the fight to take over the distribution of welfare funds among their citizens. One condition of the latest federal welfare Act is that the maximum benefit period is now two years, and people must be employed at least part-time to receive the benefit. Reservations such as Pine Ridge and rural counties like Bennett County are too remote to be able to imagine a future without some sort of assistance. Fear is growing in Bennett County that the cut in federal aid to ranchers and farmers, coupled with a loss of welfare and general assistance paid to Indians, will cause the ultimate collapse of the regional economy.

Many of those still classified as mixedbloods may take advantage of racial assumptions today as they continue to benefit from both reservation and county systems. One such benefit is their ability to return their deeded land inside the county to tribal trust status, thereby both expressing their sense of Indian identity and following a pragmatic strategy for converting property into non-taxable status. The irony is that many mixedbloods hold some of the most negative attitudes towards 'Indians' in the county, distancing themselves completely from the fullbloods except in terms of Indian entitlements based on blood quantum. Such practices have obvious negative impacts upon tax-paying non-Indian neighbours, and they fuel anti-Indian sentiment. Non-Indian land owners would also withdraw from the tax rolls regardless of the impact to the county tax base, if they too could find a legal loophole. These same non-Indian residents also fear that if too much land is returned to trust status, the county will eventually revert to Pine Ridge Reservation control.

Historically, Indian people have been construed by federal policy as 'sovereign nations' during treaty times; 'domestic dependent nations' in the Jacksonian era of removal; wards and incompetents during the years of the Dawes Act; non-Indians during the termination era; and minorities with claims to preferential hiring during the civil rights era. They are now in the process of being labelled, along with other ethnic and immigrant groups, as stubborn obstacles to the resurgence of an ideology of the melting pot, allegedly based on the principles of the founding fathers of the United States. Despite some new discussions of multi-culturalism, 'diversity' is a notion that is again being contested (cf. Glazer and Moynihan 1975).

## Consequences

Both Lakotas and their non-Indian neighbours in Bennett County have experienced many broken promises. The Dawes Act was intended to assimilate Lakotas into the dominant society by enabling them to take up the American Dream of owning private property. Lakotas were promised that their estate would be inviolate, but Americans travelling westward ignored Indian rights and entered their land to seek their fortunes in the gold mines. They built railroads and forced the government to open a corridor through Lakota land. Shortly after the allotment process began on Pine Ridge Reservation, Lakotas were told that approximately one-quarter of their remaining land base was deemed 'surplus' and would be opened to accommodate homesteaders desiring to come to the Plains. At the same time homesteaders, many of whom arrived in fear of Indians as a result of reading lurid stories about them in eastern newspapers, were told that in a mere twenty-five years they would have tax-paying assimilated Lakota farmers as neighbours. Would they have come had they known that they might be forced to relinquish the land they had worked so hard to improve?

Fear of the loss of land underlies the tensions between 'fullbloods, 'mixedbloods' and 'whites' in Bennett County and underpins most public disputes between Lakotas and non-Indians. Comments such as 'We are not going to give them one more inch' (mostly uttered by non-Indians), and 'They stole our land' (spoken by Lakotas), are 'fighting words'. Although contemporary local contestations concern relatively inconsequential issues (such as homecoming ceremonies in schools and whether or not to hold a powwow in conjunction with the county fair), undiluted anger and fear remain just beneath the surface. Identity expressed in terms of blood and 'race' is a constant reminder of a history of dispossession, both for Lakotas and those non-Indians whose land was originally made available through the practice of forcing fee patents on 'incompetent' Lakotas.

Amorphous federal policies built upon relationships to land and blood quantum as measures of competency had consequences for all county residents, but particularly for mixedbloods. On the one hand, they were able to hold elected office and garner a certain amount of personal power in the system. On the other, mixedbloods found themselves in an ambiguous position which they could not control. Many had severed tribal ties and were seen as 'Other' by fullbloods, yet they were still not seen as equals by the non-Indians with whom they had hoped to make alliances. On the personal level, the case of mixedbloods shows the limited success of federal policies designed to assimilate Indian people. They had become 'individuals' (Biolsi 1995).

Studies of settler societies and of spatially and symbolically relocated indigenous communities force a reexamination of facile dichotomies that exemplify Western oppositional thinking. By locating the field of analysis in the fluid interstices of the 'middle ground', processes of accommodation, assimilation and acculturation become salient (Spicer 1961; Linton 1940; Beals 1970: 375–95). Ethnohistorical approaches to the 'middle ground' highlight moments when groups in early contact situations are forced into tenuous alliance through 'a process of creative, and often expedient, misunderstandings' (White 1991a; see also DeMallie 1984, 1993, 1994).

Bennett County was one of the last places in the continental United States to be 'intentionally settled' through actions directly related to federal policy, and the distance between the 'established and the outsider' (Elias and Scotson 1994; Dominy 1995) was not so clearly defined. Longstanding kinship ties among Lakotas (DeMallie 1994; 1979: 221–41) that preceded their resettlement were actively manipulated by early white traders and settlers to assure some measure of social and economic security. Those alliances positioned early unmarried non-Indian men to acquire land by taking advantage of federal policies that professed to guarantee a land base, annuities and access to health care to Lakotas.

In Bennett County in the 1990s, regional psychic stresses arise when residents are confronted with unpleasant historical realities that require a conceptual move away from mythical past to ambivalent present. The myth of the west – of noble savages and fiercely independent white settlers – is easy to imagine because it is constantly reinforced through American popular culture. When these images are contextualized by historians and anthropologists, the contemporary moral order is put seriously at risk. The precarious social equilibrium that exists here is a consequence above all else of shifting federal policies concerning property relations. Each group's ancestors were 'settled' here either by federal mandate or invitation, and each is dependent on federal subsidies that bolster an unviable economy. Residents on this unsettled frontier have more in common than they may wish to see, and the history of the region discloses less independence than they care to admit. A deep, though differently articulated, love of the land, is fundamental to group identities and their awkward symbiosis.

# 7   Property values: ownership, legitimacy and land markets in Northern Cyprus

## *Julie Scott*

In 1974, following a coup engineered by Greece and then a decisive military intervention by Turkey, the island of Cyprus was divided. Populations were exchanged between the north and south of the island, the northern third becoming predominantly Turkish Cypriot and the southern two-thirds Greek Cypriot. In 1983 the north declared itself an independent state with the title 'Turkish Republic of Northern Cyprus' (TRNC), but it is recognized only by Turkey; the south is known as 'the Republic of Cyprus', and has international recognition.

Partition created both Greek and Turkish Cypriot refugees, even though Turkish Cypriots were intended to benefit from the Turkish military intervention. Turkish Cypriots who moved north and Greek Cypriots who moved south all left behind them ancestral land and property: the villages and landscapes where they had grown up, and goods which might represent a lifetime's work and saving. They had to start afresh with the land and property allocated to them, sometimes temporarily, on 'the other side'. The status of 'refugee' and the trauma of displacement created problems of adaptation on both a personal and a social level, as Loizos (1981) has documented in the case of Greek Cypriot refugees from the village of Argaki. The process of adaptation among Greek Cypriots was made more difficult by government propaganda which encouraged people to believe that they would soon return 'home' (Ladbury and King 1982).

The Turkish Cypriot position, on the other hand, has always been that partition in some form is permanent. People have been encouraged to think in terms of *compensation* for what has been lost in the south, and to create a new home in the north. In order to achieve this, the Turkish Cypriot authorities have adopted a unilateral policy on refugee property. Newly created TRNC deeds can be obtained for abandoned Greek Cypriot property on payment of an agreed number of points representing an equivalent value of Turkish Cypriot-owned property in the south. Turkish Cypriot refugees are required to forfeit their claim to what they left in the south in order to have the means in the north for

142

getting on with the business of everyday life and fulfilling social obligations based on having land as property to cultivate, build on, sell,
mortgage and pass on to children as dowry or inheritance. The transfer
of ownership from the south permits property to be reintegrated into the
social fabric of life in the north, thus underlining the finality of the break
with the past. However, it also highlights a marked lack of consensus
over the value and meaning of property, and how ownership is conceptualized and legitimized. The authorities in the north operate with
the notion of 'equivalent value', which implies that all forms of property
are reducible to one standard measure of commodity economy. This is a
notion which is frequently resisted by Turkish Cypriots. From the Greek
Cypriot point of view, pre-1974 Greek property still belongs to its
original owners, and tourists visiting Northern Cyprus at the end of the
1970s were threatened with prosecution in the British courts for use of
stolen goods and trespass (Matthews 1987).

Hann has discussed how the process of decollectivizing land in
Hungary highlights differences in the concept of 'property', as people
seek to legitimize their claims with reference to one of two competing
ideologies of ownership: one based on the rights of producers who have
worked the land, the other on the rights of the original owners (Hann
1993a). Both claims are rooted in a set of preexisting social relations. In
the context of Cyprus, I see discourses of 'ownership' as 'legitimizing
systems' for the two communities on the island. The extremely complex
land markets which have developed in Northern Cyprus reflect property
values which pertain not only to the price of a commodity, but to specific
cultural and historical meanings of ownership. In the second part of this
chapter I explore Turkish Cypriot concepts of property and their social,
cultural and political implications by examining how these land markets
operate. First I take a brief look at the historical circumstances in which
a number of conflicting legitimizing systems have been developed by the
Greek Cypriot and Turkish Cypriot communities.

### Land and historiography

In the Lusignan and Venetian periods which immediately preceded the
Ottoman conquest of Cyprus in 1571, most of the land was owned by
the Latin church, the king and members of the foreign ruling elite.
The Orthodox peasantry consisted of slaves, serfs and freedmen who
paid tributes of money, produce and forced labour to the fiefholders.
This system was transformed by the new Ottoman administration
according to Islamic principles governing conquest. Many of the new
settlers from Anatolia were allocated and given title to land which had

been confiscated from the Latin feudal lords and church. According to one German geographer, the dispersed pattern of Turkish Cypriot settlement throughout the island before 1960 can be traced back to the landholding pattern of the Lusignan nobility (Wellenreuther 1993: 34).

The Ottoman administration distinguished between land ownership and rights of use. *Öşriyye* (land owned by Moslems before the conquest or given after occupation) and *haraciye* (land left in the hands of Christian owners after conquest) were considered to belong to the owner with full rights to bequeath and alienate (Gazioğlu 1990). However, private ownership played only a small role in Ottoman land tenure, probably amounting to only 5–10 per cent of the land area of the island. All rural agricultural land was owned by the state as *miri* land. This was held by various categories of official, who derived an income both for themselves and for the state from their tenant farmers. The tenants' right to usufruct was recognized through the issue of temporary deeds, and could be inherited. Under the Tanzimat reforms of the nineteenth century, new title deeds were issued for *miri* land, allowing it to be mortgaged and inherited in the same way as *mulk* (buildings, trees, gardens, vineyards and wild trees). Other categories of land were wasteland, common land and *Evkaf* (land dedicated to pious and charitable purposes and administered either directly through the Islamic office or through trustees).

According to one Turkish Cypriot writer, the new system of land registration introduced by the Ottoman administration was 'so efficient and successful that, even after the British took over the island, the system remained in use without major changes for many years' (Gazioğlu 1990: 124). However, the Greek Cypriot author of the World Land Use Survey's monograph on Cyprus saw the situation rather differently. In his view, 'The chaos and vicious system of land registration and tax assessment was to bedevil Cyprus and its government far into the twentieth century. The efficient collection of taxes by the British administration helped to make the inequities more flagrant' (Christodoulou 1959: 73).

The British land reform of 1946, coupled with the water law of 1954, extended the agricultural area under irrigation and created the conditions for a new market in land. The modern thrust of the reforms was to halt the trend to fragmentation of landholdings and the practice of multiple ownership, which was a consequence of the system of bilateral partible inheritance, compounded by a common subsistence strategy of spreading landholdings over a variety of types of land. The British also created new tenancies on some of the large Turkish-owned estates (*çiftlik*), which contained some of the best agricultural land on the island.

From the 1950s, increasing urbanization and the trend towards part-time farming raised the value of urban land. By 1959, land around Nicosia was commanding 'fantastic' prices, as a result of rural in-migration, loose money in the economy looking for investment, and the relative lack of other lucrative investment opportunities (Attalides 1981). The appearance in the villages of large, urban-style houses alongside traditional rural dwellings showed the growing importance of income derived from outside agriculture. Traditional priorities, as expressed in the saying, 'a house as small as can accommodate you, and land as much as you can see', were rapidly modified in this period.

However, Turkish Cypriots were largely excluded from these developments in the land and property market, both for economic reasons and, after 1963, for political reasons (Wellenreuther 1993: 62). Turkish Cypriots tell many stories about the cheap sale of their land to more prosperous Greek Cypriots. The picturesque coastal town of Girne (Kyrenia) was formerly an Ottoman garrison, surrounded by large Turkish-owned estates. With the advent of the British in 1878, the new rulers took over Girne Castle and the Turkish Cypriots dwindled to a small minority of the townspeople. People in Girne told me that a large area of Turkish land had been sold to Greek Cypriots to cover gambling debts. They also said that, as tourism began to take off, intimidation was used to force Turkish Cypriots to sell land abutting the coast. Those few Turkish Cypriots who were in a position to buy often found Greek Cypriots unwilling to sell to them.

In 1963, the constitution of the independent republic of Cyprus broke down after only three years. The withdrawal of Turkish Cypriots into enclaves as a result of the violence of 1963–4 changed the dispersed pattern of settlement and resulted in the exodus of the Turkish population from more than a hundred previously 'mixed' villages. Turkish Cypriots fleeing from attack congregated initially in nearby Turkish Cypriot villages, before finding shelter in more permanent refugee camps or in the Turkish enclaves of the towns. Many Turkish Cypriot dwellings and belongings were destroyed. The cultivation of the associated plots was taken over by Greek Cypriots. In a few cases, Turkish Cypriots were able to obtain a nominal rent for land which they were no longer able to farm.

Estimates concerning the aggregate land ownership of the Greek Cypriot and Turkish Cypriot communities vary widely. The variations can be explained by the politically inflammatory nature of the land issue, particularly after 1960. Wellenreuther suggests that some Turkish Cypriot claims that 30–33 per cent of the land was in Turkish ownership are an overestimate which is intended to compensate for the injustices suffered after 1963.[1] There is a sub-text in all accounts of earlier periods, in which a moral standpoint is applied to the issue of land and ownership. The Ottoman administration's land policy, as explained by Gazioğlu (1990), had a two-fold legitimation: the right of conquest, and the ending of an onerous and unpopular feudal system. By conquest, all land became the property of the sultan. It was then redistributed according to Ottoman principles. Underlying Christodoulou's (1959) account, on the other hand, is the issue of restitution to the original and rightful owners of land, from whom it had been appropriated under the oppressive regime of the Latin Lusignans and Venetians. According to his account, land in the early Christian and Byzantine era belonged largely to the state or to the Orthodox church, and only part of this land was returned under the Ottomans. As legitimating systems, rights of conquest and rights of original ownership stand in opposition to each other; the former gives a moral underpinning to the rights of the newcomers, whilst the latter emphasizes the continuous historic existence and rights of the island's 'original' inhabitants.[2] Another recurring theme is that of 'productivity' versus 'neglect'. Gazioğlu's depiction of the efficient and rational Ottoman land code contrasts with the story of corruption and neglect which characterizes the Greek Cypriot accounts (cf. Catselli 1974). Whilst Ottoman reforms recognized usufruct rights, according to Christodoulou these were not legally enshrined until the 1946 British land reform. Many rentier landlords let their unproductive land fall into ruin.

'Purchase' and 'inheritance' have been the principal means by which rights to land and property are established. In terms of the relationship with the land, these represent countervailing trends. They do not necessarily come into conflict, but whilst inheritance is based on a continuous relationship over generations and blends closely with the idea of 'original ownership', purchase is more likely to mark a discontinuity and change of direction.

The issue of compensation cuts across all these categories. It cannot be seen strictly in terms of restitution of property: the right to compensation is based not just on the principle of original ownership, but takes other moral issues into account, such as suffering or injustice. Apart from the loss of life suffered in the 1960s and early 1970s, the gap between Turkish and Greek Cypriot per capita income widened considerably in this period, when the Turkish Cypriot enclaves were deprived of infrastructure and amenities. The alienation of much Turkish Cypriot land through sale is retrospectively viewed as unjust, since unfair advantage was taken of the weak position of the seller.[3] The 30–33 per cent land share estimate quoted by Wellenreuther coincides approximately with the land area of Cyprus currently within TRNC borders. This is disproportionately large for a population which represents approximately 18 per cent of the total population of Cyprus. However, Turkish Cypriots often argue that the proportion is fair because of the large amount of land previously in Turkish ownership and alienated following the British land reform. At the same time, a common objection to the Greek Cypriot demand for the 'three freedoms' of movement, settlement and property ownership in any future settlement is that 'the Greeks will buy all the land off us for peanuts and we will be left without anything again'.

Original ownership, conquest, productivity, purchase, inheritance and compensation are the core concepts of six competing legitimizing discourses of land ownership on Cyprus. I now turn to the situation in Northern Cyprus since 1974: I shall consider in turn the processes of settlement, the allocation and registration of land and other property, and the development of property markets.

### Resettlement and the allocation and registration of property

The exchange in populations between the north and south of the island did not occur immediately after the Turkish intervention in 1974, and took place under different conditions for the Greek Cypriot and Turkish Cypriot populations (Loizos 1981). Whilst the Greek Cypriots in the north fled before the advancing Turkish army, it was not until a year later that agreement between the Greek Cypriot and Turkish Cypriot leaderships was reached and the bulk of the Turkish Cypriot population in the south moved across the Green Line to the north. The resettlement of Turkish Cypriots in the north was, therefore, a more organized operation. The plentiful availability of empty property which had been abandoned by Greek Cypriots meant that Turkish Cypriots did not face the pressures of overcrowding experienced by Greek Cypriot refugees in the south. Rather, the population was insufficient to maintain the productivity of the resources in the north.[4]

As far as possible, the integrity of communities from the south was preserved in the resettlement process. In an effort to maintain continuity in social structure and economic activity, rural communities were settled in villages, and urban Turkish Cypriots were relocated in towns. However, since a large proportion of the Turkish Cypriot population had traditionally been urban it was not always possible to maintain this pattern.[5] On arrival in the north, the newcomers were allocated housing by the authorities. Despite the degree of organization, the resettlement process was still a traumatic experience. Many Turkish Cypriots pre-empted the exchange agreement and crossed the border in secret at night. Others crossed through the British bases, leaving their home in slippers and apron as if going to the shops in order to avoid suspicion. It was not possible in the early days to operate a system based on criteria of equivalence for the property left behind. People therefore had to take whatever was available. One woman described the process as a 'lottery'. 'When we arrived, everything else had been taken, this was the only place left.' Another, indicating the small house in front of which she sat, concluded her account of those days: '*Kaderim buydu*' ('This was my fate').

In contrast to the south, which had far greater numbers of refugees to accommodate, the selection of abandoned property for resettlement in the north was governed by criteria of 'quality' (Wellenreuther 1993: 76). By the time the newcomers from the south arrived, much of the better property had been appropriated by Turkish Cypriots already living in the north, who moved out of their poorer dwellings into higher standard Greek Cypriot accommodation. Many Turkish Cypriots from the south also found that settlers from mainland Turkey had got there before them. The issue of mainland settlers in the north has always been highly sensitive politically, and their numbers are hard to ascertain. Well-enreuther (1993: 42–9) argues convincingly that the early influx of mainland settlers diminished substantially after 1979, and estimates their numbers to total about 40,000 (in contrast to Greek Cypriot estimates of 80,000–100,000). The early settler policy was dictated by the need to maintain the productivity of resources in the north, but it contributed significantly to conflict and resentment over the distribution of those resources, particularly with the subsequent arrivals from the south of the island (Morvaridi 1993: 232).

Newcomers to the north were allocated a place to live and orchards and land to cultivate in order to feed their households. Land and other property were also allocated for commercial use, including hotels, shops and business premises. Individuals applied for a lease from the Turkish Cypriot government to manage *tahsis* (allocated) property, which carried no deeds of ownership or security of tenure. Because of the delay in the arrival of Turkish Cypriots from the south, the allocation of such businesses in practice favoured those who were already on the spot, and who still had the financial wherewithal to run the business – another drawback for those who had left everything in the south. The allocation of hotels was supervised by the State Tourism Enterprise, a parastatal organization established in November 1974. In central Girne, one of the north's prime touristic sites, the hotel stock amounted to eight hotels which had previously been in Greek Cypriot ownership. Of these, five were allocated to mainland settlers, one was run by the state, and the oldest and most famous of Girne's hotels, the Dome, was allocated to *Evkaf*, i.e. the Islamic authorities.

Political patronage influenced the distribution of *tahsis* properties, and they became an important means for the ruling National Unity Party to consolidate its hold. Supporters of the opposition left-wing Turkish Republican Party experienced particular difficulty in obtaining property. The registration of property was managed by the Ministry of Resettlement (*Iskan*), established in 1976. In accordance with legislation enacted the following year, it allocated points to Turkish Cypriot refugees according to the value of the land and other property they had left in the south. These points could then be exchanged for certificates of ownership for Greek Cypriot property in the north. This has been a slow and painful process, with the result that in 1993 nearly one third of applicants were still waiting for certificates of ownership to be issued (Morvaridi 1993). Disputes frequently arise over the valuation of the land left behind in the south and the number of *eşdeğer* ('equivalent value') points received. Furthermore, developments in the property markets in the north in the intervening years often produce a situation in which the points awarded are not adequate to secure title to the allocated property in which people have been living and working since 1974. In the next section I look more closely at the relationship between compensation and property markets.

## Land and property markets in practice

Land and property markets in Northern Cyprus are highly fragmented. Market information is difficult to obtain and highly sought after. The classification of the land, who is buying, who is selling, and the type of transaction, are all complicating factors. These are reflected in the variety of social networks operating within the market, as well as prices and the outcome of transactions. It is possible to distinguish four major types of activity: the conversion of points into certificates of ownership; cash transactions for land which has either pre-1974 Turkish deeds or post-1974 TRNC deeds; speculation (the acquisition of land and property in expectation of rising prices in the future); and the purchase of points. These are not rigid, but overlapping categories. Nor are the values involved all monetary. Some idea of the range of issues involved in property transactions can best be conveyed by a detailed examination of a particular case.

The case concerns the Riza family from Larnaca who settled in a village near Gazi Mağusa (Famagusta). In the south they left behind sixty *dönüms* of agricultural land and trees, a house in the village which they had fled in 1964, and a house in the town which they had completed just before 1974 (and on which they continued to pay their outstanding debt until it was finally cleared in 1982). In return for their deeds, which they submitted to the government office in the north, they received two million *eşdeğer* points, of which 450,000 were for the house in town. The property they were allocated in the north comprised a plot with two small houses in twenty *dönüms* of irrigated land. They planted fruit trees, cultivated a variety of vegetable crops, and carried out small-scale animal husbandry. The original Greek Cypriot owner of the land had sent a message to the Riza family through an intermediary working on the British base – a fairly common occurrence – in which he urged them to look after his land, and keep it all together.

The certificate of ownership for the land was due to be issued early in 1993. The parents decided to split the land between their five children, by now all married.[6] A daughter and her family had moved into one of the houses, and the house in which the parents were living was to be left to the youngest daughter. The remaining land was to be divided between the other children, with two small plots going to the daughters in the two houses. On receiving the certificate of ownership, however, it was discovered that the family's points were insufficient to acquire their *tahsis* land. Because of its proximity to the town and to the touristic area of Salamis, the land was classified as development land. In fact, the rural aspect of the area around the village was already changing with the building of hotels and villa-style accommodation. The Riza family had to buy an additional 250,000 points at a cost of approximately £1,200 sterling to make up their *eşdeğer* points.[7]

The two *dönüms* of land at the side and back of the house which were to have been given to the youngest daughter, and which the Riza family had been cultivating for eighteen years were excluded from the property they obtained. This land was joined to the deeds of the neighbouring property. The neighbours offered to sell it for £7,000 sterling. As the Riza family could not afford to pay this, and considered it overpriced, they decided to wait for the price to drop. The land was eventually sold to a young professional couple from the town. The matter did not, however, end there. A dispute arose over the position of the well. The purchasers maintained that the well was on their side of the boundary, and erected a wire fence around their property taking in the well. The Riza family maintained that the well was within their land, and the fence was removed by two of the sons-in-law. Relations between the three parties (the family, their neighbours and the new purchasers), became increasingly acrimonious and culminated for the Riza family in the traumatic experience of seeing the boundary fence re-erected and set in concrete, whilst their cow-sheds and by now mature fruit trees were razed to the ground by a bulldozer.

The bitter episode affected the family's father, a man in his sixties, particularly badly. The Rizas felt a strong sense of injustice for a number of reasons. Firstly, they felt they had not been compensated for their original property '*öbür tarafta*' (on the other side). The Resettlement Office had disputed their claim that half of their land in the south had been irrigated land, which had reduced the number of points they had obtained for their deeds. The classification of their land in the north as development land had further reduced what they had been able to acquire. Whilst the evaluation of the land in the north takes account of changing urban and touristic land values, it does not take into account the effects of the land market in the south on property left behind, that is, what the Riza family would have been able to realize on their original property. Their house in the centre of Larnaca was valued at 450,000 points, but an 'equivalent' house in the centre of Girne would now cost two million points. Secondly, they were sure that the new purchasers had obtained the well through *torpil* – through powerful contacts in the office of land registry, who had adjusted the boundary of the property in their favour. This suspicion was confirmed when the family managed to get the Nicosia office to look into the matter, only to discover that the file had been 'mislaid'. Despite their efforts, the family were unable to muster sufficient *torpil* (literally, 'torpedoes', i.e. social clout) to have the matter thoroughly investigated.[8]

The issue of *hak* (right), i.e. what rightfully belongs to somebody, was touched on constantly in discussions about the family's problem. It was clearly associated with the idea of 'original ownership', but several different models of original ownership emerged. First, there was the matter of what the Riza family had originally owned in the south. Second, there was the question of the property of the original Greek Cypriot owner which had been entrusted to their care, the integrity of which had been breached. Third, there was the issue of the rights generated by the family's labour over the years, in relation particularly to the planting and nurturing of the trees and the construction of the outhouses which had been destroyed. These rights they felt were more legitimate than the rights of the new purchasers. The latter considered that they had bought the land at a fair price, and denied tampering with the boundary. The relationship with the land which comes from working with it and living from it was tacitly acknowledged by the new owners, who came out every Sunday to clear the ground and prepare their garden for landscaping by a landscape designer. During their early visits they were conciliatory, backing their right to the land as purchasers with an appeal to a common rural ancestry: '*Biz de köy çocuklarıyız*' ('We too are village children'). This was derisively dismissed by the eldest of the Riza family daughters, who retorted that the only soil they had seen before had been in a plant pot. Although all the parties believed in their right to the disputed land, their claims were based in competing beliefs about ownership and the 'meaning' of the land. This is changing with the effects of urbanization and tourism development, but the new owners nonetheless felt compelled to augment their purchase rights by harking back to a rural identity.

It should be noted that throughout the course of the dispute the idea of *öbür taraf* (the other side) was an important point of reference, especially for the father of the Riza family. He continually stressed the fecundity of their old land, the crops they had grown, and his success in irrigating it. The 'other side' began to assume 'other worldly' associations, as he dismissed '*bu dünya*' (this world) and the land on 'this side' as '*yaramaz*' (no good). He said that he had given up, and entrusted the fate of himself and his family to Allah. The episode was a painful reminder of the first time the family had lost everything, when they fled their village in 1964. It led to the reflection that 'what EOKA [the Greek Cypriot paramilitary organization] did to us then, our own people are doing to us now'.

This case encapsulates four of the main issues involved in transactions over land and property. A decisive factor in the resolution of the boundary dispute in favour of the new purchasers was their superior *torpil*. This mobilization of social capital which constitutes *torpil* is not to be confused with *rüşvet* – bribery, or the buying of favours for money – which is universally condemned by Turkish Cypriots and, furthermore, regarded as 'uncypriot'. *Torpil* is a double-edged weapon. Its use is widely acknowledged and decried, but at the same time it is recognized as a valuable way of getting things done. Because the Turkish Cypriot community is small and close-knit, almost everybody has some access to kin or political networks which can be mobilized in support of a particular goal. Achieving a favourable outcome brings not only the satisfaction of attaining the desired objective, but also confirmation of one's place in society, proof that '*arkamızda var*' (we have force or people behind us). Whilst the successful mobilization of *torpil* reinforces a sense of social integration, the effect for those who do not have access to, or lose a contest of, *torpil*, is one of demoralization and alienation, as they are brought face to face with their powerlessness and lack of capacity. This is a sentiment which was forcefully expressed when the

Riza family's father compared their current situation to what they had suffered at the hands of EOKA.

A second point is the way in which, quite apart from the matter of territory debated at a formal macro level between governments, the land and property issues still cut across the division of the island. The contact established in this case with the original Greek Cypriot owner of the land is not unusual. Greek Cypriots and Turkish Cypriots continue to meet within the Cypriot diaspora. Several hundred Turkish Cypriots cross to work in the south every day, and some continue to be employed on the British base of Dhikkelia, which straddles the Green Line. The exchange of news and photographs of property left behind, directly or through intermediaries, is a common feature of such contacts. The son of the Riza family had in his possession a photograph of their house in Larnaca, taken by a Greek Cypriot friend whom he had asked to visit their old home. He kept the photograph from his parents as he thought they would find it too upsetting. It should be remembered that this family had continued to pay off the debt on their abandoned house for eight years after their move to the north. They conceived of their *tahsis* land not just in terms of a number of *dönüms* of ground, but also as an entity forged by the previous Greek Cypriot owner, the impersonal commodity aspect taking second place to a model of property formed by a previous set of social relations.[9]

The idea of the island of Cyprus as a 'whole' is frequently asserted. People are aware of the impact of tourism and urban development on prices in the south. This is relevant to my third point, which concerns the role of the state in the redistribution of land. The new arrivals from the south had to lodge the deeds to their former property with the government in order to obtain equivalent value points and receive land and property in the north. This implies that any future negotiations with Greek Cypriots over compensation will be conducted by the government on a collective basis, rather than between individuals. It also means that the state will reap the benefit of the increase in land values in the south, rather than the original owners. It is a common complaint that the points system and land distribution has favoured only a political elite and those with powerful *torpil*. People say that it has resulted in a class of *nouveaux riches*, often referred to as '1974 millionaires', and the relative impoverishment of a significant portion of the Turkish Cypriot population.

Finally, attention should be given to the number of land markets involved in the transactions outlined in this case study. The family obtained certificates of ownership for most of their *tahsis* property by paying *eşdeğer* points, awarded on the basis of their property in the south. They then had to buy further points to obtain the outstanding land which their equivalent value points did not cover. Meanwhile, a certificate of ownership was granted to the neighbours on the basis of their *eşdeğer* points for the two *dönüms* of land which had been cultivated by the family. These were subsequently sold for cash. Three different types of transaction occurred within three different markets: the exchange of points for land, based on equivalent value of land in the south; the 'points market', in which top-up points are purchased to make up the value of allocated land; and the cash market, for land with a clear certificate of ownership issued by the government. Whilst values in the first two markets were determined by the government, the third category of transaction fell outside the government's ambit and approximated the 'free' market. The land values involved varied dramatically. Allocated land theoretically represented an equivalent 'land for land' value. The outstanding two *dönüms* were purchased with approximately £1,200 sterling worth of extra points, a rate determined by the government. However, the two *dönüms* alienated by the neighbours fetched approximately £7,000 sterling on a competitive real estate market.

## 'Notional land': the market for points

*Tahsis* property previously belonging to Greek Cypriots was allocated to Turkish Cypriots from the south and to mainland settlers for accommodation and cultivation, and to both these groups and Turkish Cypriots already living in the north for tourism, commerce and agriculture. Certificates of ownership had to be acquired through the exchange of points. Whilst only settlers from the south were entitled to *eşdeğer* points, others were eligible for another category, *mücahit* points. These were given to those who participated as fighters in the Turkish Cypriot struggle. Unlike *eşdeğer* points, they did not represent land in the south, but could be considered as reward for service, or compensation for additional suffering. A nominal rent was paid for *tahsis* property by occupants without points. A group of apartment blocks just east of Girne was leased out in this way. Settlers from Turkey were accommodated in half-finished flats which they had been completing over the years, whilst paying an annual rent in 1993 of 350,000 TL (about £20 sterling). Turkish Cypriot refugees from the south living in the same apartments paid nothing because they had deeds to property in the south and hence an entitlement to *eşdeğer* points.

The release of land in packages (1993 saw the release of the sixteenth package) provided the opportunity for points to be cashed in for land. At this point, people who have been occupying or running property on a lease from the government can apply for permission to buy points to secure a certificate of ownership. Normally, points may only be bought from relatives, but the dense pattern of family relationships among Turkish Cypriots means that this is not much of a restriction. In any case, special permission can be obtained (possibly using *torpil*) to waive the requirement that points can only be bought within a kinship network.

Buyers and sellers of points are brought together either through personal or family contacts, or through *aracı* (middlemen). People may want to sell their points for a number of reasons. Some may have small amounts of points left over after securing their *tahsis* property. Some cannot find any property which they consider suitable, while others may simply need the cash. However, the fall in the relative value of points (which has not kept pace with inflation: see Morvaridi (1993: 227)) causes many people to consider that it is not worth their while to sell their points. One family with some points left after acquiring ownership of their *tahsis* property in a residential neighbourhood of Girne, decided to save the remaining points to divide between their two sons. A Turkish Cypriot who had come to Girne to retire after living in London for forty years chose to buy property with his savings rather than use his points. He explained that he did not want the bureaucratic aggravation of exchanging his points, and in any case he did not possess enough points to buy anything worthwhile. He added that people had offered to buy the points from him, but that the price he was offered was so low that he preferred to hang on to them. In both these cases, it might seem that the decision to keep the points implies retention of a depreciating asset, but behind the decision is the thought that the *eşdeğer* points represent land in the south which is gaining rather than losing in value.

Once points have been purchased, they may be exchanged for property and converted into deeds of ownership which can then be bought, sold and used as collateral for raising loans. It follows that the points market occupies an intermediate position between land exchange and money transactions. Dealing in points is dealing in land as an abstraction: notional land in the south is converted into property in the north, but its value is frozen, and cannot keep pace with the dynamic market which is developing in the north. Because of the relative decline in the value of points, the market favours those with the liquid assets to buy points and hence to benefit from the rise in value which accompanies the acquisition of deeds. However, the association of the points with the original property they represent does linger. It was suggested to me that it might be possible to buy points from refugees who had owned land in the Kouklia district near Paphos in the south, where a major holiday complex was planned. This would increase the value of that land significantly. Although this in itself would not affect the value of the points in the north, in the event of a later political agreement the owner of the rights to the land in the south might be able to realize the appreciation in its value. This was certainly considered to be a theoretical possibility, and it illustrates the creativity in the ways people conceive of land and property in Cyprus. Some of these ways run counter to the intention underlying land distribution policy, which is to anchor people in their new environment. Similar notions, though not so clearly formulated, lie behind the decisions not to sell points. If points represent land as pure commodity, divorced from the social relationships attached to a particular place, there still persists in the minds of many point-holders a model in which the link between property and place, embedded in the history and social relations of the owner, is paramount.

## Speculation, political uncertainty and *hava parası*

The land and property market presents an opportunity to make significant windfall gains for those who have cash resources for speculation, and particularly for those with sufficient *torpil* to obtain land through the points market for packages which have yet to be released. Prices continue to fluctuate once certificates of ownership have been issued for property. The designation of an area as a tourism development area brings an automatic rise in prices. Properties with *kesin tasarruf* (clear deeds of ownership) may be bought for development or parcelling, or merely for further resale in anticipation of future price rises. The area around and to the west of Girne commands particularly high prices because of its tourism value. However, another factor in land deals is a strategic element which is based on a political assessment of the likely consequences of a settlement to the Cyprus issue. Some people say that they would only buy land to the north of the Girne range of mountains, because this area will never be ceded to Greek Cypriots in any political deal.[10] The mountains are thought to be an effective barrier in the case of any future attack – security is of paramount importance. Others are attracted to the region close to the town of Mağusa, because they anticipate a boom in prices in the event of the reopening of the resort of Maraş.[11] At the moment prices around Mağusa lag behind the prime Girne region, and the potential future gain would therefore be great. However, there is also felt to be a greater risk that a deal with the Greek Cypriots might mean the loss of part of this area. Despite low prices, the main citrus growing region of Güzelyurt (Morphou) is considered too risky by most potential buyers, because it has been openly talked of as a possible area for the resettlement of Greek Cypriots. There is little or no tourism development there. On the other hand, one hotel owner in Girne told me that he had been buying land around Güzelyurt for cultivation, pointing out the UN undertaking to ensure that any future solution will preserve the economic balance and viability of the two communities. As Güzelyurt was the most productive agricultural area in Northern Cyprus, this man argued that it would have to be retained by the north if total dependence on tourism was to be avoided. Furthermore, as he was paying cash for land which has clear deeds of ownership, in the event of an agreement which ceded Güzelyurt to the Greek Cypriots he could expect to receive good compensation, either in money or land.

The delay in the issuing of certificates of ownership has meant that 'some of the occupiers of land and property are not in a position to sell, if they should want to do so' (Morvaridi 1993: 227). This is a particular problem for settlers from Turkey, who have no idea what their rights would be in the event of a political resolution to the problems of partition. Mainland settlers are often censured by Turkish Cypriots for the dilapidated state of the houses in which they live, particularly in many of the villages which are falling into decay: 'When they get a hole in the roof and the water comes in, they just move everything to the other side of the room and live in that.' Many Cypriots believe that the Turkish settlers do not want to spend money on repairs and improvements because they send all their money back to Turkey to build houses there. This would seem a sensible strategy in view of the uncertain position of the mainland settlers. One family of four in Girne had one income, from the father who earned the minimum wage of approximately £100 per month working for a taxi firm. He had incurred substantial debts in improving their one-bedroom flat, which they had taken over in a half-completed state. To the constant anxiety over money was added the uncertainty about the future. In a conversation about the UN-sponsored talks on Cyprus which were going on at the time, the mother expressed considerable unease. 'Do you think there will be a settlement? What do you think will happen? Surely we'll get something back for the money we have put in here?' Some express the fear that, if they do make improvements to the property they occupy, a Turkish Cypriot with points might come and take it from them.[12] Settlers from the mainland also believe that the dilapidated state of the villages is in part the fault of the Turkish Cypriots, 'because they own several houses which they don't live in and just let them fall into ruin'.

Although land and property cannot be bought and sold without certificates of ownership, this problem is largely circumvented by the trade in *hava parası* ('air money'). The sums involved can be substantial, hence it is sometimes said ironically that so-and-so '*havadan zenginleşti*' (has got rich from the air). In conventional business dealings, *hava parası* approximates to a consideration for 'good will'. In the Northern Cyprus property market, it comes close to the idea of 'key money'. Outside the rented sector, what is actually being traded is the future right to acquire property. An old stone house in a ruined state in the old Turkish quarter of Girne which was allocated to a mainland settler was sold cheaply for *hava parası* to another mainlander. He later bought the deeds with points, and then placed it on the market for a much larger sum (£38,000 sterling). *Hava parası* enables those with no immediate prospect of acquiring ownership to make a quick profit by passing it on to someone who is in a position to realize that asset.

### Conclusion

Turkish Cypriot resettlement policy, unlike Greek Cypriot policy, has been to anchor refugees in their new 'home' in the north. Full property rights – that is, ownership and title rather than just use and possession of land – are considered to be important in giving people a stake in their new 'country'. Ownership is legitimized at the level of public ideology by reference to territorial and historical arguments hinging on the concepts of original ownership, conquest, productivity, purchase, inheritance and compensation. The combination of these discourses is intended to appeal to a Turkish Cypriot national identity. The state has assumed responsibility for compensation by encompassing ownership at the level of private citizens within the macro-political issue of territory. It has attempted to sever the link between social relationships and property, replacing it with points which represent property in a notional or commoditized form. Nevertheless, people continue to assert a model of property as embodying particular places, social relationships and personal histories in which Greek Cypriots, the 'other side', and the idea of the island 'as a whole' play a part. They tend to do this in two different contexts, and to mean two different things.

   In one context, the local model takes the form of an idealized nostalgia for property in the south, as a way of expressing frustration at the handling of resettlement and compensation in the north. The long delay in regularizing the status of allocated property has meant that for two decades people have been living and working on land, only to find, when they receive their points, that in many cases the boundaries have been changed, or the price demanded is above their means. Resentment is further fuelled by what is widely perceived to be the suspect affluence of the *nouveaux riches*. Many feel that they have done badly out of the compensation process. The bureaucratic valuation of property as a commodity is countered by recourse to alternative legitimizing systems, which reflect the tension between official and unofficial ideologies of property. Original ownership is invoked both in terms of the property boundaries of the original Greek owner and the 'real' value of the property left in the south, while the labour which has been expended on the property is the other major legitimizing principle. In invoking these alternative legitimacies people are also invoking another moral code, and 'the other side' often takes on other-worldly connotations, particularly when actual outcomes do not match up to profoundly felt *values*.

At the same time, reference to these various models of property and to the island 'as a whole' can also be part of a pragmatic response to the commoditized property market. Many people try to keep abreast of commercial developments in the south and of the strategic value of land in the north, with an eye to securing investments and maximizing profits in the event of a future political settlement on the island. The principle of impersonal commodity equivalence is built into these notions of property. It fuels markets which reflect and respond to the complexities and uncertainties of ownership, with regard both to the general terri-torial issues and to changing social, political and economic relations in the north. Most people demonstrate in their everyday lives a creative capacity to inflect the logic of markets by invoking differing, and even conflicting, models of property and place, and even sometimes invoking the same model for quite different purposes.

# 8    Property and power in Transylvania's decollectivization

*Katherine Verdery*

An especially challenging area of transformation in the former socialist world – challenging for both social policy and social theory – concerns privatization, the (re)creation of private property rights from the collective property of socialism. Hann (chapter 1) points to the world-historical significance of this process by labelling it, with a bow to Polanyi, 'the Second Great Transformation'. The literature is growing fast, treating such issues as the theoretical relationship between private property, markets and democratic politics (e.g., Comisso 1991); the means used for transforming public property into private and the consequences of this for economic development and state power (e.g., Staniszkis 1991; Stark 1992); the justifying ideologies of transformed property rights and their social effects (e.g., Appel 1995; Verdery 1994); and the nature of the new rights being exercised (e.g., Hann 1993a, 1993b). Among the main questions concerning privatization are the following. How will goods and resources formerly managed by the Communist Party in the name of 'the entire people' become either state property *sensu stricto* or the possessions of jural persons? Will socialism's complexly overlapping and often vaguely defined rights of use, ownership and transfer be rendered the 'exclusive individual property' of the neo-liberal theory that underlies privatization programmes, and if so, how?

Analyses of post-socialist property transformation so far find the evidence equivocal. Stark (1996), for instance, writes of 'recombinant property', rather than a wholesale shift from 'public' to 'private' ownership. He finds mixes of ownership by the state, private firms and private individuals, with different social actors holding different bundles of rights and the definitions of the status of property being blurred and ambiguous. In his view, these forms are far more adaptive, in the climate of tremendous uncertainty following the collapse of socialism, than more exclusive individual ownership would be. Thus, he believes, over at least the medium run powerful economic actors will resist the disambiguation of property rights that Hann, in this volume's introduction, sees as a dominant model for modern industrial economies; instead such actors will profit from leaving property rights unclear. Cornea (1993) agrees, as does Staniszkis (1991), for somewhat different reasons.[1] What, then, is happening with plans to create individual private property in this region?

In the present essay, I pursue two questions, one raised directly by the post-socialist situation and a broader one concerning property as a concept. The first question is: through what sorts of social struggles are actors striving to carve individual ownership rights from the collective property of the socialist period, and in whose interests (if anyone's) is it to clarify these, reducing ambiguities and rendering rights more exclusive? To elucidate this matter, I present some examples from my research in a Transylvanian community. The second, larger question is: how should we *conceive* of ownership, in seeking to follow the transformation of 'socialist property' as privatization proceeds? What conceptualizations enable us to catch the most significant aspects of this process? Anthropological observers (along with lawyers) are unlikely to follow the common practice of seeing property as a 'thing' or 'object', or even as a relation of persons to things; we tend to see property, rather, as relations among persons with respect to things (cf. Strathern 1988; Hann, chapter 1; Macfarlane, chapter 5), often emphasizing the rights and obligations that ownership entails (e.g., Gluckman 1965a; Malinowski 1935). I follow Hann as well as Ghani (1996), however, in suggesting that property is best analysed in terms of the whole system of social, cultural and political relations, rather than through more narrowly legalistic notions such as 'rights' and 'claims'. We probably do better to speak of property as a bundle not of rights (which may be moot – see also Howarth, chapter 9) but rather of *powers*. For those who would study post-socialist privatization as nothing more than a respecification of the locus of ownership rights, I offer a complex – if murky – picture centring on power relations.

### The setting

How is individual ownership being chiselled from formerly socialist property? My data on this question come from Aurel Vlaicu, a Transylvanian village undergoing decollectivization.[2] That process, which I have described in other publications (see Verdery 1994, 1998), was launched in 1991 with the passage of Romania's Law on Agricultural Land Resources, known as Law 18/1991. As of 1996, decollectivization in Aurel Vlaicu had produced individual titles to land for about 90 per cent of villagers, but this land was arrayed in various property forms and subject to conflicting claims, antithetical to what I believe the neo-liberal architects of privatization had in mind. Particularly significant among them was a new organizational form, the agricultural association. Throughout Romania (and some other countries of the region as well), the liquidation of collective farms (in Romanian, *cooperative agricole de productie*, or CAPs) and the return of land to its former owners was accompanied by the creation of associations (*asociaţii*).[3] These are a kind of producers' cooperative whose *raison d'être* is that very few of the new proprietors own the equipment necessary for cultivating their newly returned land, and many of them are too old to carry out the work of farming it. Moreover, in the Romanian case, many new land owners do not even live in villages at all, for the restitution process permitted *all* heirs of former owners, even those living in distant cities, to claim family land. In order to ensure that newly private land does not go uncultivated, thus requiring massive food imports, the government encouraged people to form associations.

Legally, an association takes a form that is neither a limited liability nor a joint-stock company but a 'commercial society'; it has a different tax regime from those other, more explicitly profit-oriented forms. In some Romanian settlements, villagers chose to transform the CAP directly into one or more associations without first dividing the land among former owners. In Vlaicu (as in many other villages), however, before an association could organize, a few people occupied the land they had once owned and began to work it. This set off a chain reaction that ended in reassigning private property rights to all former owners in the location of their old plots. About half of all recipients then joined the Aurel Vlaicu association, giving management of their land to it. Members are free to exit at any time, taking their land with them.[4] It is understood that the owners hold and retain ownership rights to the land placed in the association; they transfer only managerial rights over cultivation in exchange for a payment from the harvest.[5] Thus, a given object – a piece of land – has different claimants to ownership rights and use rights over it: different sets of rights overlap.

The process of land restitution proved extremely complex and resulted in considerable ambiguity in the ownership status of land (see Verdery 1994 for a detailed description). The titling process, to begin with, was very slow: although Law 18 was passed in February 1991, three years later less than a quarter of Romania's entitled households had received their property deed (*titlu de proprietate*), a figure that had increased to 63 per cent by mid-1996.[6] In consequence, for many villagers in Vlaicu and elsewhere, even by that year it was still not clear exactly who 'owned' which parcel. Differences of opinion and overt conflicts persist; legal challenges hold up the process of clarification, for one can go to court only when one has a deed, but it is precisely over who should have the deed that many parties want to litigate. While villagers fight over these questions, local officials often usurp the contending owners' usufruct rights, cultivating the land and disposing of the product themselves.[7] Additional complexities lie in the ambiguous status of land while it is in titling limbo. All claimants received in 1991 a temporary property affidavit (*adeverinţă*), but this did not endow them with full proprietary rights, which were to follow only with subsequent registration and titling. Bearers of an affidavit held only rights to use the land and take its fruits; they could not sell it or use it as collateral on a loan (although the affidavit did obligate them to pay taxes on it). Strictly speaking, then, until villagers began to obtain title in 1995, those who placed their land with the association did so as not-yet-owners, allocating rights of control that they did not technically have full capacity to cede.[8]

Following Romania's 1989 revolution, then, 'ownership' contained ambiguities that had a number of sources. Different people might contest ownership of a single object, complicating the assessment of use rights, obligations and claims to revenue. Alternatively, ownership was ambiguous because different social actors held overlapping claims to a given parcel: for example, the state held rights of eminent domain, enabling it to preempt the rights of owners to land located in the state farms, but the owners nonetheless had a claim on state farm revenues. Similarly, the rights and claims of individual owners and associations as managers often overlapped. Even in cases where the hierarchy of rights and obligations is in fact quite *un*ambiguous, in the context of privatization programmes like those being implemented in the former socialist bloc they appear indistinct, because of their complex interrelations and the multiplicity of actors holding them. In the sections to follow, I explore these several sources of ambiguity and overlap, as people in Vlaicu struggle to become owners in various ways. I also ask who, in this environment, presses for clarification of ownership as against persistent uncertainty, and I find that it is generally the less powerful who strive to individuate their holdings against the predation of the stronger.

### Contested ownership

The overlapping rights that accompanied association membership resulted, first of all, from the fact that most villagers lacked means of cultivation. For example, in the first year after property restitution, one woman I know tried to work her land as an independent farmer. She described her experience to her neighbour (who had joined the association, and from whom I have the anecdote) as follows. After a season of racing around to arrange for tractor drivers who did not show up or showed up drunk, to find fuel when they claimed not to have any, to line up a harvester when her crop was ready and hoping it would come before the crop was ruined, to find fertilizer and herbicides, and so on, she said to her neighbour, 'Never again! Who has this kind of energy and time to arrange for ploughing and harvesting? With the association, they come to you with 1,000 kg of wheat for each hectare you give them and you haven't lifted a finger for it.'

As long as villagers lack means of production, all but the most recalcitrant see definite advantages to the overlapping property rights and obligations of the associational form. The association obviates their having to maintain or acquire their own storage spaces and implements, yet they retain some say in how their land is to be used. Although they are at the mercy of the association's leaders (and, of course, the weather) for the revenues they will draw from their land and will almost surely get less output value from it than they could if they farmed it themselves, they are saved tremendous effort and expense. Particularly for elderly villagers, this is a great advantage. It serves as adequate incentive for people to press for at least minimal clarification of their property rights, in the form of the affidavit. To have an affidavit did not guarantee, however, that one would know exactly where one's land lay. Such uncertainty posed no problem for owners who gave their land to the association, but it did pose a problem for the association's managers, who could not effectively work a piece of land if they did not know its boundaries. They thus had an incentive to clarify that, even if an owner was not concerned to do so. Let me show this with a specific example.

Week after week during the winter and spring of 1994 I heard complaints from each of three sets of cousins concerning their seeming inability to fit peaceably into a stretch of land that had been divided among them. Ill will focused on the person in the middle, who seemed to be squeezed too tightly and kept encroaching on one or the other of his neighbours. 'He's nuts!' complained one of them. 'He's so bent on enriching himself with his land that he's prepared to throw away a half century of good relations!' 'She ploughed too far away from the edge!' he defended himself to me. 'There's a strip that hasn't been ploughed for years, and she just left it and came in on my land. What am I supposed to do?' In reply she alleged that not she but the other set of cousins had ploughed too far from the edge. During my earlier visits these three families had been the closest of friends. Now I heard nothing from them but disgruntlement and carping.

In April, at sowing time, I learned to my surprise that the cousin in the middle had given his piece to the association. This was particularly remarkable inasmuch as he had expressed nothing but contempt for that organization and had been one of the first to withdraw his land and farm on his own. He had changed his mind, he explained to me, because he thought the association would work to clarify the boundary dispute so as to obtain more land for its own use. That is, where two villagers contest land and neither is in the association, if one puts his land into it the association will strive to resolve the conflict so as to increase the certainty and extent of its managerial rights. I heard exactly the same motivation concerning other problematic land cases. A variant on the theme appeared when someone challenged the amounts received by one of the richest villagers, who immediately put his land in the association until his title could be confirmed.[9]

Thus, whenever someone's property right is questioned by someone else – whenever we are dealing not with overlapping rights but with conflicting claims to a given surface – one solution is to let the association handle the problem. In this way, the association becomes a parking place for property of dubious ownership status, exclusive rights to which are claimed by more than one person. If for any reason 'owners' are unable to establish the bounds of their property and the legality of their title, then the association may step in to help them: its managers need to clarify ownership rights at least sufficiently to know whose land they are empowered to work.

We see in a different example a rather different source of ambiguous or overlapping property rights. The example concerns not land but other things that once belonged to the collective farm, and the agent of persistent ambiguity in ownership in this instance was a court decision. A villager I will call Ionescu sued the association over an outbuilding he had tried to buy at auction, as required by law for disposing of collective farm property.[10] Leaders of the association had, in his view, corrupted the procedures of the auction and illegitimately acquired the building over his bid. Having lost his first lawsuit, he appealed (I was present for the second trial), but the appeal failed as well. As a result, an object to which a single individual had attempted to secure exclusive ownership rights remained, instead, collective property, owned jointly by all the association's members in common. Their rights to it as individuals were limited to storing their share of the grain taken from everyone's fields together (that is, one could not store in the building anything one had planted and harvested oneself), and there were no provisions for recovering their quota of its value should they resign from the association.

There were two interesting features to this case. First was the reasoning offered by the judge who rejected Ionescu's appeal, a woman with a lengthy career as a judge during the socialist period. What was decisive for her was the question of what constitutes 'the public good', which she saw as her job to defend – especially in these uncertain times, when, she said, morality should play an even stronger role than usual in deciding cases. In this case she did not believe the plaintiff could claim to be defending the social interest himself, for a larger social interest was represented by the defendants; they were far more numerous than he, and it was in their interests to keep the outbuilding available for general use rather than to have it become the property of 'a single individual'. To my suggestion that in the new Romania the public good might best be served by promoting private ownership that would contribute to solving the country's economic crisis, she agreed that this was in principle true. But Ionescu was not, she thought, the kind of person to act in that way. Thus, through a legal decision, a quasi-collective property form took precedence over exclusive individual possession.

Second, although what was decisive in the outcome were the values of the judge, a large number of villagers (especially those who had formerly owned land, as opposed to post-collectivization in-migrants) agreed with her. They, too, saw it as unacceptable to have something built with villagers' labour become the property of a single individual, particularly an in-migrant whose family had not contributed to building it. Central to their reaction was the idea that one should possess what one works, and neither Ionescu nor his family had worked on building this object. Nor did he intend (or so it was said) to work with it now: he was going to rent it back to the association and become rich without doing any work at all. The widely held view was that the community, which had laboured on the building, should remain its 'owner'. The values informing this view were not just 'communist': they had been part of village notions of personhood before the socialist period as well (cf. Lampland 1995).

In this case, an effort to disambiguate the property status of an object – to reduce the overlapping claims that individual owners and organizations might exercise over its possession and use – was launched by someone relatively powerless in the village social hierarchy, a low-status in-migrant, against the state-supported quasi-collective form, the association. Defeating the effort was a coalition of officials at the local level (including the association's leaders) and in court, backed by locally born villagers relatively better situated in the village hierarchy. All these groups found it to their advantage to maintain overlapping property rights, rather than permit individual ownership. If, in my first example, it was the actor with relatively greater institutional and social power – the association, as against the individual member – who saw it as advantageous to clarify ownership rights and claims, in this second example it is the person with relatively *less* social power – Ionescu – who sought to do so. The chief difference is that the association was clarifying the ownership status of land so as to subject it to further overlapping claims (see final section below), whereas Ionescu was seeking to individuate an object for his exclusive ownership. Something like the same result appears in a third case, that concerning the superimposed ownership claims of two sets of Vlaiceni to a single surface area in the village.

Among the persons whose land was expropriated in 1945 and redistributed to others were families of German ethnicity, resident in Vlaicu since the late 1800s and, until their expropriation, owners of its largest farms.[11] As of 1945, they lost all their land and were deported to the Soviet Union for war reparations labour; their fields were redistributed to Romanian veterans of the war who had little or no land (I call them '45ers'). When the CAP was formed, it was these Romanians who gave the land to it, and by the provisions of Law 18 they were the ones to receive the land back at the CAP's dissolution. In 1991, therefore, the former German owners and their heirs were outraged to find that they had received not land but shares in a nearby state farm.[12] Since Germans had never had land in that part of the village, they challenged the decision in court, winning the right to receive a total of seventy hectares altogether. The commune's mayor gave it to them in precisely the place where Germans had owned land before.

Unfortunately, restoring ownership to the Germans meant throwing off that same land all the Romanians who had been impropriated on it in 1945 and briefly *re*impropriated after 1991 (fifty-nine families). But where to put them? For two and a half years, this problem was left unsolved. The '45ers' could not bring suit because few had property deeds. Initially, the mayor asked the association to distribute some produce to them (this effectively diminished the take for other members), but they continued to agitate for return of 'their' land received in 1945. One or two filed suit against the mayor; he responded by giving them land on a state farm from which still other villagers were supposed to be paid – in short, further complicating the set of persons having a claim to that state farm land (which now had to pay two sets of masters) in the name of simplifying the superimposed ownership claims to the fields of the Germans. A group of '45ers' finally took matters into their own hands: they threatened the Germans and forced them to stop ploughing the contested area, then ploughed and occupied it themselves. The consequences were a lawsuit that the Germans won, considerable wasted time, the loss of fifteen hectares' yield where ploughing had never resumed, and much escalated friction between the two ethnic groups.

In this example, two sets of people – the German owners/heirs and the Romanian '45ers' – came into conflict for title to a single surface area. The set that prevailed represented more 'collective' interests, in two senses, than those who lost. First, the Germans brought their initial suit *as a group*, arguing that the local implementation of Law 18 had discriminated against them as Germans; the '45ers', by contrast, failed to produce a collective counter-response, striving to resecure their ownership rights by arguing with the mayor as individuals. The results of their one collective action – breaking in on the Germans' ploughing – collapsed as soon as the Germans took the case to court; they named a particular '45er' as defendant, at which point all the other '45ers' abandoned ship. Second, the Germans did not attempt to individuate themselves as owners, but rather argued to receive their land *in a single block*, which they would work collectively as an association. Indeed, they did not carve out individual parcels until forced to do so in 1995 in order to receive title (and even then, they assigned each family a plot that had no necessary relation to that family's prior holdings). Here, again, as in Ionescu's case above, we see the legal process favouring actors who are constituted as collectives.

Those who are pressing for exclusive *individual* ownership, in this instance, are once again the relatively less powerful: Romanian families of poor background, most of them entitled to only fractions of a hectare, as against the six to ten hectares of several German owners. When the Germans won their suit, twelve owners replaced fifty-nine on the same surface; retaining their collective character, the twelve faced the fifty-nine who as individual families sought – and failed – to reestablish their claim. This same pattern of the more powerful preferring non-individuation of rights appears in my final example, in which political officials profit from ambiguities and uncertainty in ownership rights so as to enrich themselves.

A villager I know bought a tractor and offered to plough the land of his elderly aunt. She went with him to the place she knew to have been hers but, to their astonishment, they found the land already ploughed and planted with wheat. Others working nearby told them it had been ploughed by the vice-mayor of the commune, someone who was not from Vlaicu and had no rights to land anywhere in it. Some time later, as I walked through this same area with members of the Vlaicu land commission, I learned from one of them that it has the most confused property situation of any in the village. Much of it had belonged to a wealthy land owner and had been nationalized in 1948, some of it becoming state reserves and some entering the newly established state farm; parts of it that had not been cultivable before had been cleared and turned into arable land; large sections of it had been administratively detached from Vlaicu and given to the CAP of neighbouring Gelmar; and substantial chunks had also been eaten away by the river and deposited in yet another village on the opposite shore. The area was often referred to as 'la Jigoaia', after the person from whom it had been nationalized.

As we talked about the area, my interlocutor suddenly said, 'This should all have been for the land commission to redistribute. But who do you think was the first person to come in here after the revolution, before he became mayor . . . The old mayor ordered him to get out, but he said "Forget it. I'm here to stay." Then he stood for election, and won. There's no getting him out now!' I spent considerable time trying to verify this statement – speaking with the heir of 'la Jigoaia', who was having tremendous difficulty getting any of the land back (among other things, she found that the crucial file in the Land Registry Office was inexplicably missing), and asking others who worked in the area or knew something about it. I heard the same story repeatedly, but the murky state of the property boundaries in this area defeated all my attempts to prove or disprove it. I am inclined to believe the story, however, and proceed with my account as if it were true. Like the case in my very first example, this one involves conflicting ownership claims to exclusive rights on the same surface. But in the first case above, the claims were to parcels that had the same status: they had belonged to the villagers who donated it to the collective and had remained collective property until returned by Law 18. But in the area being putatively usurped by commune authorities, the property had belonged to someone long ago expropriated. 'State property' that is still in state farms has custodians – the IAS directors – but other forms of nationalized property, especially that which entered into collectives by fiat rather than by the owners' donation, lie at dead centre of socialism's 'property vacuum' (cf. Campeanu 1988). 'The commune' is supposed to administer them, but 'the commune' can act only through its administration; and those in this particular commune's administration would seem to have their own ideas as to how 'state property' should be used. As the most powerful local authorities, they are in an excellent position to keep the definition of these properties unclear. The mayor is president of the local land commission; he can encourage it to avoid a piece of land in which he has an interest. The commune's administrators have privileged access to documentation; they can identify the areas in which ownership rights will be most difficult to untangle, such as 'la Jigoaia', and they can find proofs 'missing' when heirs come to call. Long years of friendship with party officials in the county capital – some of whom are still in power,

but now as appointees of the Iliescu government – assure local authorities that complaints from villagers wanting to clarify their rights will be
met with a yawn. Their connections and their local power make other
lesser authorities (such as those in the association) hesitant to expose
their usurpations.[13] Unlike the land contested by the three cousins in
case 1, the status of this land cannot be resolved by putting it in the
association. At best, it can be resolved only when the usurpers secure
title to the land and can be sued by those who want to claim it. In this
most confused of all lands in Vlaicu, clarity may therefore be postponed
indefinitely.

This example is directly related to the case of Germans and '45ers' –
and in a disturbing way, for the social conflict of that example results
directly from the usurpation suggested here. Law 18 provides that each
village should constitute a 'reserve fund' from lands that are not claimed
by former owners or their heirs, or from farms in excess of ten hectares.
'La Jigoaia' is one such farm, having consisted of about forty hectares
when it was nationalized.[14] Those parts of it that had not been disposed
of otherwise would have formed a substantial reserve for resolving
problems of property restitution. The problems might include finding
land for people whose old parcels had disappeared when an embank-
ment was built to contain the river or when the CAP buildings were
constructed, as well as for cases in which more than one owner had a
rightful claim to a piece of land – as with the land given to the Germans.
Law 18 states clearly that when ownership is restored to the members of
'national minorities' expropriated prior to 1948, they should receive
land from the 'reserve fund'; the mayor's award of a block of land on
their original site blatantly contravened this provision. And no wonder:
to have given them a comparable block in the 'reserve fund' would have
meant displacing the powerful people already working there, first among
them himself.

In sum, the power of the local authorities enables them to maintain
uncertainty of ownership in an area that should go to other users. To
keep their own cultivation of this area from being uncovered and
stopped, they allocate exclusive ownership rights to surfaces where such
rights have already been given to others, thereby producing ethnic
conflict and litigation that distract attention from their own misdemea-
nours. To prolong their usurpation of good land, they procrastinate in
solving these conflicting claims, taking advantage of continued ambiguity in the nature of land still held in state farms. Because the claims to
state farm land are only to its *revenues* and not to usufruct or disposition,
state farm directors can be strong-armed into paying out dividends to
people beyond those whose ancestral land is actually within their

perimeter. Although this reduces the profits these farm directors can claim for the actual former owners and themselves, they are reluctant to take on the local authorities who oversee many aspects of their life chances. Here we see it advantageous to local power-holders that ownership remain unclarified, but at the cost of interethnic harmony and other villagers' livelihoods.[15]

We might push this conclusion further, seeing in local authorities' preference for ambiguous property rights a continuation of socialism's widespread resort to social networks, as directors of firms and local officials parlay the resources they control *by virtue of their institutional positions* into ever greater success for their firms and themselves. It may be that because the party-based hierarchy of responsibility and subordination has weakened, making horizontal networks relatively more significant than they were before relative to vertical ones, it is now more important than ever to have an institutional vantage point – that is, a set of resources *defined as collective*, rather than exclusively individual – as one's base of operations. In this environment, property rights emerge as decidedly ambiguous and, in Stark's (1996) terms, 'recombinant', with mixes of individual and collective rights, capacities, and claims that permit a flexible exploitation of those having less power by those with more.

### Hierarchies of rights and powers

In the above examples, I have shown how ownership of a piece of land may be contested among social actors, both equal and unequal. Even if ownership is clarified, however, the resulting situation is not necessarily unambiguous. The reasons include a political context in which 'the state' plays a significant ownership role and the political process has continued to bias outcomes in the direction of collective as opposed to individual ownership rights. Law 18 set fairly stringent constraints on an individual's private property rights – that is, it instituted a hierarchy of prior rights and claims, similar to what Gluckman in his work on Barotse land owning describes as a 'hierarchy of estates of administration' (1968, 1965a). For instance, it constrained the land's use: owners of agricultural land do not have the right to leave it uncultivated, on penalty of a fine; those holding use rights and not cultivating the land lose those rights after two years (Law 18/1991, Art. 53–5). Nor have they the right to change the category of its use – say, from vineyard to pasture, or arable to houseplot – except under certain conditions, and only by permission of the Ministry of Agriculture (Art. 56, 57 and 69). There are constraints on acquisition as well. Persons who in 1991 failed to register their claim to land within a specific time (initially thirty days, extended to forty-five) lost their right to claim ownership altogether – property rights reverted to the state. No one was permitted to claim the return of more than ten hectares per family (Art. 8 and 9) nor to acquire thereafter more than a hundred hectares total (Art. 46). Finally, although the wording of the law is unclear on this point, it appears to make all sales of agricultural land contingent on the prior exercise of rights of preemption by the state, through an organization called the Agency for Rural Development and Planning (Art. 48).[16]

Such provisions, together with the fact that anyone wishing to regain property title to earlier-owned lands had to file a *request* (*cerere*) to this effect, suggest that 'the state' holds the most inclusive, prior rights over disposal and use, the top level in a hierarchy of administrative estates. This set of state powers is not unique to post-socialism: many legal systems empower the state to limit property rights (though the content of those limitations varies). Nor are these state powers in practice absolute: Law 18 specifically allocates to 'common law', for instance, the division of a holding among its rightful heirs (Art. 12).

Law 18 not only made the state preeminent landlord; it predisposed subsequent property rights at levels below this in a collective rather than individual direction, by giving associations as jural entities the edge in acquiring property from moribund CAPs. Consider the following provision:

Zootechnic constructions, workshops for small manufactures, machinery, equipment, and other such fixed means belonging to the disbanded CAP, as well as the land underneath these and the land necessary to using them, and also vineyards and orchards and animals all become the property of the members of associations of a private nature having the status of jural persons, if these are established. The rights of former CAP members to the above-mentioned goods will be set as a value proportional to the land area the CAP received from them and the volume of work they gave the CAP (Art. 28).

In a word, CAPs would 'morph' into associations, the capital of which was assigned as shares to the members by an algorithm linking one's total land and labour contributions to the CAP.[17] Only those villagers who chose not to belong to the association were to be separated out fully from the collective and paid in money or kind for their share of the fixed capital. Thus conceived, the law presents the continuation of a quasi-collective form (the association) as *un*marked, to use a linguistic term – or, in computer jargon, as the 'default option' – while transformation of CAPs into individual property was *marked*, requiring extra work to effectuate. We see clearly in this a systemic bias towards collective forms.

So far I have indicated the advantage accorded to the upper tiers in the hierarchy of administration over land. I now describe the intricately overlapping rights, obligations and claims exercised by individual owners and the association's managers concerning the land given into the administration of the latter. Let us take as example a widow who is too old to manage the work on her newly acquired three hectares. Theoretically, as holder of title to the land, she exercises rights to use, benefit from, and transfer it. If she turns it over to the association, she loses the right to farm her land on her own or allocate its use to a third party, and she alienates most (but not all) of the rights to its day-to-day management; still, she can tell the agronomist what crops she wants as payment, and in what proportions. She can specify, for example, that she wants some sugar beets, potatoes, corn and wheat in specific proportions, and cash instead of barley. That is, she has the right to influence the use of her land even if she is not farming it directly. Her choices obligate her to pay certain amounts of money (according to the areas being sown with particular crops) for the cost of ploughing and to provide the necessary labour for the labour-intensive tasks such as hoeing and weeding corn, since the association does not have an independent labour force for this work.

Although our widow can specify the *proportions* of various products and cash that she will receive as revenue from her land, she has lost virtually all control over the *amounts* (except for the rows of corn she hoes, where her effort and timing do affect the outcome). These enter into a complex politics within the association leadership. One agronomist of the Vlaicu association, for instance, wanted to be popular with villagers and prove that he was as good as the previous fellow, even at the expense of the association's long-term prospects; after the harvest, he paid for the inputs and salaries and then divided the entire remainder among members (each received about 1,000 kg per hectare given to the association), reserving nothing to renew production the following year – by which time he had left the village. Two and three years later, members received only 400 and 550 kg per hectare, for the new agronomist had persuaded its council to buy two tractors and related equipment with the association's income, docking members' pay for the cost and interest on the loan. If our widow were clairvoyant, she might have taken her land out of the association so as to avoid having to contribute to the future purchase of tractors; otherwise, she has lost income and automatically become part-owner of the tractors, since she helped to buy them.[18] On the other hand, should she decide – as many Vlaiceni do – to keep, say, a hectare of her land out of the association and work it herself, she might (if her timing and connections are right) now use an association tractor to plough that hectare.[19]

The association to which the widow gives her land acquires rights to manage and use it and to take its fruits, some of which must be redistributed to her. That is, by taking the land, the association incurs obligations to cultivate it and generate revenue for redistribution. In summer 1994, the Vlaicu association ran out of money to pay for the ploughing, sowing and harvesting of about twenty-five hectares for which it was nonetheless obligated to deliver a product; the agronomist cast about for someone else who would do the work and pay the owners in a sort of sub-contracting arrangement. Because everyone giving land has a claim on revenues, every member of the association would have received less had the twenty-five hectares gone uncultivated. That is, the rights of each member limit the rights of others to the product from their land; or, to put it differently, people share rights to the revenues with other members. In the following year (1995) a similar sub-contracting solution resolved the problem that, for rotational purposes, the association needed to plant more corn than members were prepared to work; a third party contracted to plant the difference.

These two examples show several tiers of overlapping rights and obligations with respect to both revenues and use. At the top (tier 1) is the state as preeminent landlord; below that are individual land owners (tier 2), who allocate use rights to the association (tier 3). In order to fulfil its obligations to owners, the association has the right to sub-contract further the use rights allocated to it, thus producing a fourth tier and an alternative form of 'estate of production', in the terminology of Max Gluckman. Each tier of claimants expected revenues from that surface, and in 1995 tiers 1 and 2 also exercised certain rights to the product that constrained managerial decisions at tier 3 below it. From the viewpoint of a Western ideology of exclusive individual ownership, this hierarchy of rights ambiguates the property status of land. The allocation of rights, however, although complex, is by no means chaotic.

Although the individual holder of title to a specific surface area of former CAP land theoretically holds all the rights of use, enjoyment, and disposal not constrained by the state, there are serious contextual constraints on the exercise of these rights. One concerns the possibilities for disposing of their products, owing to inadequate channels for distribution. A household of two or three people will use about 600 kg of wheat a year for its own needs; anything over that amount will be useful only if it is sold – and the cash from sale will be necessary to paying for next year's ploughing and harvesting. But without a vehicle or a cart to drive to market and the time to go and stand there to sell, one may have difficulty exchanging the product for cash. One alternative has been to contract part of the product to a state monopoly organization called Romcereal, but this means accepting the state price for grain, which has been considerably lower than the market price. A second alternative is to give one's land to other, landless villagers in share-cropping arrangements for half the harvest; this economizes on the cash needed for production and disposes easily of half the product. That alternative is limited, however, by the lack of tools, farm equipment and cash among landless villagers, and by their loss of interest in share-cropping once they secure land of their own. Thus, a rudimentary distribution infrastructure limits property-owners' possibilities for dis-posing of the fruits of their possessions – not just for individual owners/ farmers but for the association and its members as well.

A more important constraint concerns production, for few of the people who obtained land owned other means of production necessary for cultivating it: the implements they had donated to the collective in the 1950s had long since rusted away. Those who had given cattle to the CAP received in 1991 an equivalent number, which they might use as draft animals, but to profit from their animals they would have to acquire ploughs, harrows, seeders, threshers, fertilizer and all the other means that go into a cycle of agricultural production. Ideally, they would buy tractors and combines as well. In the early 1990s, however, the price of agricultural implements increased much faster than the prices of agricultural produce.[20] Actions of both government and banks made the conditions for credit to purchase equipment very unfavour-able, interest rates approaching or even exceeding 100 per cent. Without cold cash it was hard to acquire implements or get one's land worked, and without these it was hard to acquire cold cash. This simple conundrum caused many to give some or all of their land to the association, rather than attempt to work it themselves as exclusive private owners.

The association, for its part, enjoys rights to manage and use the lands given into it; its members collectively 'own' the buildings and imple-ments in its care, which its leaders manage. As with individual owners, however, the association's managerial rights and its control over the product are circumscribed in a variety of ways. These include the property structure that associations inherited and their relations both with members and with the state. The association is obligated to cultivate the land it has taken in; it must create enough revenue to pay the members. But the conditions under which it is to do this are far from optimal. The structure of the fields worked by associations such as that in Vlaicu is unconducive to rational cultivation. The land commissions that restored land to owners failed to consolidate fields;[21] even worse, the return of *people's original plots* meant breaking the association's holdings into myriad small parcels, scattered among the parcels of non-members. Because the association finds it technically impossible to work very tiny parcels, it cannot accept every piece of land people want to give it, and this reduces the scale of its operations.[22]

Constraints inherent in the association's relationship with its members come from such factors as the members' rights to withdraw their land at will, their claims on revenue and problems with labour. As owners, members have the right to withdraw their land – indeed, some did so once their pay dropped following the purchase of tractors. In order to form a rational cultivation plan, in 1995 the association was beginning to press for three-year contracts, which would restrict owners' rights to withdraw. Members resisted the contracts, however, fearing further erosion of their receipts. Their rights of withdrawal were in turn limited by the availability of other ways of getting their land cultivated. In Vlaicu, several people bought tractors and a few of them would plough for others, but in many other villages alternatives were few: there, associations could control their members by threatening expulsion, which might mean not being able to have one's land worked at all. Rights to allocate land use thus became an important locus of struggle between individual owners and associations, the outcome being much affected by villagers' wealth and by conditions in their external environment.

Problems with the labour supply, coupled with members' rights to determine their crop profile and form of payment, placed further checks on the association's exercise of its managerial capacities. The generally low technical and financial endowment of agriculture means that, like CAPs before them, associations must rely on the manual labour of their members to carry out labour-intensive tasks such as hoeing and weeding. Many members are not physically capable of doing this work, or not locally resident for the purpose; they tend not to ask for payment in crops whose hoeing and harvesting requirements they cannot meet – especially root crops and maize. This is particularly true of members residing in cities, who hold three-fourths of the Vlaicu association's land and, according to the agronomist, generally want payment in wheat and cash only. No farm can plant wheat year after year on the bulk of its surface area without crop rotation; nonetheless, the Vlaicu association has been forced to err in that direction. In the summer of 1996, the condition of the soil and the cost of fertilizer drove Vlaicu's agronomist to increase the amount of maize beyond what local members could hoe and harvest, risking large expenditures for day labour to do so. Therefore, members' rights to determine their revenue and to dispose of their land put pressure on the leaders not to manage optimally and not to take risks that might reduce income and provoke departures.

Aside from constraints inherent in their relations with members, the association's managerial rights have been limited by its dependency on the state for mechanized inputs, prices and credits – a dependency that, in the view of this farm's agronomist, is much greater now than it was for CAPs. The right of associations to inherit the fixed capital of CAPs did little to endow them with tractors and combines, for CAPs in Romania, unlike other socialist countries, generally did not have this equipment: it was provided by machinery stations (SMAs) on the Soviet model. After 1989 the SMAs changed their names to 'Agromecs' but remained state institutions, slated for eventual privatization. Associations lacking equipment were compelled to use their services. The fees, however, were exorbitant, set so as to support the leftover bureaucracy of paper-pushers and the antiquated machinery that tractor-drivers still treated carelessly (using it to moonlight for side income, as well). In Vlaicu, it was precisely these fees that pushed the agronomist to persuade members to buy tractors and other implements. (They remained dependent on others, however, for harvesting.)

Finally, the association's rights of control have been limited by government policies relating to pricing and credits. Problems of obtaining enough money to start the production cycle and of disposing of large crops pushed associations toward dealing with state agencies such as Romcereal. The fact that the state initially allocated credits for agriculture only through Romcereal meant that cash-strapped associations were forced to enter into contracts with it. Moreover, the alternative of getting a bank loan and repaying it by more lucrative sales on the open market was foreclosed for many associations because they did not have enough fixed capital to stand as collateral (see Verdery 1994: 1087). When credits became available through banks, the often crippling interest rates made them inaccessible to barely viable associations. Banks, for their part, have been notorious for offering friends (as opposed to solvent clients) the cheapest loans. Thus, government and bank policies produced a dearth of credit that is the biggest obstacle to associations' enjoyment of their property rights.

In this section I have discussed the hierarchy of administrative estates, emphasizing particularly the overlapping rights of association and individual owners that constitute 'private land ownership' as something rather different from the exclusive individual possession of neo-liberal theory. While underscoring the rights and obligations that supposedly accrue to owners and managers, I have found it increasingly necessary to qualify those rights by noting the systemic constraints on people's exercise of them. In so doing, I support Hann's observation that to consider property only as a matter of rights and obligations is inadequate.

'There are many persons and families in Hungary today for whom the current rhetoric about widening choice and extending property rights must seem a sick joke . . . they cannot become entrepreneurial farmers because they lack the basic capital resources, and their social rights are being whittled away all the time' (Hann 1993a: 313; cf. Anderson, chapter 3).

Thus ownership, in the examples given above, consists of complexly overlapping use and revenue rights lodged in external conditions that give many of the holders of these rights incomplete powers for exercising them. Exclusive individual ownership rights to land, which many in both Eastern Europe and 'the West' see as the goal of decollectivization, are effectively constituted only within a total field of relations among institutions, policies and social actors. These relations shape what actors are *able* to do with property, modifying the 'rights' to which they may be entitled. For something more closely approaching exclusive individual proprietorship to emerge would require not so much clearer legal specification of who has what rights – these rights are fairly clear already – but modifications in the surrounding economy, modifications that would permit individuals to acquire the means of cultivation affordably and to dispose profitably of their product while outcompeting quasi-collective associational forms. That, in turn, depends on various parties' electoral fortunes, intergovernmental relations, decisions by international lending agencies, and other conditions not usually included in discussions of property.

## Conclusion

The above examples show various individual and collective claims jostling and interfering with one another in Aurel Vlaicu in such a way that clear and exclusive ownership rights to land have not uniformly emerged. Even where they do, this is not necessarily the solution everyone adopts. The elderly who have no hope of acquiring farm equipment, people who live in cities, or all who for one or another reason cannot work their land, find it preferable to perpetuate a mix of individual land owning with quasi-collective production forms that rest on overlapping rights, claims and obligations.

Who, in this environment, strives for clarity and exclusive ownership rights? On occasion, I have suggested above, it is the association – paradoxically, since that entity benefits from the collective wealth of the CAP, is premised on overlapping rather than exclusive rights and claims, and maintains itself in part through some degree of collusion with local authorities who like situations that are unclear. Nonetheless, the association's staff want sufficient certainty concerning their members' ownership rights to be able to plan. They also want to reduce their organization's dependence on the external environment and escape the predation of state institutions that are more powerful than they – such as the state monopoly Romcereal and the machinery Agromecs, whose pricing policies can intersect to squeeze an association's budget dry. They want to have 'their own' tractors to which no one else will have a claim. Indeed, as time has passed the accountant of this association has seen ever more reason for them to strike out on their own, clarifying the overlapping rights and claims that define their internal organization and striving to limit claims from outside.

As this wording implies, and as I have also indicated above, striving to clarify one's ownership rights is sometimes a weapon of the relatively weaker trying to protect themselves from abuse by the stronger.[23] Those who want to be sure they get what the land can yield them will press to reduce other claims to it. But this exposes them to the problems of arranging for its cultivation; hence, many of the weakest prefer the quasi-collective association, which solves these problems for them. The villagers more likely to succeed in benefiting from exclusive rights are those who have managed to buy a tractor or have easy access to one, have reliable call on a harvester, have transportation and cash enabling them to buy fertilizer and herbicides and to market their produce, dispose of a labour force, and have outbuildings for storing their crops. Without such resources, exclusive ownership rights avail them little. This is a description of someone who is already somewhat well-to-do by village standards – in land, in savings from prior income, or in post-1989 opportunities.

For villagers who lack these resources, the system of overlapping claims and rights provides a far more satisfactory ownership arrangement than would exclusive and individual ones. The reasons are the prior set of social arrangements that denuded them of productive means; the present arrangements for working the land and obtaining credit; and the destruction of a village community that renewed its commitment to farming across the generations: most of these old people do not have children who want to farm. In order for exclusive property rights to exist, it is not enough to legislate property restitution: the entire configuration of villagers' external relations would have to be different. These external conditions include, as of this writing, a systemic bias against individual ownership and in favour of state or quasi-collective forms, and the power of local officials to keep the ownership status of some parcels obscure. They also include the tendency of banks and other institutions to allocate favourable credits to collective forms (IASs, associations) over individuals, and the consequent obstacles to individual cultivators who want to buy a tractor or take out a loan to renew production. They include the balance of political forces that keep nationalized property in legal limbo, postponing the dissolution of the state farms containing 30 per cent of Romania's agricultural land. In other words, the system of interests and ties in which exclusive, individual private property might be constituted is biased against it, in favour of communal property relations, the claims they permit, and the opportunities they afford.

This observation reminds us of the truth, easily forgotten, that 'property' is about social relations. These include both relations among persons and the power relations in which persons act. The evolution of a post-socialist property regime involves complex interactions between macro-systemic fields of force and the behaviours and interconnections of people caught up in them. In other words, for property to crystallize as individual, exclusive private ownership requires a very specific field of political, social and cultural relations, and that field does not (yet) exist in post-1989 Romania.

As villagers described it to me, when decollectivization was launched everyone said they had no use for recovering private ownership of their land; they would simply let the old CAP turn itself into an association. Then a few families began pulling their land out and striving to define it as solely 'theirs'. Following them, ever more villagers decided to claim the land their parents had worked, perhaps giving some of it back to the association, but now conditionally. Their accounts suggested to me the image of a forming snowflake, which begins solidifying around one tiny core. From it develops a lattice that draws neighbouring crystals into the emerging pattern, until what had been liquid or gas has hardened into a solid with fixed shape. But just as the crystallization of water into snow depends on the ambient temperature, the crystallization of exclusive private ownership depends on the ambient conditions and the relations among actors in an overall field of power. To see the snowflake itself as representing 'property', then, is not enough: we might say it is just the tip of the iceberg.

# 9    Property rights, regulation and environmental protection: some Anglo-Romanian contrasts

*William Howarth*

The main purpose of this chapter is to consider the relationship between property rights in land and environmental protection and, specifically, to consider to what extent private, rather than state, ownership of land is conducive to effective protection. A secondary aim is to contrast the role of property ownership in environmental protection in the United Kingdom with the emerging situation in the former socialist countries of Eastern Europe with particular attention to the situation in Romania.[1] A central thesis to be scrutinized is that of inherent 'ecological proprietorship', whereby it is supposed that private ownership of land creates a vested interest in preventing environmental damage to that land.[2] The most extensive system of private land ownership, combined with the greatest possible rights of owners, and minimal state intrusion upon those rights, is thought to secure the best possible mechanism for environmental protection. Stated in the converse, the thesis is that the widest possible state ownership of land will result in the worst possible protection of the environment, since the state will lack the supposed inherent concern of a private owner for environmental protection.

The historical experience of the United Kingdom, where private ownership of land has been the norm for many years, is that private land ownership, and the rights and remedies to which this gives rise, provides no guarantee against environmental degradation. Broadly, the progression of national environmental law shows an increasing shift of emphasis from private rights and duties to increasingly sophisticated public regulatory mechanisms of control, to the point that regulation has become the dominant mode of environmental standard-setting (Steele 1995: 238). This regulatory approach has been found necessary to meet the shortcomings of a private ownership and private rights approach to environmental protection. Put concisely, the sum of private interests which exist in the environment fall far short of the collective or public need for environmental protection and, over time, public regulation has increasingly been necessary to meet this shortfall.

By contrast, a prevalent popular perspective from the former socialist countries of Eastern Europe, where private ownership of land has been unlawful or discouraged until recently, comes close to an affirmation of inherent ecological proprietorship. A widely held view is that state ownership of land and industry has proved to be environmentally detrimental and that restoration of private property rights will greatly assist in solving the significant environmental challenges facing these countries. For this reason or, more likely, because the restitution programme is likely to involve the transmission of land from the state to many ordinary individuals, the programme is generally popular. Despite this popularity, however, land restitution is proving problematic to implement (Verdery 1994; see also chapter 8).

The disparity of perspectives upon the role of property ownership in environmental protection between the United Kingdom and Eastern European countries is remarkable. It brings into question fundamental and longstanding assumptions. Is the relatively limited role of private property ownership and rights of property owners in environmental protection merely a contingent feature of the law and history of environmental protection in the United Kingdom, or does it illustrate a broader or even a universal necessity to subsume private environmental interests under broader public concerns? Alternatively, the private versus public ownership debate may be seen as a misleading distraction from the more critical issues concerning the rationale of regulation. Perhaps the solution to the problem of environmental protection lies in genuinely effective regulation, and the effectiveness of regulation should be judged independently of whether the activity being regulated is being conducted by a private or public body, or on private or public land. The difficulty lies in testing this hypothesis by comparing 'regulation' in jurisdictions where the concept is so greatly different as to make comparisons difficult or impossible. In the former socialist countries of Eastern Europe, past state ownership and operation of industry has meant that 'regulation', as understood in the Western sense, has been unnecessary. Whilst industries were both owned and operated by the state, control of their activities was complete. It is only when private ownership exists that new mechanisms for control become necessary. This facility to exercise legal control over areas of activity independently of their ownership is the distinctive rationale of regulation. However, recent changes in Eastern Europe have brought about a significant shift away from a centrally planned economic order towards the increasing adoption of market systems. This transition will involve the progressive

from it, its future use is also to the benefit of the original producer. Such property is culturally validated as extensions of persons, often in quasi-procreative idiom, as in the appeal to the moral right of creators to their creations or to the paternity of the author. Indeed, the language of kinship was an important source of analogy in early struggles to establish the recognition of authorial copyright (see Coombe 1994). A background question in the Tennessee case was the extent to which the couple's previous procreative intent was to continue into the future.

From a Danish perspective on embryo disposal, Nielson raises two questions. One concerns the disposition of embryos in other than a procreative context; who then has the entitlement? If, for example, someone consents to the embryo being used for research, the entitlement cannot be on grounds of the future parenting or custody of a child. In her view that is the point at which 'it becomes clear that the embryo is treated as property' (1993: 219). The other more general question explored by Nielson is the right to become a parent. This the US legal theorist Robertson pursues in terms of procreative liberty – the extent to which interference in people's reproductive choices is warranted. The right to reproduce he sees as a negative right, that is, against interference, rather than a positive right to the resources needed to reproduce (1994: 29). The correlative right not to reproduce can be asserted before pregnancy insofar as it is already legally protected by the courts in upholding the liberty to use contraception. However, other issues come into play when a couple are in dispute.

Robertson also refers to the problems posed by frozen embryos and introduces the concept of dispositional control: who has the authority to choose among available options for disposition. 'The question of decisional authority is really the question of who "owns" – has a "property" interest in – the embryo' (1994: 104). He then qualifies his terms:

However, using terms such as 'ownership' or 'property' risks misunderstanding. Ownership does not signify that embryos may be treated in all respects like other property. Rather, the term merely designates who decides which legally available options will occur . . . Although the bundle of property rights attached to one's ownership of an embryo may be more circumscribed than for other things, it is an ownership or property interest nonetheless (1994: 104).

Dispositional authority might rest with an individual in relation to his or her gametes, to a couple jointly, with the physicians who create the embryos and so forth, but the persons who provide the sperm and egg probably have the strongest claims.[3] It can be exercised in and of itself and thus would not require coming to a decision about other claims to ownership, nor indeed a decision as to whether the entities at issue were 'property' or 'people'. The concept enables a further principle to be brought into play. Robertson recommends that the best way to handle a dispute is to refer back to the dispositional agreement made at the time of creation or cryopreservation of the embryos (1994: 113). In other words, rather than considering afresh the procreative desires of the parties as they have developed in the interim, and perhaps having to balance their interests anew, it could endorse their intent at the time of first determining to procreate – always provided that was made explicit.

The Tennessee Supreme Court upheld the principle of advance agreements for disposition, but in the absence of such an agreement rejected the idea that freezing alone constituted an agreement to later implementation. In the end it weighed up the relative burdens on the two parties, and found in favour of the husband's desire not to reproduce.

I have borrowed this case from another context (M. Strathern 1996) for the issues it raises about sources of interpretation. The dispute between former husband and wife necessarily mobilized different arguments to litigious effect. Interests at stake were expressed through appeals to interpretations evoking different domains of reasoning (property/people). In academic arguments interpretative choice becomes equally explicit: disputes are often *about* the relevance of the domains from which analytical constructs come. One learns in any case to be self-conscious about the choice of analytical vocabulary; it does not emerge from inspection of data unaided. This is a point on which James Carrier has commented and on which I construct something of a rejoinder to his own arguments in this volume. I propose to endorse his observation that the Melanesian debates about gift exchange are also debates about property relations. Given, however, that the concept of 'gift' was borrowed from Euro-American discourse in the first place, and with political intent, we might consider what parallels we wish to be drawing in the late twentieth century. This is not just an academic matter. I take the view that the way in which people organize their relations to one another as a matter of control not just over things ('property' in the Supreme Court's sense) but over aspects of life and body (that define 'people') will loom large on the world agenda over the next decade. We can expect an explosion of concern with ownership.

New resources are coming into being all the time, through the invention of objects of knowledge and utility, as well as new contests over existing resources, and in their wake new negotiations over rights, as the Tennessee case shows.[4] The anthropologist might well be interested in the accompanying cultural search – in the exploration of the domains from which reasons are drawn, in the metaphors, analogies or precedents being pressed into service. Here, the claims were over products of the body for which no prior transactional idioms existed, and the mental intentions of the parties in producing them had to help define what they were. The language of intellectual property rights itself shades into other languages, such as those of cultural rights and all the questions of exportability that they raise (e.g. Gudeman 1995), including reformulations of practices of reproduction never indigenously conceived in terms of (property) rights at all. Thus Coombe (1996: 217) writes of the descendants of Crazy Horse, 'upset to learn of the appropriation of the identity of their revered ancestor as a trademark by a manufacturer of malt liquor' who 'find themselves compelled to claim that they hold his name and likeness as a form of property'.[5] Anthropologists need to know how and why they might use the language of property and ownership themselves.

Pannell provides a very explicit statement on this from Australia. A particular vocabulary of ownership and repatriation which once shaped debates over the restitution of cultural property (as held for instance in museums) was swept aside by the proclamation of the High Court judges in the 1992 Mabo case. Pronouncing on the death of the legal fiction of *terra nullius*, they also pronounced on the 'corresponding common law recognition of native title [as having] implications which extend beyond so-called "land-management" issues' (1994: 19). These extend into the possibility of legal protection for other forms of cultural and intellectual property, inviting a new interpretation of repatriation as reappropriation, that is, making something one's own again.[6] Pannell (1994: 33) also offers a persuasive case for considering possessory rights; one might indeed (after Annette Weiner) wish to reinvigorate the concept of possession, though we should be watching what the concept of possession is doing elsewhere. Like any other construct, it needs debate, especially if it is to be appropriated to demonstrate universal human needs for possessions. The point is that Pannell's argument explicitly addresses the displacement of one set of analytical terms by another.

I follow the contributors to this volume in deploying property relations as a general analytical construct. Its reference to disposable resources embraces both more than and less than its phenomenological or experiential counterpart, owning/ownership. This is as apparent in Robertson's elisions, and in the reply of Christopher Hann's son (see p. 2), as it is in the proprietorial but not property connotations of owning as belonging (Edwards and Strathern, in preparation). A further qualification is that a property relation may or may not be construed as one of possession, that is, as an extension of or gathering into the self.[7]

In contributing to the division of analytical interests in the concept of property, I wish to point to certain situations where we are made aware of relational preconditions. The Tennessee embryos were in dispute precisely as the product of a relationship between former conjugal partners. An abstract understanding of property as a set of relations is thus explored through concrete instances where relations are presented twice over, as the (invisible) conceptual precondition of there being any claims or rights in dispute in the first place, and as the (visible) social grounding of the particular dispute at issue. In English one can thus say that all property claims engage relationships; only some are about 'relationships'. One can say the same for ownership: any property claim can be perceived as implying ownership (of rights, interests, etc.), but only some imply 'ownership' (possession, certain kinds of title, or whatever).

In discussing the management of knowledge, and envisaging new proprietorial forms, Harrison (1995: 14) specifies the contribution of anthropologists, 'namely their own knowledge of the culturally diverse ways in which knowledge can be "owned"'. I introduce this reference to culture not to detract from social analysis but to sharpen up the conceptual tools on which such analysis relies, not just to elucidate 'meaning' but to understand the categories of action people mobilize in pursuing their interests. It is probably redundant to say that anthropologists' own management of knowledge already inheres in the concepts they choose to use.

### Varieties of timelessness

What connotations does Carrier (chapter 4) give to the concept of 'ownership'? In his account of Ponam, where Carrier focuses largely on property embedded in kin and other relationships, he starts with a description of patrilineal *kamal* groups as land *owning*. I wonder how the account might have looked if he started with the statistical fact that land is held through numerous transactions which link persons to numerous others; among these others is also a group that lays title to it. If this title constitutes 'ownership', it does not imply that enjoyment of the land and its products inevitably follow. So what does title entail? We know from the detailed ethnography (e.g. Carrier and Carrier 1991) that *kamal* are prominent in political life and were in the past important channels for the inheritance of assets. Are continuing claims to land a matter of dispositional right, to borrow Robertson's term? Or should one be thinking along the lines of intellectual property claims asserted by the originators of places? One would then be drawn into comparative analysis with, say, title to ritual performance or rights held in images or designs, as in New Ireland *malanggan* statuary (see Harrison 1992: 234), while recognizing that in the Ponam case the assets in question were material – not the intangibles of the kind often associated with ritual (Carrier and Carrier 1991: 42). That would make them more like property that can be enjoyed by a third party while at the same time conserving a value for the original 'owner'. Whatever way, one may add, contests of power were likely to be built into the claims. How then can such contests be a qualification of or deviation from them? To oppose 'practice' to 'formal rules', as Carrier does, is to beg the whole question of what contests of title or usufruct are about, that is, what they bring about for the people involved. In short, Carrier reifies the notion of a rule or principle, finds it in Ponam land titles, links these to a concept of order, not to speak of propriety, and projects the whole idealist bundle on to a 'Maussian model'! Having located power and interest *outside* this model, he then attributes them to other 'forces'. That is, he divides the material up into domains and then shows how one of them does not encompass the whole.

I certainly could not defend the model that he puts forward as Maussian; nonetheless there remains an interesting question to ask about the story of the free trader (see pp. 98–100). The story is intended to trump any analytical claims that people can only transact in the context of enduring relationships. Should the question not be whether such actions are a resource for thinking about social relationships? What use do Ponam people make of this act? Does it become a paradigm for other solitary ventures? Consider a Hagen woman going off to a birth hut by herself. Birth may take place in isolation; but when the act of birth becomes a metaphorical resource, an image of productivity or creativity for instance, with the social resonances of regeneration those carry, the hut becomes peopled with others. The mother is not alone: ancestral ghosts affect the ease of labour; the child she bears is already in a relationship with her; all kinds of consequences follow for her kin. At the same time, the act is accomplished in solitude because in another sense only she can effect the birth, and seclusion also signals autonomy of personal action. Acts have to be intentional, purposive; without such personal action there would be no relationships. And without knowing how such acts are imaginatively appropriated, economic analysis cannot begin. For all kinds of values can become present. Battaglia (1994) makes the point through a story about a wealth item, an axe which played a determining role in a set of urban transactions without ever appearing; it was (however/only) potentially there.[8] One might ask what is present and what is absent in the actions of the Ponam trader. Among the reasons for his treatment was the islanders' view that he was no kinsman of theirs, that is, they summoned up 'other' kinsfolk for him. It is not immediately clear why the transactions therefore resemble those of an 'urban, capitalist economy'.

This is a question of description: what analysis makes meaningful. It is also a question of what the object of study is. My own interest has been in forms of sociality developed without regard to the European/ Enlightenment distinction between individual and society that has driven much anthropological enquiry. So whatever uses that distinction might have for organizing social analysis, there were bound to be some things it left unexplained. The question became how to construct an analytical vocabulary that would make evident those elements previous analyses had hidden. Any choice would entail its own concealments in turn, and I have been conscious of the fact that exactly the kind of study in which Carrier is involved (the study of economic forms) is concealed by that strategy. But there was nothing surrogate or covert about the antinomies I used; they were deliberate artifice. Nonetheless they do, as Carrier correctly notes, make assumptions about timelessness.

Carrier and I both deploy timelessness, though Foster's (1995) *rapprochement* renders the observation somewhat out of date. I hold that the knowledge anthropologists have made out of their encounters with Melanesians poses all sorts of questions about the way they (the anthropologists) might wish to think about human relations. The knowledge does not cease to become an object of contemporary interest simply because practices have changed. I would indeed make it timeless in that sense. Carrier's argument is that historical change is crucial, because among other things that shows up the social and conceptual location of previous practices, and this must be part of – not excluded from – the knowledge with which one works. Yet from another perspective his own categories of analysis remain timeless, as in the very constructs of 'property' and 'ownership', and in his notion that there is such a thing as '*the* relationship between people and things'. By contrast, my interest is directed to the historical location of analytical constructs, for none of the major constructs we use is without its history. Let me make this last issue explicit.

I remember at the time of writing *The Gender of the Gift* that I did not want to 'go back' to Mauss. In the end I noted one or two places where others had drawn on his work, and the absurdity of no acknowledgement at all to the inventor of 'the gift' in anthropology led to another reference. But while one might say all this comprised a salient background, in the foreground was a recent study, Gregory (1982), and contemporary interests in the then influential field of Marxist anthropology. Gregory's composite model drew on Marx, Morgan and Lévi-Strauss, as well as Mauss; I thus drew on Mauss's work principally as it was filtered through Gregory's. Economist as well as anthropologist, Gregory had a grasp of the economic theories of development being applied to Papua New Guinea at the time, and a lively and informed interest in economic change, and I thought that his appraisal of what was wrong with prevailing economic categories demanded attention.

That is why I followed Gregory in my definition of the 'gift economy'.[9] I used this as a shorthand reference 'to systems of production and consumption where consumptive production predominates' (1988: 145). The issue was laid out in ongoing critiques of private property: if the idea of property as a thing conceals social relations, then what is gift exchange concealing? (It conceals its own conventions of reification.) Hence the debate with Josephides was concerned with what gets concealed or mystified and what is made overt. It was she who stimulated me to consider the conversion process by which wealth is transferred from one domain to another. For the ethnographic problem was that, when pigs are taken off by men, women's efforts and the conjugal relation in which production was embedded are *not* disguised. Returns on work are simply made at a later date. In the meanwhile the man gets out of the transaction power and prestige the woman never does. The theoretical problem became how to understand that conversion.

That led me into an analysis of gender relations. The man only takes off the woman's pig in one sense! He is also appropriating his own efforts. To understand the power he has to do this, one has to understand that the husband is taking out of a domestic sphere the pig jointly produced from the work of both of them into a sphere which he alone controls.[10] This is a conversion from multiple relations of interest in the thing to singular ones. A specific instance that unfolded in Hagen recently will flesh out these observations. But, first, a further observation about the historicity of analytical constructs is in order. Which historical epoch is going to supply the anthropologist's comparative vocabulary?

I take Carrier's chapter as raising two important issues for historical understanding. The first is obvious, that all accounts are contemporary. That is, they can only come out of the present in which they were written; at the same time that present includes diverse pasts and theoretical antecedents that appear to be for the choosing, as one might for example construct an intellectual pedigree. The second is that the anthropologist searching for an analytical vocabulary may be as much drawn to particular cultural domains as to other theorists, going to some field or area of knowledge for potential connections. This 'spatial' effect may be literalized in cross-cultural comparison when a society in one place is described from the vantage point of another elsewhere. But suppose we also thought about historical epochs as domains from which to draw resources for analysis?

This has been made explicit in anthropology from time to time, as in Gluckman's (1965a: 86f.) critical appraisal of feudalism in interpreting land tenure systems in sub-Saharan Africa, fuelled by his interest in hierarchies of estates. Europe remained the reference point, but the observer pursued constructs from a former era. One wonders what fresh purchase starting out 'now', at the end of the century, would yield the Euro-American anthropologist interested in describing Melanesian societies. Anyone drawing on the reach of theoretical resources available from a post-industrial economy might find themselves choosing between modernist, post-modernist and realist approaches to 'contemporary' material. Alternatively, in certain respects 'traditional' Melanesian societies belong much more comfortably to some of the visions made possible by socio-economic developments in Europe since the 1980s than they did to the worlds of the early and mid-twentieth century. Euro-Americans live these days with the idea of dispersed identities, of traffickings in body parts, but above all what perhaps one could call new divisions of interest in familial and conjugal relationships. Some of these are laid out by Jack Goody in the previous chapter. Monetary interpretations of kin obligations and new forms of procreative assets hardly turn Euro-Americans into Melanesians. But perhaps they have turned some of the ways in which relationships are contested in late capitalist society into a new resource for apprehending Melanesian social process. Let me advance this supposition through the specific instance already promised.

### Dispute

The following sequence of events took place in Mt Hagen in the Western Highlands Province of Papua New Guinea.[11] Kanapa had two children, a boy and a girl; she was looking forward to the day when the bridewealth was assembled for her son. It is the groom's kin who assemble wealth items, including pigs reared by his father's and brothers' wives. So that would be the occasion on which Kanapa's pigs would be on public display, and people would see what she had raised. However, one particularly large pig that she had intended as the special 'mother's pig' (for the bride's mother) had been taken off a couple of years previously by her husband for a funeral prestation (when a big man of the clan died), and her anger with him was one cause of a long illness.

Discharged from hospital in a weak state, for a month or so she did little more than creep outside to sit in the sun. Her husband complained several times that she did not take the medicine he had paid money for, and had brought the sickness on herself. The routing of her anger through ancestral ghosts (who in the past would send sickness to make the victim's suffering visible) had been diverted by charismatic Christian teaching which held that one should not get angry at all. Local Christian leaders came on three or four occasions to exorcize the bad spirits that were fighting with her good spirit, and the senior co-wife and other women of the settlement frequently said loud prayers over her. However her sickness persisted, and several relatives became implicated. This included on occasion her long-suffering daughter who had moved in to care for her. They bickered, and some blamed the continuing sickness on the daughter's getting cross with her mother. The daughter was married into a locally wealthy family, but the initiative that gave her husband's brother a good job with a national company had not passed on to her own husband, a youth who contrived to do no work except mind their little boy. He had a small supply of cash coming from his brother, but his father-in-law saw him only as a drain on resources, contributing neither money nor labour. There were complaints about his not using his education. The same could not be said of Kanapa's now adult son, Kitim, who was employed in the coastal capital Port Moresby. The father calculated what it had cost him in school fees over the years to put him through secondary education. There was astonishment that he rarely sent money home, and when he occasionally did visit he failed to help in the gardens or contribute money to buy in labour, which would have been as acceptable.

Kanapa loved Kitim but was agitated about his bridewealth. He showed no signs of making a match, and parental promptings had fallen on stony ground. The mother was burdened with the thought of his bridewealth going to waste, all the work she had put into rearing pigs, and – with the pride women take in the size of their pigs – her need to show not just that she was but how she was a mother. Relations with her husband were also involved. The prospect of the son's marriage would galvanize the husband into thinking about the pig he had taken from her. In being the principal person to assemble and dispose of the bridewealth, he would have to make good his promise to the wife to replace the large animal he had taken. At one stage he had promised a sum of money in lieu, and her illness was put down by some to the fact that he had never produced this.[12]

There were various small reasons for displeasure with Kitim; for instance, he had left the rebuilding of her house to her elder brother, and then given presents to this man rather than to herself; this turned into a quarrel between sister and brother. But Kanapa generally accepted the fact that the son lived away, since it was assumed that one day he would come home to claim his inheritance in land. Had the woman been well she would have taken her part in helping to plant new garden land being developed at the time, as well as clearing the scrub, burning off the rubbish and tilling the soil, while the men did the heavy work of cutting the bush and digging ditches. The men included her husband, her co-residential brother and workers – 'cargo boys'. Youngish men, these latter were recruited from the settlement area on an ad hoc basis, prepared to work for immediate cash but not, as might have been the expectation in the past, for food or for the credit of having helped their seniors. These particular gardens were destined for the market, and men and women alike had cash yields in mind. Having to spend on cargo boys was a monetary investment for monetary return. This was work Kitim himself might have done but either could not or did not.

As her illness wore on it became a source of general anxiety, and Kanapa's husband decided there had to be sacrifice. The only way to get the ancestral ghosts to release their hold on her was to give them something in return, and that had to be one of her own pigs.[13] An animal she had reared from a piglet was selected, for her work was evidently in it. Some would take the killing as an offering to God while others would understand the silent invocation of the ancestors. The husband held the sacrificial pig rope and then handed it to his wife's brother, both of them making short speeches about dispatching the sickness. At that stage they had identified two ghosts as responsible, the dead mother of Kanapa and her brother, and the dead mother of her husband. When she did not get better immediately, suspicion fell on the latter alone as having a longstanding grievance against the living and fertile alike. It was she who had prevented Kanapa from bearing more children and had made her sick on numerous occasions in the past. People concluded that the ghost was reminding Kanapa that in fact the husband did care for her; she should be content and not allow herself to get carried away by jealous co-wife gossip.

Sickness is thrown away or detached from the afflicted person in the same way as a man gives away a pearlshell/money in exchange, or a woman a child in marriage (whether it is a daughter who leaves her mother's house or a son whose mother-in-law will receive the large bridewealth pigs she has intended for her). Living people used to fear the too close attachment of the dead who would hang about; at the same time such ghosts can also afford protection, if only from themselves. Kanapa's husband was already planning a public payment of pigs and money to his maternal kin in order to elicit the positive support of his matrilateral ghosts and perhaps (he did not say this) keep them at bay at the same time. Such payments come under the general rubric of payments for the 'body'. The rationale is recompense for the mother's breast(milk) that is regarded as a source of nurture in counterpoint to the nurture derived from paternal food from a person's lineage land. (There is a direct equation between the 'grease' of breast milk, semen and fertile land; cf. A. Strathern 1972; Carrier and Carrier 1991: 218.) Maternal nurture from the lineage of a person's mother, anticipated at the bridewealth that establishes the marriage in the first place, is paid for again once a child is born, especially at the birth of a first child, and subsequently according to people's inclination or conscience, not terminating until mortuary compensation at death. The special bridewealth pig destined for the bride's mother thus acknowledges the social origin of the girl's nurture, and a division of interests between maternal and paternal kin. Thereafter, the girl's paternal kin become assimilated to 'maternal kin' of her children, a relatively smooth transition, and one that 'new' maternal kin are ready to exploit since they can expect a small stream of gifts in recognition of their special status. The social divisions are thus acted out as connections to be pursued. One man told me that it was always worthwhile investing in daughters, because a married daughter thinks of her own parents all the time (wants to send things to them), whereas a married man must think of his parents-in-law. He had adopted two daughters in prospect of the flow of money that would come to him by this route. In short, the 'work' that goes into making a child comes from both parents, but only paternal kin reap axiomatic benefit. So the (already separated) maternal kin have to be specifically recompensed for their lost nurture. It should be added that maintaining connections with maternal kin (and thus the division between sets of kin) is itself 'work', the work being manifest in the swelling and rounded body of the baby and the stature of the adult. A person's spiritual welfare is taken care of by the ghosts, or by God. In fact God has rather upset most such payments, including ones given at death; the missions are said to disapprove of such child payments on the grounds that God makes the body not the mother's kin. The arrangements are also somewhat upset by the capriciousness of modern marriage, women not necessarily having the input into their husband's land and labour that would be the basis for their kin to claim payment.

This is the view Kanapa would have had from the house where she lay sick. Tethered at the end of the courtyard, in the two or three pigs churning up the soil they stood on, tended by her daughter and chased by her husband when they broke loose, she would see some of her years of work, planning and care – a throng of persons, relationships and events. She would see the division of tasks, and her husband's work on the cleared land in which the tubers grew, the hours of tracking down animals when they strayed, the discussions about how they should dispose of them, the promise to replace particular pigs taken off for an exchange partner. The size of the pigs and their fatness were prime testimony to the abundance of the staple starch, sweet potato, that she cultivates and they eat, and to the fertility of the soil in which it grows. They were also testimony to her intellectual application to her tasks, and the purposefulness of her work. Kanapa wanted to hold on to the pigs long enough to be able to get rid of them at her son's marriage, in a gesture that would make evident her motherhood. If she could not expend them this way, then she intended to realize them for herself by selling them! For she also saw the division of interests between herself and her husband.

## Reproduction

This took place 'in Hagen' but what time is the anthropologist in – from what historical epoch should I be drawing the tools of analysis? In one sense the events are reassuringly coeval (after Fabian 1983; cf. Dalton 1996: 409–10) with diverse late twentieth-century global Northern European or American cultures. While bridewealth and the mother's pig, the need to sacrifice and prospective payments to maternal kin were all in existence in Hagen before people ever set eyes on the money that enables them these days to discharge their obligations, I was assured of their contemporary saliency. I was told that looking after kin on the maternal side was the one distinctive 'custom' (*kastom*) of all Papua New Guinea. It was what marked them out in the modern world, the sign of common identity or national community. But interesting as it would be to join the many commentators on the description of con-temporary culture as *kastom*, including Carrier's analysis of commodities and markets, I choose another route.

One of the times Euro-Americans may find themselves in has so to speak only just happened for them. But it may have 'happened' long ago in Papua New Guinea. I wonder if some of the considerations voiced by Kanapa – especially those with their roots thoroughly in Hagen's past – might not *anticipate* certain future economic directions in Euro-American quests for ownership. I refer to the economics of new reproductive forms, of rights established through (pro)creativity, bodily and mental.

Some years ago now, Weiner (1980, 1982) called for the anthropology of Melanesia to look not to reciprocity as a model for gift-based or exchange relations but to reproduction. Although her own model has been criticized for serving the old tautologies of structural-functionalism in new guise (Carrier and Carrier 1991: 110–13), its reference point was not simply the replication of social categories but reproduction in the sense of bodily procreation. She dwelt on Melanesian images of the individual life-cycle, of birth and decay, and the circulation of exchange items in relation to these, as generative extensions of body processes. Since that was written, *recent* developments in the Euro-American anthropologists' society of origin are beginning to provide a vocabulary of 'reproduction' that could inform contemporary analysis with the same kind of effect that an economically interpreted inflection of reciprocity once did. In Hagen, the right to the mother's pig is long established – it has historical antecedents that have nothing to do with reproductive technology and Euro-American legislation and litigation. Yet the emergent quasi-legal concepts that accompany these applications of technology invite Euro-Americans to think of property in persons and property in life forms (Franklin 1995). There is analytical mileage here. One example must suffice: the recently invented concept of procreative intent. It renders some of the enduring forms of Hagen social life newly coeval with some from the anthropologist's world.

Kanapa's final defiance says it all: the dispute between husband and wife was not between keeping and giving but over the contexts in which either of them could dispose of the products of their joint efforts. Carrier is right to emphasize the work that goes into keeping debts alive in people's minds. Yet it is not just transactions that create debts. Maternal nurture also makes persons indebted to their maternal kin. However Kanapa's husband tried to avoid making good what she thought he owed, he could not avoid the long-term consequences of neglect, his own dead mother's ghost being a ready reminder. Bride-wealth has a special poignancy for women, as we have seen, for it is the moment at which the mother's part is made manifest. Indeed, the occasion of marriage is the public 'birth' of parents and children alike, and thus the culmination of a procreative process. One might almost speak of Kanapa, in her deep-felt frustration, articulating the right to be a parent. This means that it is not just, as Sillitoe reminds us (1988: 7), that men need women to produce pigs, but that women need pigs to produce men. That is, they need a medium which will make visible their maternal care, and then of course for their children to get married. What holds true for both groom's and bride's mother is culturally explicit in the case of the bride's mother. Bridewealth goes to the girl's kin because they are her originators, those who produced her, and this is the point at which the bride's kin will utter remarks – as the adopting father did – that could well be glossed in terms of procreative intent. Procreative intent is expressed in people's desire for daughters who will bring their parents (bride)wealth.

This is an openly reproductive system geared to producing persons through the production of things. Yet to locate the principal analytical vocabulary in terms of production and consumption would be to privilege one kind of body product, namely labour, over others. Anthropologists are used to debating the general applicability of market models or the capitalist mode of production to their materials. As I have indicated at several points, here is another debate: the extent to which the technology released by post-industrial/late capitalist institutions has given us new economic forms, including new body products, to think with. The latter includes both body parts previously inseparable from human activity or embodiment, but now capable of externalization, such as the pre-implanted embryo, and products of the intellect previously embedded in their realization, but now valued in the way that the potential of inventiveness is valued, such as procreative intent.

The large pig that Kanapa had in mind for the bride's mother was one she had reared, we might say, with such intent. That is, she foresaw the day when it would appear at her son's bridewealth. It would appear both as the product of joint work bestowed on it by herself and her husband *and* as the embodiment of her own actions which subsumed her intentions for it. Like the question of the disposition of embryos in an other than procreative context, the husband's taking it off instigated a conflict over the respective interests of the spouses. We might consider, then, the further concepts that Robertson develops: dispositional authority and dispositional agreements. The issue is not that these are necessarily new in American legal thinking but that they are these days being applied to products of the body. Something of a parallel is offered by Sillitoe's discussion (see n. 10; and cf. Salisbury 1962) of personal possessions owned by Highlands men and women and the pigs and shell valuables that circulate in exchange. In relation to valuables he notes that the rights at issue are those of disposal, and that this is a right that only one person at a time may hold, though the item in question (the rights in it) may pass serially between persons. No one can own valuables exclusively (as 'private property'), but people may enjoy custody of them for a while. He thus disputes the relevance of inalienability as a concept; people may cease to have rights in particular items while continuing to have rights in relation to the recipient by virtue of the transfer of those items.[14] What is helpful in Sillitoe's contribution is his focus on the right to dispose not as a concomitant of preexisting or already established property rights but (precisely as suggested in the case of the Tennessee embryos) as a form of property relation itself. Recall Ponam land titles.

One might elaborate: disposability begins to appear as an outcome of social context, an entitlement to be exercised in the appropriate milieu. Like the Tennessee woman who wished the embryos to live so that she could complete her motherhood, in however removed a form Kanapa wanted to complete her motherhood with the disposal of her pigs at her son's marriage. By the same token, the Hagen woman's entitlement to dispose of the mother's pig is dormant until bridewealth mobilizes it. The conventions of marriage prestations here provide a kind of tacit dispositional agreement. In the meanwhile, the potential 'mother's pig' is prey to all sorts of other demands. Until it is realized as such, like the unrealized embryo, other claims may come to the fore. In the Hagen case men have an interest in deferring that particular realization because they have other uses for the valuable items; in the Tennessee case the man who had no other uses for the embryo simply wished to block that realization, for it would have made him the father he did not wish to be.

Now through their own exchanges Hagen men create a separate domain of entitlements for themselves; they belong to this social domain by the authority of the dispositional control it enables them to exercise. We may further note that it defines desire as desire for valuables to dispose of and identities as relations made present through the dispositional acts of others. In short, what keeps men's commitment to their collective exchanges is the same as the commitment of husbands and wives to their joint work: a division of interests. For any or either party to pursue their interests, such a division must be made visible.

### Languages of property

Macfarlane's analysis (see chapter 5) of the varying divisibility and indivisibility of resources (things) on the one hand and on the other of rights (distributed among persons), at different times and places in Europe, becomes germane at this point. Partibility and impartibility may rest either with the object of the property claim or with the subjects making the claim. Suppose the focus were not on things or rights but on persons as such? They could be divided both as subjects (anthropologists have always argued for a theoretical construct that defines persons as social bundles of rights and duties distributed between various relationships) and as objects (their body products, the objects of other people's interests, and with value attached to intent and potentiality of their own as well). In one sense there is nothing new here. In another sense, to think of *divisions* at all is prompted by novel partitionings of bodily material. This is often interpreted, in Euro-American experience, as fragmenting what was formerly considered whole. But that does not give us much of a comparative tool. A formula apposite for Melanesia might be: relationships entail *divisions of interest.*

This construct does not map in any simple way on to the difference between inclusive and exclusive relations.[15] Rather, inclusivity/exclusivity seems a particularly apposite dichotomy for the analysis of one type of property relation, namely possession, which resonates with the community/individual axis engrained in European thinking. A renewed anthropological concern with the concept of possession may be a response to a late twentieth-century cultural re-embedding of personal desire and identity in indivisible things, resisting exactly these new perceptions of divisions of body and body products. Perhaps it challenges exactly those emergent quasi-legal constructs of dispositional control being developed to deal with divergent interests in life forms.

But the case does not have to be made with selective generalization, or 'idealist' supposition, about an indeterminate Euro-American culture. Let me point to practice and give an example, to supplement Jack Goody's in the previous chapter, of the way in which one scholar has deliberately sought to construct a critical vocabulary drawn from another epoch, and with resistance in mind. Battaglia (1994) considers how Trobriand Islanders in Port Moresby drew attention to axe blades, a class of valuable called *beku*.[16] These were analysed by Weiner (1976) as significant for the beginnings of new reproductive cycles, affirmed in the words of an urban Trobriander that they 'represent life'. If one wished to use the terms, they are both alienable (bestowed on recipients without creating continuing partnership) and inalienable (a man hopes eventually to walk after his *beku* and follow its path through successive villages in order to buy it back). 'It would seem', Battaglia adds (1994: 637) 'that possession, while an important issue for users, is not the only . . . issue . . . Property models are outdistanced by the way people operate the object and by their quest for it along the path of remembered (or fabricated?) "owners".' This is the juncture at which she draws attention to an article by Rosalind Petchesky (1995) on the conceptualization of property in relation to the body: the problem is not the language of ownership but the reification of property as possession. Note that the language of ownership is thus rendered 'unproblematic' through a deconstructive division (on Battaglia's part) that produces a counterpart query, as here in the query about reification, possession conceived as a thing; without that kind of division, one may add, there is no analytical position to take.

Petchesky wishes to recover political purpose for the construct of 'self-propriety' or self-ownership specifically in relation to the body as a point of feminist resistance to other, private, exclusive, conceptualizations of ownership. Against those who decry the language of property altogether she wishes to open up the range of conceptual resources from which we might draw our models.[17] Her inspiration is a moment of resistance that she identifies as having taken place some three hundred years ago. This was a moment at which 'self-propriety' summoned a 'concept of property that is inclusive rather than exclusive and a model of the body that is extensive rather than insular' (1995: 400). (Protest was against the enclosing of the commons, property imagined as a shared rather than a private resource.) It was inclusive from the connections that were established with the community, evoking a vision of an 'extended or communally embedded body' as a 'normative ground in the process of self-creation and self-engagement' (1995: 400). The embedding of self-creation *in* community rather than against it echoes Gudeman's (1995) analysis of what he calls 'the community economy' as a 'reproductive system'. He draws on Latin American ethnography in order to make a point about the embeddedness of innovation in social practice.[18] It is a specifically 'Western' proclivity, and a late one at that, to treat innovation as a product of the intellect and the products of the intellect as separate from other aspects of the person. He thus asks, apropos the foundations of formal economic knowledge in common practice, at what point it would have made sense to treat innovations in practices and knowledge as clearly independent products of the mind. A historical question about the development of modern European institutions again asks us to historicize our analytical vocabulary.[19]

Petchesky deliberately searches for a conceptualization of ownership in relation to the body that will be relevant for contemporary feminist practice. '[O]wning our bodies depends integrally on having access to the social resources for assuring our bodies' health and well-being; self-ownership and proper caretaking go hand in hand with shared owner-ship of the commons' (1995: 403). She finds the construct she is looking for in the writings of Leveller tracts, as well as later slave narratives, of the seventeenth century. The concept of self-ownership, or property in one's person, was being promulgated among folk who were collectively opposed to market relations, not defending them. The promulgation, pre-Lockean, summoned a notion of rights in the body that were free from state interference, especially in sexual expression.[20] Early modern radicals were, in her view, taking an oppositional stance against interference by public authorities in sexual and bodily functions, much, we might add, as Robertson would like to see procreative choices constitutionally protected against restrictive legislation on the grounds that legislation interferes with reproductive liberty.[21] With Locke, Petchesky argues, the radical idea of self-ownership fell away before a new and individualistic interpretation of property in the person founded on rights to one's own labour. There is no 'one' epoch here. It would be interesting indeed to know how these diverse formulations related to the seventeenth-century beginnings of intellectual property rights (copyright) and the emergent idea of authors' proprietary rights in their work.[22]

Here we find in miniature a recapitulation of the European history of inclusive and exclusive notions of ownership ('possession') that have been developed at various points in this volume, and a suggestion for a creative re-use of them. The need comes from the pressure of contemporary social change. Against the background of an emergent Euro-American discourse about property in persons and body products, especially in the context of kinship created by transactions, it is not only anthropologists who are thinking anew about what 'ownership' entails. The current language about reproductive rights is also developing in conscious collusion with and contest against commercially driven definitions of body products. It may endorse or defeat other connotations of proprietorship, for instance in Britain those evident in indigenous kinship thinking. It may find an echo in the indigenous comparison of socio-economic systems, prompted for instance by the Melanesian way in which commerce and *kastom* are played off against each other in radically different trajectories of commoditization. These all afford analytical choices. In devising their own contemporary lexicon of property relations, anthropologists need to know the lexicons developing around them.

# Notes

## 1 INTRODUCTION: THE EMBEDDEDNESS OF PROPERTY

An earlier draft of this introduction has benefited from the comments of several contributors to this volume, and also from those of Chris Gregory, Keith Hart and Ildikó Bellér-Hann. They are not responsible for the views expressed or any errors which remain.

1 Paul Bohannan recognized this point explicitly in the context of land tenure in Africa. He distinguished between the 'man-man' unit, where rights and social relationships are of the essence, and the 'man-thing' unit , which is the '"relationship", so-called between a person (be he individual or social group) and a "parcel of land"' (1963: 102).

2 I am grateful for the guidance of Paul Mellars on this point.

3 The fieldwork on which this summary is based was carried out in Xinjiang Province in 1996 jointly with Dr Ildikó Bellér-Hann. It was supported by an ESRC research grant (R235709 'The historical and contemporary anthropology of Eastern Turkestan').

4 As a final example of how the dominant liberal paradigm of property has been extended we may note that, in some universities, academic departments are told that they must now 'own' the programmes they teach, as part of a new 'culture of accountability'. (Of course, like other authors, anthropologists are also keen to protect their intellectual rights, and so all the standard conventions apply to the citation of material from this volume!)

5 In this same passage Hume also draws attention to '*symbolical* delivery' in cases where the transference of the full object of property is impractical. For example, 'the giving the keys of a granary is understood to be the delivery of the corn contained in it' (1962: 228). Hume goes on to describe this as analogous to Catholic religious superstition. My thanks to Ekkehart Schlicht for drawing my attention to these observations.

6 See Reeve (1986) for an interesting discussion of property and liberty, and for an introduction to political theory frameworks more generally. See also Ryan (1984).

7 I thank Roy Ellen for drawing my attention to this point.

## 2 'SHARING IS NOT A FORM OF EXCHANGE': AN ANALYSIS OF PROPERTY-SHARING IN IMMEDIATE-RETURN HUNTER-GATHERER SOCIETIES

This paper has benefited greatly from comments by Jonathan Parry, by Maurice Bloch and also by Chris Hann and other participants in the University of Kent

Seminar for which it was written. None of those who so helpfully commented can be held responsible for the inadequacies which remain.

1 For the distinction between immediate-return and delayed-return systems see Woodburn (1988a: 31–3). Sharing appears to be much stressed in all hunter-gatherer societies. But in hunter-gatherer societies with delayed-return systems, where long-term rights over certain material goods, over religious knowledge and over women are more elaborated, the contexts within which sharing operates are more restricted and forms of sharing are more differentiated in terms of the specific relationships between those who share.

2 This concept is explored in an important paper by Nicolas Peterson (1993), which gives particular attention to delayed-return Australian Aboriginal cases where demand sharing is in some respects different from the instances considered here.

3 For example, we certainly do not regard English mothers who feed their children well or English citizens who pay their taxes in full as being generous even when these actions involve considerable self-denial. This is because both types of action are perceived to be, in their different ways, obligatory.

4 I should perhaps make explicit that I am objecting here to a number of different things. Firstly, I disagree with the notion that the phenomena described should be treated as any form of exchange or reciprocity as these terms are understood by social anthropologists. Secondly, I disagree with the notion that the transactions I discuss more or less balance out in the end for the various participants. This latter view is held by some social anthropologists but also by many other researchers on hunter-gatherer societies who would not consider themselves to be social anthropologists. The fact that the transactions do not balance out would not, of course, in itself, demonstrate that we are not dealing with some form of reciprocity or exchange.

5 It could be argued that what I describe here is indeed not exchange or reciprocity, but is also not sharing. Certainly Hadza or !Kung sharing does not map neatly on to English sharing. In using the English term here some extension and change in meaning is involved, just as it is in other anthropological uses of familiar English terms such as 'clan', 'descent' or 'gender'. The two crucial points are: (i) Is the English term misleading? Does it tend to distort our understanding of the issues being investigated? (ii) Do the various phenomena to which the term is applied have enough in common for it to be appropriate and useful for the purpose of analysis to apply the same term to them all? I suggest that for the matter which I am considering in this chapter the term 'sharing' succeeds on both counts while the terms 'exchange' and 'reciprocity' fail on both counts.

6 Concepts of ownership and rights over property in hunter-gatherer societies are discussed at some length in Barnard and Woodburn (1988: 12–32).

7 Dowling (1968: 505) and Testart (1987: 289, 291) are both mistaken in their suggestion that defining a person as the owner of the kill implies that this person controls the distribution of the meat of the kill.

It may seem puzzling that an individual is recognized as owner and yet has so few subsequent rights over what he owns. But this is entirely normal in many hunter-gatherer societies (see Barnard and Woodburn 1988) and also occurs in some contexts, often restricted contexts, in most other human societies. As Gluckman pointed out for agricultural tribal societies, individual and group rights often exist in the same item of property (1965b: 36–43). Sometimes such rights exist concurrently, sometimes sequentially. Even in Britain, land which is notionally held individually is subject to important enforceable community rights, some of which are expressed through planning permission procedures which greatly constrain land use; and in the recent past in Britain certain forms of individual money income were subject to government taxation at rates of well over 90 per cent. Richard Lee, in a fascinating paper (1988), has sought to revive the Marxist term 'primitive communism' for the systems of property rights in most hunter-gatherer and non-centralised tribal societies. He is right to stress the particular importance attached in these societies, and especially in hunter-gatherer societies, to access by all, or by all members of the local group, to key resources including land and food. But I would not accept that the term 'primitive communism' is appropriate for the complex combination of individual and community rights held in property in these societies. This combination is well illustrated by the individual ownership of a hunted animal and the obligation to share it with members of the community in immediate-return hunter-gatherer societies.

8 There are differences in cooking style. Roasting directly on the hot embers of a fire is more immediate and individual. Boiling is the focus for consumption by a wider set of people.

9 The Batek of Malaysia go further. They believe that anyone whose reasonable request for something – food or tobacco for example – is refused is endangered by the refusal and is likely to suffer some misfortune (Endicott 1988: 117).

10 I have never seen women gambling with men. Women do occasionally gamble with other women but this is regarded as unusual and the quantities of objects that change hands are insignificant.

11 There has been a decline in the frequency of gambling in recent years. My description relates to the period 1957 to 1969 and particularly to 1957 to 1960 when my most intensive field research was carried out.

12 In recent years the Hadza have been visited by many researchers and other outsiders, some of whom have sought bows and bird arrows. This has given them a value which they did not have in the 1950s. There were other factors in addition to the restriction on transferability which limited their value in the 1950s. All of these objects are made directly from materials available in every part of Hadza country. In contrast, the objects which are used in the gambling game include scarce materials – traded materials such as metal, cloth or beads or materials such as arrow poison or the stone for making stone smoking pipes which are only available in some places in Hadza country.

13 The procedures at death among the Hadza and three other African hunter-gatherer societies with immediate-return systems are discussed in Woodburn (1982b).

14 A Hadza man called Naftali Z. Kitandu who came to the Fourth International

Conference on Hunting and Gathering Societies at the London School of Economics in 1986 gave a spontaneous and passionate speech about the importance of sharing in human societies. He brought out very clearly how strongly people feel about sharing as a universal moral imperative.

15 An interesting exception here is that it is acceptable during the *lukucuko* gambling game to exchange a high-value arrow for two or more of lower value in order to obtain gambling stakes of appropriate value.

16 This paragraph and the four which precede it are drawn directly from a passage I wrote for Barnard and Woodburn (1988: 22, 23).

17 With rapidly increasing land loss to neighbouring pastoral and agricultural groups, adequate nutrition may well become a problem in the near future.

18 In recent years land loss to neighbouring pastoral and agricultural peoples has become so serious that the Hadza, especially the small minority with some formal education, are now asserting property rights over their land. With the help of a Canadian NGO, they have so far succeeded in obtaining government recognition of their rights over a small part of their land (Woodburn 1995: 16). Access to this area of government-recognized land remains open at present to all Hadza and not just to those particularly associated with it. Access to land by individual Hadza is still obtained automatically and is not controlled by the senior generation.

19 Interestingly, unlike Sahlins, Karl Polanyi classifies meat-sharing in the 'primitive hunting tribe' as a form of redistribution (Polanyi 1977: 40).

20 Sharing is, of course, not always redistributive. The extent to which it is redistributive differs from one society to another and from one context to another in each society. It would be reasonable to say that the emphasis on the redistributive character of sharing is particularly great in the case of the Hadza and other hunter-gatherers with immediate-return systems.

## 3 PROPERTY AS A WAY OF KNOWING ON EVENKI LANDS IN ARCTIC SIBERIA

This chapter was composed in dialogue with colleagues in a number of forums. It was first presented and critiqued at the Writing-Up Seminar at the University of Cambridge in 1993. It was later presented more formally at the University of Kent in 1994. The range of cross-cultural comparisons was suggested by my students in the seminar on Aboriginal Rights at the University of Alberta. The most significant contribution to my understanding of post-socialist economic forms came from my apprenticeship on the Number One Reindeer Brigade of the state farm Khantaiskii in 1991 and 1992, where the languages I used were Russian and Evenki. I have made two brief visits since, most recently to Dudinka in October 1995. I am grateful for the hospitality and companionship of Nikolai Savel'vich Utukogir and his family, as well as the helpful insights offered by my colleagues in Cambridge, Canterbury and Edmonton. This research was made possible by a generous grant by the Social Sciences and Humanities Research Council of Canada.

1 In Evenki there is no word for 'property' in the exclusive sense in which it is used in English. The Russian word *sobstvennost'* is understood but rarely used. When Evenkis signal appropriation in either Evenki or Russian they

tend to prefer possessive pronouns (*nash* (Rus.) 'ours'; *mende* (Ev.) 'mine'), adjectival forms of proper names indicating possession (*brigadnyi* (Rus.) 'of the brigade'; *oron nunganngiin bihin* (Ev.) 'The reindeer is his'). Russian–Evenki dictionaries commonly give the Evenki word *meendykee* as a translation of *sobstvennost'* (property). This is a complex expression made up of the particle *meen* ('to oneself or themselves') with an added possessive suffix -*dy*. I did not note this cumbersome expression during my fieldwork. Boldyrev (1994: 44), however, notes that the word also carries the connotation of to 'wield' or 'know' in some dialects.

2 Vasilevich (1969: 220–2) writes that the spirit of the home camp is an old woman (*babushka*) who lives in the hearth. In order to have good luck she is expected to be fed and not to be given rubbish or sharp objects (like fishbones). The 'spirit of the fire' can foretell the future of a hunter. The *pastukhi* of Number One Reindeer Brigade were very generous to their fire, offering her vodka and meat, and avoiding burning the remains of fish. They did not speak of the fire as having any presence or human attributes other than hunger or an ability to speak.

3 Nurit Bird-David (1990) has proposed the metaphor of the 'giving earth' as a central philosophical idea for hunter-gatherers. The images of reciprocity and hunting for circumpolar societies can be found in Feit (1994), Tanner (1979) and Henriksen (1973) for Crees and in Ridington (1990), Sharp (1988), Nelson (1983) and Osgood (1936: 155, 161) for Athapaskans. These images, as well as those of other peoples from Australia, have been thoughtfully compared by Ingold (1994) in order to develop a relational understanding of personhood which goes beyond Western ontological dualism.

4 It might be said when fishing that a desirable fish 'came to me'. Very successful fishermen are said to 'love the fish' or to be 'good men'. The proper way to treat a fish after it has been consumed is to break the skeleton into pieces 'so that the fish come back'.

5 In the Evenki sentient ecology the prime non-human actors are wild deer, bears, fish, mountains, lakes, rivers and trees. Ingold (1994) draws on a wide range of ethnography from the circumpolar region to Australia in order to demonstrate that representations of a hunt need not be classified as either naively natural or abstractly cultural. He coins the term 'inter-agentivity' to denote a complex social system where animal and human persons 'attend' to each other. I see Ingold's terms as consistent with Bateson's (1972: 454–71) argument for an 'ecology of Mind', which encourages would-be individual agents to recognize the links of communication which tie them to 'the environment of other social units, other races, and the brutes and the vegetable' (*ibid.*: 468). My use of the term 'sentient ecology' combines Evenki stories of the wild deer hunt with Ingold's work on perception and Bateson's definition of ecology.

6 The gift of twenty Finnish snowmachines to the state farm by the Noril'sk nickel plant, as a sign of its goodwill to the native hunters who were forced to consume its airborne pollution, provided an invaluable opportunity for the director to strengthen his position. The machines were 'given' to those who signed contracts pledging to market a certain number of furs per year

exclusively through the state farm. Similarly, during one inspired evening the director explained to me over vodka and raw sturgeon how he had calculated that though the money price of furs in the newly deregulated market had tripled, one could still encourage a hunter to surrender two sable furs for one snowmobile transmission belt (as during Soviet times).

7 People often amplified this idea of a 'birthright' by pointing out the fact that most place names on the maps were of Evenki origin.

8 The Volochanka rebellion of 1932 involved approximately forty representatives of Evenkis, Sakhas and Ngos. It claimed the lives of twenty Party workers and injured fourteen. The rebellion was instigated by attempts to create a single reindeer herd in Taimyr of over ten thousand head. The rebels fought under the slogan 'Why should we take reindeer from our relatives?' This rebellion and others led to the first official guidelines for collectivization in Siberia (O Rabote 1932).

## 4 PROPERTY AND SOCIAL RELATIONS IN MELANESIAN ANTHROPOLOGY

As ever, work on Ponam Island reflects the influence of Achsah Carrier. I thank Marilyn Strathern for providing a copy of her chapter draft: as so often happens, her work has stimulated and challenged me. I have revised my chapter slightly in light of her draft but have not addressed the basis of our disagreement, which is less about social life in Melanesia than about how anthropologists might think about and carry out their work.

1 I develop this model more fully, and indicate why it is 'Maussian' rather than 'Mauss's', in Carrier (1995a: preface, ch. 1).

2 Strathern (1988, ch. 8) is dubious of the degree to which her model is Maussian, and points out that it draws heavily on Indianist work. Whatever its origins, her model does approach objects broadly in the way that I have described as Maussian.

3 Briefly, I think Strathern takes too idealist a stance, neglecting the ways that the meaning structures she describes are a subject of dispute in Melanesian societies and do not apply uniformly in all areas of people's lives (Carrier 1992a). Equally, and like many others, she draws an artificial contrast between Melanesia and the West (Carrier 1995a). I return to both these points later in this chapter.

4 The anthropological convention of writing in the present tense about events the researcher observed in the past lends ethnography a timeless air that can be deceptive. Here I write of Ponam in the past tense, to describe what was happening during the period of fieldwork. Ponam had changed before then, changed during that time and continued to change thereafter.

5 *Kamals* were also the central institutions in the ownership of reef, sea and fishing techniques. In spite of Ponam involvement with the sea, I ignore marine ownership here for two reasons. First, it was managed very differently from land (see J. and A. Carrier 1989: ch. 3). Second, marine ownership was much less contentious than land ownership, probably because an area of the sea could be used by different sets of people in a way that a piece of land could not.

6 The Ponam stress on rights shapes my orientation here. Equally, it brings to the fore a key element in most anthropological renderings of people's lives and thoughts (including Strathern's rendering of the Hageners). Such accounts, implicitly or explicitly, involve generalization and hence the generation of rules about thought, behaviour and the links between them, be they derived retrospectively, descriptively and tentatively by the ethnographer or asserted prescriptively and forcefully by those being described.

7 Those making a distribution were careful to select the appropriate site, normally the distributor's dwelling house or men's house. However, distributors could choose a different site if they wanted to make a particular comment about the state of their relations with their kin (A. and J. Carrier 1991: 178–84).

8 For other treatments of the need to compare models with social practicalities, see the discussion of Melanesian kinship studies and of Weiner's model of social reproduction in A. and J. Carrier (1991: 8–22, 110–13).

9 In 1979, in the midst of a marriage prestation on Ponam Island, the father of the groom began to shout out his anger about the proceedings and took an axe to the bed that was part of the prestation. An on-looking islander turned to Achsah and me and said, 'Don't write this down. It's not true.'

10 Such an argument also begs the question of just what it is that constitutes 'Ponam' or 'Melanesia' from an anthropological perspective (see Carrier 1992b).

11 This dissension resembles the sort of conflicts inherent in the multiplicity of ways that land ownership can be claimed or justified in most cultures (cf. Scott, chapter 7).

## 6 AN UNSETTLED FRONTIER: PROPERTY, BLOOD AND US FEDERAL POLICY

Funding for the research on which this chapter is based has been provided by the National Science Foundation, Law and Social Sciences Programme (no. SBR 9410504), the John D. and Catherine T. MacArthur Foundation and the Philips Fund of the American Philosophical Society. I am grateful to all these bodies for their support.

1 There is an ongoing debate regarding the proper way to refer to American Indians. This essay deals primarily with Oglala Lakotas (Teton, or Western Sioux). In local context they are referred to as 'Indians,' which is in no way a derogatory term. The word Sioux is a Cree corruption of a French word meaning 'adder' (a snake or an enemy). Lakota (Teton), Nakota (Assiniboine) and Dakota (Yankton) linguistic variations made up the L/N/Dakota language family that is glossed as 'allies' or 'friends'. Locally, Lakota people refer to themselves as Lakota, Indian or Pine Ridge Sioux. The choice of terminology is, in many cases, a generational one with elderly people calling themselves 'Sioux' or 'Indian' and younger ones calling themselves 'Lakota', 'Oglala' or a 'Pine Ridge Indian'.

2 Quoted from Governor William Janklow's remarks to the Martin Commercial Club, 17 October 1996.

3 See Matthews (1992) for a discussion of local residents' attitudes concerning

arguments that the Great Plains should be turned back into the 'Buffalo Common', that they were before non-Indian farming practices wreaked havoc upon this environment.

4  Figures and statistics provided by the Bennett County Assessor in November 1995.

5  For a detailed discussion of cultural difference in the perception of land in colonial New England, see Cronon (1983).

6  This term was coined by Chief Justice John Marshall in *Cherokee Nation* v. *Georgia* 30 US (5 Pet.) 1 (1831). The term referred to the unique status of Indian tribes which were determined to be neither a state of the United States nor a foreign state. He concluded that Indian tribes 'may, more correctly, perhaps, be dominated domestic dependent nations . . . in a state of pupillage [whose] relation to the United States resembles a ward to his guardian' (cited in Cohen 1982: 220).

7  The problem of fractionated allotments was not remedied until the Indian Land Consolidation Act of 1982 (25 USCA ss. 2201–11).

8  For an economist's perspective on allotment policy see Carlson (1981).

9  The term 'Indian Country', defined in 1948 (18 USCA ss. 1151), refers to federal jurisdiction over certain land within individual states, including land within Indian reservations (whether or not a patent has been issued), and rights of way running through reservations. Federal jurisdiction also applies to 'dependent Indian communities', whether within or outside the original or subsequently acquired reservation borders. The most pertinent definition for Bennett County is that federal jurisdiction extends to unextinguished Indian titles on all Indian allotments, including rights of way running through them.

10  The original six districts were White Clay, Wakpamni, Porcupine, Wounded Knee, Medicine Root and Pass Creek. Bennett County was once included in the Pass Creek district but subsequently the boundaries have changed and Eagle Nest and LaCreek districts have been added. Bennett County is now in the LaCreek district (One Feather 1974).

11  Letter from John Brennan to Hon. E. W. Martin, Washington, DC, 1 February 1909. Brennan Family Papers (H72.2), Letterbook 1906–9, South Dakota State Historical Resource Centre.

12  'Proceedings of Council held by James McLaughlin, Inspector, with the Indians of Pine Ridge, South Dakota, with reference to opening the south-eastern portion of the Pine Reservation, as contemplated by Senate Bill No. 2341, 61st Congress, 1st Session', 1 September 1909. Brennan Family Papers.

13  Council Proceedings, 9 September 1909. Brennan Family Papers.

14  The Bennett County Historical Association's account states that the meeting was held in 'about 1910' in Allen and that 'there was a 100 per cent vote in favour of the proposition'. However, according to the minutes of the meeting, which was actually held on 15 September 1909, that assessment was far from correct. For a good collection of life histories of the early Lakota and non-Indian settlers in Allen, SD, see Lewis (1980). This volume is important because it relates stories of everyday life that are not 'political'.

15  Council Proceedings, 1 September 1909. Brennan Family Papers.

16 *Ibid.*

17 *Ibid.*

18 Of the 762,698 acres, 548,229 were held in deeded status, and 198,442 were held in tribal trust status. A 1935 Executive Order set aside 16,027 acres for the LaCreek Wildlife Refuge. See Bennett County Historical Society (1981: 63).

19 *Bennett County Booster,* 28 February 1912: 1; 17 January 1912: 1.

20 The officers were elected to serve only until 1 January 1913. While the vast majority of officers were mixedbloods, in the election held the following year many were replaced. By World War I, there were few mixedbloods left in power. See Bennett County Historical Society (1981: 6–7) and *Bennett County Booster,* 10 April 1912: 1; also 17 January 1912: 1.

21 For detailed discussions of the Indian Reorganization Act, see Biolsi (1995); Cohen (1982); Getches and Wilkinson (1986: 122–9); Philip (1986).

22 In 1980, after a thirty-five-year court battle, the Sioux won a cash settlement for the illegal taking of the Black Hills. It was, at the time, the largest claim case in US history. Some Sioux had signed the Act of 1877 under threats of starvation from agents of the government. The Supreme Court awarded them a $106 million award, which the Sioux refused to accept. It is collecting interest in a bank, and the total now stands at over $300 million dollars. Despite their poverty, they refuse to accept cash for the land they consider sacred. This is a case in which the federal government set the terms for compensation in terms of cash only. They ruled out the return of the land, which is what the Sioux requested. It should be noted that the Homestake mine brought out $500 million dollars in gold from the Black Hills, and has been the most productive gold mine in the United States. The three lawyers for the Sioux received $11 million dollars for their efforts and the fee was taken out of the Sioux account. See Lazarus (1991).

## 7 PROPERTY VALUES: OWNERSHIP, LEGITIMACY AND LAND MARKETS IN NORTHERN CYPRUS

Fieldwork in Girne, Northern Cyprus, was carried out between 1989 and 1994 with the aid of an ESRC research studentship. Full acknowledgements can be found in my doctoral dissertation (Scott 1995).

1 According to figures from the 1960 Census of Population and Agriculture, the Turkish proportion of property owners with holdings of between forty and eighty *dönüms* (i.e. medium-sized landholdings – one *dönüm* = approximately one-third of an acre) was roughly equivalent to the Turkish proportion of the population (about 18 per cent). For landholdings smaller than this, the proportion of Turkish owners was lower. It was higher for larger landholdings, reaching a proportion of 42 per cent of landholders with 500–1,000 and above 1,000 *dönüms* (Wellenreuther 1993: 62).

2 Cf. Papadakis (1993) on the importance of the 'continuous Greek presence' for Hellenist historiography.

3 In contrast to the Turkish Cypriot account, for Catselli Greek Cypriot purchases of Turkish Cypriot property were a demonstration of Greek

industry and thrift, in contrast to Turkish neglect/laziness. Similar views
were advanced by Greek Cypriots in the village of Argaki, where most of the
Turkish land had been bought by Greeks. Loizos comments: 'This view so
obviously fitted some of the Greeks' more general attitudes to the Turks that
it might have been little more than a rationalisation of the 1968 *status quo*'
(Loizos 1981: 40).

4  As with so much of the statistical information relating to the Cyprus conflict,
figures given for refugees tend to be obfuscated for political and propaganda
purposes. The estimated numbers of refugees vary from 150,000 to 200,000
Greek Cypriots, and from 32,000 to 80,000 Turkish Cypriots. Wellenreuther
(1993) argues that the most realistic figures are about 160,000 and
40,000–50,000 respectively.

5  At the time of the first British census of 1881, 25 per cent of the Turkish
population of the island lived in Nicosia, reflecting the numbers employed in
government and administrative positions. In 1960, 40 per cent of the Turkish
Cypriot population were urban-dwellers (Attalides 1981). According to
Wellenreuther, the resettlement processes in the north after 1974 slowed
down the Turkish Cypriot rate of urbanization (1993: 76).

6  Turkish Cypriots like Greek Cypriots, practise bilateral partible inheritance.
According to the Ottoman Land Code which remained in force in Cyprus
until 1946, 'Children of both sexes had equal rights in property transmitted
as inheritance' (Sant-Cassia 1982: 649). Unlike the situation in Turkey
(cf. Starr 1984) legal and customary rights in Cyprus do not appear to
conflict: women both inherit and dispose of property in their own right, and
married women also receive and hold in their own right *eşdeğer* points for
land in the south. Land and other forms of property are regularly transmitted
as *inter vivos* gifts as well as *post mortem* inheritance.

7  The 'market' in *eşdeğer* points had come into being as soon as this compensation scheme was introduced in the 1970s. I discuss this market in more
detail below.

8  Variations on *torpil* exist throughout the Mediterranean region; e.g. Sicilian
*fuerza* described by Schneider, Schneider and Hansen (1972) and *mesa*
amongst Greek Cypriots (Attalides 1981). *Torpil* can be understood as
forming part of that complex of behaviour, based on networks of social
obligation amongst 'insiders' and constructed in opposition to the formal/
monetary transactions characteristic of relations with 'outsiders', which
defines who is and who is not 'one of us' (cf. Herzfeld 1991: 195).

9  The feelings of many Turkish Cypriot refugees for place, property and home
and the personal histories and relationships they embody closely parallel the
attitudes of Greek Cypriot refugees as recorded by Loizos (1981).

10  The Girne region has enormous symbolic importance because it was here
that Turkish troops landed in 1974, sustaining many casualties.

11  Maraş (Varosha), a Greek Cypriot suburb of Gazi Mağusa located outside
the walls of the old city, was the focus of tourism development before 1974
(cf. Andronicou 1979). Since 1974 Maraş has been a 'ghost town' under
Turkish military control, and the Greek Cypriot and foreign-owned hotels
have remained empty. However, the possibility of its opening was being
discussed in 1993 as part of the 'UN confidence-building measures'.

12 Some Turkish Cypriots have experienced the opposite problem – of land which had been allocated to them being taken away and reassigned to a mainland settler.

## 8 OWNERSHIP, PROPERTY AND POWER IN TRANSYLVANIA'S DECOLLECTIVIZATION

I owe special thanks to the following people for valuable comment on this paper: Michael Burawoy, Elizabeth Dunn, Gail Kligman, Mary Poovey and Kim Scheppele.

1 These authors also disagree on whether such mixed, ambiguous forms are a good or a bad idea. For Staniszkis (1991), they are the route to a Polish capitalism; for Cornea (1993), they are a ticket to economic stagnation and communist restoration.

2 I specify 'Transylvania' because the property regime differed in Romania's other regions in ways that make some of what I learned in my Transylvanian research not completely applicable elsewhere in that country. See Verdery (1994: 1077–8).

3 I note that land restitution in Romania affects only the land formerly in collectives (CAPs), not the land in state farms (IASs). State farms were run as state enterprises with salaried labour and an appointed director. Much – but by no means all – state farm land came from expropriating large land owners, political prisoners or 'war criminals'. Collective farms, by contrast, were formed from 'voluntary' donations of land by villagers who thereby became their members and their labour force. Members were not paid a fixed salary but various forms of remuneration in cash and kind. The two kinds of farm had differing jural statuses. Before 1989, about 60 per cent of Romania's agricultural land was in collective farms and 30 per cent in state institutions, with the remainder in individual private farms.

4 At exit they may take all their capital, provided they leave behind a minimum value of 10,000 lei. When the association's statute was written, in August 1992, members' minimum required contribution was set at 10,000 lei, 'taken as the value of one hectare of land'. By summer 1996, however, a hectare of land was being valued at around three to three and a half million lei, but the statute had not been rewritten.

5 This payment was partly negotiated between the association and each member, partly fixed by the association independently as a function of its financial needs and the decisions of its leadership council. Such decisions varied widely from one village to the next.

6 It was only in autumn 1995 that anyone in Vlaicu acquired one. My figures for the percentage of property deeds given out come from the Romanian Ministry of Agriculture.

7 For details, see Verdery (1994).

8 Some villagers understood this technicality when pressed about it, but many did not. One man asserted to me that from the moment he planted his land, it was 'his' whether he had a piece of paper or not, and thus he could do whatever he wanted with it, including placing it with the association. In his view, property rights did not require ratification by any

superordinate authority but only (in Lockean fashion) the mixing of one's labour with an object.

9 The same principle works in reverse: the director of a nearby state farm, hearing that two Vlaiceni were deadlocked over ownership of some fields, offered to work them and pay the litigants in kind until the conflict was resolved.

10 This incident is described at greater length in Verdery (1998).

11 As of 1993, Germans made up 3 per cent of Vlaicu's population of 915 – twenty-four resident individuals in eleven households. Unlike some of the Romanians, whose families have resided in the village for centuries, ancestors of the Germans only settled in Vlaicu in the 1890s. See Verdery (1983: ch. 5) for details on this group.

12 Law 18/1991 disbanded only the *collective* farms, not the *state* farms. The reason was that while ownership was changing in the former, the latter would continue to produce food for the population, in case decollectivization caused a drop in production. People who had land in the territory of a state farm would receive a certain sum of money as annual dividends – initially set by the Ministry of Agriculture at the financial equivalent of 300 kg of wheat per hectare owned. In 1994 a Law on Land Rental was passed, according to which people with land in state farms would be able to reclaim it at the end of five years.

13 I suspect that this land's ambiguous status owes something to the association: in my conversations with people on its leadership council, they responded uncomfortably to my questions about the status of this area: 'Uh, we don't ask too many questions about that land.'

14 I say 'about' because no amount of diligence enabled me to determine its size with certainty; even the heir who was trying to repossess part of it did not know how big it was, owing to the missing Land Registry file. 'Jigoaia's' ancestors a century earlier (in the lists noted with the abolition of serfdom, in 1848) had an estate totalling nearly a hundred hectares, but this must have been divided or sold before 1945 – otherwise the Communists would not only have expropriated 'Jigoaia' but also sent her to hard labour on the Danube canal, along with everyone else who owned over fifty hectares. Forty hectares was the estimate of her heir, and I adopt it as well.

15 More than just adequate livelihood is at stake. One '45er' explained to me that he had taken out a bank loan to buy a tractor, expecting that he would have the harvest of seven hectares to use in paying the loan back on time. But he had managed to cultivate only four hectares, owing to the machinations of the land commission and the mayor. He risked being unable to pay off his loan, which was rising exponentially at 76 per cent interest, and ultimately losing his tractor.

16 As of mid-1996 this did not yet exist, though the law creating it was at last moving through parliament. Until this agency comes into being, however, owners have been unable to dispose of their land as they please within a legal framework; they do so through informal means whose durability is questionable, such as handwritten contracts with two witnesses. As of my research in summer 1996, many persons who had bought or sold land informed me that they had done so in exactly this way, without registration in the new cadastre

because 'it's not possible' (*nu se poate*). Notaries with whom I discussed the problem claimed that no official transfer could be recorded in the absence of the Agency for Rural Development and Planning; the wording of Law 18, however, states that circulation of land is free with certain exceptions, noting only that land 'may' be sold via the rights of preemption exercised by the state through this agency, giving first refusal to relatives and neighbours (Art. 48).

17 Law 18 does not specify how these two quantities are to be linked. The Vlaicu CAP liquidation commission, following instructions from the county capital, weighted people's donated land as worth 40 per cent and their labour in the CAP as 60 per cent of their claim on the goods of the old CAP.

18 To my knowledge, the Vlaicu association has no provision for returning to members their share of these fixed means if they decide to withdraw their land; it simply restores to them the land's use.

19 In conversation with the association's agronomist and chief accountant, I learned that they view the new implements as belonging to the members and will rent them out at low cost once the work of the association itself is completed. So far, those who have benefited the most from this possibility tend to be people on the association's council, but other members also reported having ploughed with an association tractor.

20 In June 1996, the agronomist of Vlaicu's association told me that she would need the wheat harvest of a hundred hectares to buy a tractor she could have bought two years earlier with the harvest of fifty hectares.

21 The reasons given for this included the refusal of many owners to accept land on any other place but the spot where they had had it before, even if this meant repossessing a two-hectare farm in ten tiny parcels (cf. Hann 1993a).

22 Some associations did consolidate fields, while others gave to those who wanted to farm independently parcels other than the ones their families had owned before.

23 The same principle applies further up the social hierarchy as well. Others who press to disambiguate claims on the property they manage and have not been considered here are directors of certain state farms, which would be profitable if only the entire bureaucracy of the state farm system did not scoop up their earnings. State farms are grouped in county-wide farm networks that include farms specializing in dairy cattle, others in grapes, others in hops, still others in wheat and corn. While one farm in the network may make substantial profits, these will be averaged in with the enormous losses of others in the network. The hard work and savvy of that one farm director thus support all those other directors who are running down their farms. When the profit-making director tries to pull her farm out and privatize it, however, she will discover just how little interest her superiors have in assisting her: her necessary deliveries of fuel, fertilizer and herbicides will suddenly cease, and she has no independent budget to acquire them on her own. Her attempt to individualize her piece of state property – written as a theoretical possibility into various privatization programmes – and to disambiguate and limit the claims upon it will falter, owing to the power relations through which state property is maintained intact.

## 9 PROPERTY RIGHTS, REGULATION AND ENVIRONMENTAL PROTECTION: SOME ANGLO-ROMANIAN CONTRASTS

This chapter is a revised version of the paper contributed to the series of seminars on Property, organized during the Lent Term of 1995 by the Department of Social Anthropology, University of Kent at Canterbury. I am grateful to all who offered comments upon the original paper, and particularly to Donald M. McGillivray and Chris Hann.

1 I use 'United Kingdom' in the following discussion, although most of the national law that is considered is, in fact, the law of England and Wales. Some significant differences may exist in Scots law. My involvement in Romania follows from participation in a project providing legal expert assistance to the government of Romania in improving the management and productivity of inland fisheries, undertaken through the Natural Resources Institute and funded by the United Kingdom government's 'Know How Fund for Eastern Europe'. This project involved a study tour of Romania in 1994 and the submission of a report to the Romanian Agriculture and Environment Ministries, *The Law of Fisheries, Fishculture and Water Resources in Romania: Review and Recommendations* (W. Howarth and D. M. McGillivray). This report proposes major legislative reforms. In drawing this contrast it is necessary to acknowledge a methodological shortcoming. Whilst the account of the United Kingdom law which is given is historically presented to emphasize the transition from property rights to regulation, the discussion of the Romanian situation lacks a corresponding historical dimension and seeks merely to summarize the apparent contemporary significance of property rights and regulation as these were perceived by informants and inferred from a relatively sparse body of available source materials. Arguably, this amounts to a failure to compare like with like and the making of genuinely empirical comparisons would have involved a study of the perceptions of ordinary people in the United Kingdom to ascertain what common perceptions exist as to the role of property rights in environmental protection. It has not been possible to undertake an investigation of this kind, and I acknowledge that the comparisons made fall well short of recognized standards of rigour in legal anthropology (see Gluckman 1955, 1965a; Roberts 1979).

2 A forthright exposition of the thesis of inherent ecological proprietorship is to be found in Brubaker. 'Empowering those most directly affected by pollution, common law property rights protect powerfully, preventing polluters from arbitrarily fouling streams or spewing poisons onto neighbouring property. No longer victims, the property-rights-holders set the rules, having veto power over developments. When projects do proceed, the property-holders can ensure mutual benefit by negotiating effective mitigation measures and extracting compensation of their choosing for any damages suffered. Many environment groups prefer regulatory solutions to environmental problems. But regulations are made by remote governments who, driven by the need to create jobs or some undefined "public good", are often the least responsible stewards of natural resources' (1995: 19). 'Ecological proprietorship' is to be contrasted with normative theories which maintain

the existence of equitable duties with regard to the protection of the environment for the benefit of future generations. Examples of intergenerational duties are to be found in the *Declaration of the United Nations Conference on the Human Environment* (the Stockholm Declaration of 16 June 1972) which states, in Principle 1, that humankind 'bears a solemn responsibility to protect and improve the environment for present and future generations'. The World Commission on Environment and Development took a similar position in its 1987 report *Our Common Future* (The Bruntland Report). The idea of inherent ecological proprietorship is not concerned with the imperative nature of environmental duties to future generations, but with matters of fact, history and logic as to whether private owners of land do actually have better reason to protect land from environmental harm than would exist if the land were to be the subject of state ownership.

A further source of potential confusion which is best clarified at this point is the contrast between public ownership of land and common ownership of land. Inherent ecological proprietorship is the claim that private ownership of land is environmentally better than public ownership of land. This envisages a comparison between situations where land is exclusively owned and actively used for a particular purpose, respectively, by private or public owners. It does not involve comparisons between owned and unowned land and the respective exploitation of natural resources in such land. The problems of devising a strategy for the optimal utilization of resources available in common land is, therefore, not relevant to the issues under discussion (cf. Hardin 1968).

3 Traditionally, a legal distinction is drawn between real and personal property, so that the law of real property is 'almost equivalent to' the law of land, while the law of personal property is 'all but identical with' the law of movables (Fitzgerald 1966: 420; see also Dias 1985: ch. 14). For a discussion of the contrasting features of ownership in a command economy see Major (1993: ch. 2). On the abstract nature of property generally see Turner (1941).

4 Gray (1991) makes reference to Jeremy Bentham who pointed out that 'property' is what we have in things, not the things that we think we have; see Bentham (1948: ch. 16, s. 26). Gray himself adopts the extreme view that property 'is mere illusion . . . a vacant concept . . . rather like thin air' (Gray 1991: 252).

5 See Dias (1985: 292). This may be contrasted with a much broader conception of 'new property', encompassing such communitarian notions as environmental rights. See Reich (1964), and discussion of this in Gray (1994: 168–9).

6 See Kiralfy (1958: Part Three, ch. 2); Baker (1971: ch. 19); and Simpson (1961).

7 Most civil actions concerning pollution are brought in private nuisance and involve the plaintiff establishing that the defendant has unreasonably interfered with the plaintiff's enjoyment of land. Alternatively, some situations might justify an action being brought in trespass, where the defendant's action constituted a direct interference with the plaintiff's rights. A third

possibility is that an action might be brought in negligence where it can be shown that an injury to the plaintiff has been sustained as a consequence of a breach of a duty of care owned by the defendant. Negligence is the exception amongst the three possibilities in that it does not require an interest in land to be shown by the plaintiff. Pollution actions in negligence are, however, uncommon. For a discussion of the comparative characteristics of these kinds of action in the context of water, see Howarth (1988: ch. 3).

8 Landmarks in the history of pollution control legislation are the Rivers Pollution Prevention Act 1876, providing for a criminal offence of water pollution; the Alkali Works Act 1863, providing for regulatory controls over industrial emissions to the atmosphere; the Clean Air Act 1956, restricting the pollution of air by smoke; the Deposit of Poisonous Waste Act 1972, providing the first controls over contamination of land; and the Control of Pollution Act 1974, first providing for the general regulation of waste dumping activities. For a discussion of the disparate legislative approaches to pollution control and administration see Richardson, Ogus and Burrows (1982: ch. 3), and Vogel (1986). Although some progress towards the integration of pollution control was made under Part I of the Environmental Protection Act 1990, in giving Her Majesty's Inspectorate of Pollution responsibility for the regulation of emissions *into all sectors of the environment* from the most hazardous industrial processes, the implementation of a comprehensive regulatory approach to environmental emissions has only recently been provided for under the Environment Act 1995. This Act will establish an Environment Agency for England and Wales with responsibility for regulating emissions into *all* sectors of the environment. See Howarth (1992: 82).

9 (1498) YB Trin. 13 Hen. 7, f. 26, pl. 4; and see Fifoot (1949: 87).

10 Hence it was stated that the difference between trespass and nuisance is that if I throw a log into the highway and it hits another person this is actionable as trespass, but if it falls into the road and another person trips over it at night that is actionable in nuisance. See *Reynolds* v. *Clarke* (1725) 93 ER 748.

11 See also *Aldred's Case* (1611) (9 Coke Rep. f. 57b), in Fifoot (1949: 99) where it was said 'the building of a lime-kiln is good and profitable: but if it be built so near a house that when it burns the smoke thereof enters into the house so that none can dwell there, an action lies for it' (per Chief Justice Wray).

12 See Fifoot (1949: 9), and see Newark (1949: 480); but contrast discussion in note 22 below of the relaxation of the property interest required to sustain an action in nuisance.

13 Strictly, this discussion concerns *private* nuisance rather than the distinct kind of action referred to as public nuisance. Public nuisance is both a tortious action and criminal offence which arises where an act or omission obstructs or causes inconvenience or damage to the public in the exercise of rights common to all members of the public; see *Attorney General* v. *PYA Quarries* (1957) 2 QB 169; see also Spencer (1989: 55). On private nuisance generally see Gearty (1989) and Ogus and Richardson (1977).

14 See McLaren (1972).

15 (1865) 11 HL Cas 642.

16 *Ibid.*, per Lord Westbury.

17 (1893) [1891–4] *All England Law Reports*, 439 HL.

18 *Ibid.*, at p. 441.

19 Conversely, the lack of interest in land will make an action in nuisance unavailable regardless of the strength of the environmental concerns of the plaintiff. In relation to the difficulties of environmental groups seeking to bring legal actions generally see *R. v. Secretary of State for the Environment, ex parte Rose Theatre Trust* [1990] 1 *All England Law Reports* 754; but contrast *R. v. Inspectorate of Pollution ex parte Greenpeace Ltd (no. 2)* [1994] 4 *All England Law Reports* 329.

20 (1993) [1994] *All England Law Reports* 53.

21 In criticizing the decision, a Friends of the Earth spokesperson described the outcome as a 'blanket amnesty for polluters of ground water' and a spokesperson for Greenpeace described it as 'bad news for the environment and for the victims of pollution everywhere'; see *The Independent*, 10 December 1993: 1.

22 *Malone* v. *Laskey* [1907] 2 KB 141. However, some uncertainty has recently been cast upon the extent of this principle by the controversial decision in *Khorasandjian* v. *Bush* [1993] 3 *All England Law Reports* 699, where an action in nuisance for harassment succeeded, and an injunction was given to prevent unwanted phone calls, despite the fact that the plaintiff had no proprietary interest in the property to which the calls had been made. More recently still, the decision *Hunter and Others* v. *Canary Wharf Ltd* (see 'Important rulings on Nuisance law in London Docklands case' (1995) 249 ENDS Report 39) has reaffirmed that the need to show a property interest extends beyond establishing a freehold or leasehold interest in the property concerned and the 'substantial link' with property which must be shown by a plaintiff bringing an action in nuisance will be satisfied by showing occupation of the property without the need to establish ownership.

23 'Remediability' is here used in the sense of providing redress for interference with an interest recognized by the civil law, rather than the rectification of environmental harm, as where contaminating material must be removed to restore the environment to its former state. See Steele (1995: 615).

24 See Howarth (1988: ss. 3.18 to 3.23) on the use of injunctions in relation to civil actions concerning water pollution.

25 As Steele comments, 'The Cambridge Water case illustrates that compensating the plaintiff does not necessarily have any positive environmental consequences' (1995: 619).

26 It has been estimated that in the mid-nineteenth century only about 15 per cent of the population were owner-occupiers, and thus the great majority of the population would have been unable to bring an action in nuisance. See Ball and Bell (1995: 181).

27 Royal Commission on the Pollution of Rivers, Third Report, (1867) *Parliamentary Papers* 3850, li–liii.

28 See, for example, *National Rivers' Authority* v. *Shell UK* (1990), discussed in Howarth and McGillivray (1996: 41).

29 For an example, consider the position of the pre-1989 regional water

authorities, acting under powers under the Water Act 1973, which required these authorities both to treat effluent and to act as the environmental regulatory authority with responsibility for bringing prosecutions for the inadequate treatment of effluent. See Department of the Environment (1987: Annex A, 41).

30 For a recent discussion of this in the context of the new Environment Agency to be established for England and Wales, see House of Commons Environment Committee, First Report Session 1991–92, *The Government's Proposals for an Environment Agency*, HC (1991–92): 55; and Howarth (1992).

31 In this respect the environmental policies of international investment concerns are a significant consideration. See Murphy (1993).

32 Clear contrasts may be drawn in this respect with the situation in neighbouring Bulgaria where public protests about atmospheric emissions from a caustic soda plant on the Romanian bank of the Danube led to the establishment of the Social Committee for Environmental Protection of the Town of Ruse. Its members were later active in the Bulgarian Independent Union, Ekoglasnost, in 1989. See Baumgartl (1993).

33 Under the Romania Agricultural Land Resources Law (18/1991) land is classified according to use. The large area of land presently in agricultural use is required to be returned to private ownership and, accordingly, individuals may exercise the right to reclaim from the state up to ten hectares of land where prior legal title can be established. For a discussion of the difficulties involved in implementing this law see Verdery (1994).

## 10 DOWRY AND THE RIGHTS OF WOMEN TO PROPERTY

This chapter was first given as a seminar paper at the University of Kent, and I have not added the many references that I might otherwise have done. The general references are available from the works cited and the more particular ones from the account of the work done with Juliet Mitchell (Mitchell and Goody 1997).

1 Laroche-Gisserot (1988: 148).

2 The rest of this paper rests on research being carried out jointly with Juliet Mitchell.

3 Child benefits to single parents are only a lesser part of the total benefits for the unemployed and the elderly, but they give rise to more resentment because of the assumption of parental responsibility.

## 11 DIVISIONS OF INTEREST AND LANGUAGES OF OWNERSHIP

The National Research Institute (Port Moresby, Papua New Guinea) facilitated the field research reported here (see n. 11), but my appreciation of their good offices and of those who worked after me in Mt Hagen goes far further than that. In addition, I am most grateful to Alan Macfarlane for initial stimulus, and to Debbora Battaglia and Eric Hirsch for further comments. A version of this chapter was read as a paper to the Royal Historical Society's 1996 conference at York University, and to the Sociology and Social Anthropology seminar at Keele

University. It received some hefty criticism from which I have benefited. James Carrier has as always given me much food for thought, and I record my warm thanks.

1 The Supreme Court considered the parties' intentions in terms of their current interests in wanting or not wanting to procreate, whereas the trial court which had granted custody of the embryos to the woman, on the grounds that they were (already) children, focused on the pre-conception intent of the couple 'to produce a human being to be known as their child' (quoted by Dolgin 1994: 1278).

2 Schwimmer discusses the variables of alienation and identification, use value and exchange value, in a four-way matrix. The world of literature, music and art is a Euro-American example of identification involved in the creation of exchange values; the Melanesian counterpart he cites is contributing labour ('cargo work') to starting up businesses.

3 Robertson cites a case where a court found that embryos were the property of gamete providers against the claims of an IVF programme that refused to release a frozen embryo to a couple moving state.

4 The rights concerned neither contraception nor pregnancy but an entity only recently come into existence, a pre-implanted, extra-corporeal embryo. A quite separate source of renegotiation lies in conditions of deliberate social innovation that explicitly take property relations to be the core of social justice. One example is Verdery's account (see chapter 8) of the redefinition of property rights under changing political and bureaucratic regimes in Eastern Europe.

5 Coombe points here to the recent legal discovery in the US that litigious strategies related to trademarks are likely to be more successful than appeals to the violation of sacred emblems ('claiming that the nominations of Cherokee [et al.] . . . are already the marks of nations and were held as properties by the governing bodies of national peoples' is a powerful proprietary idiom given that assertions of theft, as she observes, seem to have greater rhetorical value in American politics than assertions of harm (1996: 218)). One should add, however, that the range of things regarded as 'stealable' is also likely to be a variable (Harrison (1990) describes how the Manambu of Papua New Guinea steal from one another's stock of names; elsewhere special practices or emblems may not be released to others without due compensation, and so forth).

6 She argues that this interpretation resonates with anthropological positions, such as those of Nancy Munn, which take sacred and other objects alongside land as phenomenal (consubstantial) manifestations and transformations of one another.

7 These overlapping denotations are typically 'merographic', that is, each appears at once to summon a whole order of phenomena and to be but parts of other orders of phenomena.

8 The two cases are not entirely parallel. In the latter, the axe had a powerful effect by being withheld and thus as something which might have appeared; in deriving, as Battaglia says, its saliency from concealment, it created an effect other than its appearance would have had. In the case of Hagen women, ancestral ghosts always remain concealed, and there is no

potential appearance at issue, while the social presences of kin have a certain constancy whether or not they are there in person. I simply draw the cases together as a further comment on analytical decisions – what the anthropologist chooses to make present *in the account or description* of the event.

9  'Economy' in quotation marks since it was a route to trying to solve general problems in the interpretation of Melanesian 'society', not an investigation into economic life as generally understood. Such interpretation remains necessary. Foster (e.g. 1995: 19) can argue that the different types of social reproduction in Melanesia 'have differently conditioned the process of commodization' precisely because of that general interpretative work carried out by many ethnographers of the region.

10 See Sillitoe (1988: 7) who, independently of Strathern, argues apropos pigs that they are 'not strictly speaking owned by the men who held the right to dispose of them. While men transact with them, women are responsible for herding these animals. The division of rights and duties results in neither owning them. They are jointly custodians, both necessary to their posses-sion. While men hold title to animals, they cannot take possession of them and exercise their right of disposal until they have made a payment, customarily in pearlshells, to the woman herding them, for her male relatives. This payment transfers the creatures from the female productive domain to the man [male] transactional one.' (In Hagen women expect pork, but at some deferred date – they look to the future.)

11 Based on events told and witnessed in 1995; some details are disguised. I am grateful to the British Academy for making the two-month return to Hagen possible. Kanapa ('sweetcorn') is not the woman's name, though she may be called this by some people. (Kanapa is a common food-name, that is, a name bestowed on someone with whom one has shared the item in question.)

12 Money would have enabled her to purchase a substitute pig, mindful of the work bestowed on the one reared earlier, and thus standing visibly for her achievements.

13 A man's pigs are given to his wife to tend, so that 'his own' pigs are also 'her own'. In this case it was important that it was a pig into which the sick woman had put her own effort – only this would sway the ghosts.

14 This is the context in which I argued (1988: 161) that Highlands people do not have alienable items at their disposal; inalienable *property* only makes sense in a context where other things are alienable.

15 Carrier refers to *objects* as being thought about in either inclusive or exclusive terms. I note the formula in English that allows one to refer both to exclusive relations and to property, apparently excluding 'relations' altogether.

16 Battaglia's argument about presence and absence is made in the context of a widely renewed anthropological interest in the material properties of objects which require, as she points out, presence for effect, a critique she extends to Bhaskar's (1989) 'critical realism'.

17 She thus offers a critique of the narrow conceptual framework adopted in prevalent feminist objections to commercial traffic in bodies and body parts. To attack 'ownership' only in its bourgeois, privatized, individualistic sense, she argues, is already to cede the ground of meaning.

18 He draws, too, on a tradition of thinking of social life in terms of 'communal' behaviour and 'communities', constructs with their own history, as Petchesky hints.

19 In order to find appropriate analogies for his argument about the ownership of ritual knowledge in Papua New Guinea, Harrison (1992) considers intellectual property (and religions as the property of groups) in a range of historical contexts, including the Protestant Reformation in Europe, Germany under the Third Reich and ancient Rome. In acknowledging the interest of Harrison's work here, I should note that he adopts a *non*-reproductive model of intellectual property in his view of such property as the ownership of classes of things (image, typification (design)). He argues for similar continuities of forms as does Gudeman, that in Melanesia ritual action and beliefs are experienced in the same way as objects, objects being understood not as what people 'own' but as what they 'are'.

20 Locke, she suggests, appropriates the radical language of the Levellers but channels it to different ends. 'It would not have occurred to the authors of the Leveller women's petition [presented to Cromwell in 1651] to see a dichotomy between individual claims to integrity and ownership in one's "person" (body) and communal claims to justice and free use of the commons . . . Only at the end of the seventeenth century . . . did "privacy" become a synonym for "freedom" and "goods" take precedence over "lives, limbs, liberties"' (1995: 393).

21 But, as noted above, p. 215, this is not an argument for claims on common provision.

22 The state conditioned its recognition of authors with 'a system of press regulation intended to hold authors and printers accountable for publications deemed libellous, seditious, or blasphemous', while authors' proprietary rights to works as commodities with an exchange value did not exist (Coombe 1994: 402, after Rose).

# Bibliography

Albu, L. and Georgescu, G., 1995. 'Problems in the Structure of Romania's Economy', in M. Jackson and W. Biesbrouck (eds.), *Marketization, Restructuring and Competition in Transition Industries of Central and Eastern Europe*. Aldershot: Avebury, pp. 285–336.

Anderson, D. G., 1994. 'The Novosibirsk Stock Market Boom: Privatisation and Accumulation in Russia', *Anthropology Today* 10(4): 10–16.

1996a. 'Bringing Civil Society to an Uncivilised Place: Citizenship Regimes in Russia's Arctic Frontier', in C. M. Hann and E. Dunn (eds.), *Civil Society; Challenging Western Models*. London: Routledge, pp. 99–120.

1996b. 'The Aboriginal Peoples of the Lower Yenisei Valley: An Ethnographic Overview of Recent Political Developments in North Central Siberia', *Polar Geography and Geology* 19(3): 184–218.

Anderson, H. H., 1973. 'Fur Traders as Fathers: The Origins of the Mixed-Blooded Community Among Rosebud Sioux', *South Dakota History* 3(3): 233–70.

Anderson, P., 1974. *Lineages of the Absolutist State*. London: New Left Books.

Andronicou, A., 1979. 'Tourism in Cyprus', in E. de Kadt (ed.), *Tourism: Passport to Development?* Oxford: Oxford University Press, pp. 237–64.

Appadurai, A., 1986. 'Introduction: Commodities and the Politics of Value', in A. Appadurai (ed.), *The Social Life of Things*. Cambridge: Cambridge University Press, pp. 3–63.

Appel, H., 1995. 'Justice and the Reformulation of Property Rights in the Czech Republic', *East European Politics and Societies* 9(1): 22–40.

Attalides, M., 1981. *Social Change and Urbanization in Cyprus: A Study of Nicosia*. Nicosia: Social Research Centre.

Austin, J., 1954 [1832]. *The Province of Jurisprudence Determined etc.* London: Weidenfeld and Nicolson.

Baechler, J. *et al.* (eds.), 1988. *Europe and the Rise of Capitalism*. Oxford: Blackwell.

Baker, J., 1971. *An Introduction to English Legal History*. London: Butterworths.

Ball, S. and Bell, S., 1995. *Environmental Law* (third edition). London: Blackstone.

Barnard, A. and Woodburn, J. C., 1988. 'Property, Power and Ideology in Hunting and Gathering Societies: An Introduction', in T. Ingold, D. Riches, and J. Woodburn (eds.), *Hunters and Gatherers*, vol. II: *Property, Power and Ideology*. Oxford: Berg, pp. 4–31.

Barnes, J. A., 1962. 'African Models in the New Guinea Highlands', *Man* 62(1): 5–9.

Barraud, C. *et al.*, 1994. *Of Relations and the Dead: Four Societies Viewed from the Angle of their Exchanges*. Oxford: Berg.

Bateson, G., 1972. *Steps to an Ecology of Mind: Collected Essays in Anthropology, Psychiatry, Evolution and Epistemology*. London: Intertext Books.

Battaglia, D., 1994. 'Retaining Reality: Some Practical Problems with Objects as Property', *Man* 29(4): 631–44.

Baumgartl, B., 1993. 'Environmental Protest as a Vehicle for Transition: The Case of Ekoglasnost in Bulgaria', in A. Vari and P. Tamas (eds.), *Environment and Democratic Transition Policy and Politics in Central and Eastern Europe*. Dordrecht: Kluwer, pp. 157–78.

Beaglehole, E., 1931. *Property: A Study in Social Psychology*. London: George Allen and Unwin.

Beals, R., 1970. 'Acculturation', in Sol Tax (ed.), *Anthropology Today*. New York: University Press, pp. 375–95.

Bellah, R., 1957. *Tokugawa Religion*. Illinois: Free Press.

Bennet County Historical Society, 1981. *70 Years of Pioneer Life in Bennett County South Dakota, 1911–1981*. Pierre, SD: The State Publishing Company.

Bentham, J., 1970 [1789]. *An Introduction to the Principles of Morals and Legislation*, (ed. J. H. Burns). London: Methuen.

Berezovskii, A. I., 1930. 'Kak Ratsionalizirovat' Rybnoe Khoziaistvo Turukhanskogo Kraiia', *Sovetskii Sever Sbornik Statei* 2: 71–160.

Berkhofer, R. F., Jr., 1979. *The White Man's Indian: Images of the American Indian from Columbus to the Present*. New York: Vintage Books.

Berlin, I., 1969. *Four Essays on Liberty*. London: Oxford University Press.

Béteille, A., 1990. 'Race, Caste and Gender', *Man* 25(3): 489–504.

Bhaskar, R., 1989. *Reclaiming Reality: A Critical Introduction to Contemporary Philosophy*. London: Verso.

Biolsi, T., 1995. 'The Birth of the Reservation: Making the Modern Individual among the Lakota', *American Ethnologist* 22(1): 28–53.

Bird-David, N., 1990. 'The Giving Environment: Another Perspective on the Economic System of Gatherer-Hunters', *Current Anthropology*, 31(1): 189–96.

Blinderman, A., 1978. 'Congressional Social Darwinism and the American Indian', *The Indian Historian* 11(2): 15–17.

Bloch, Marc, 1935. 'Feudalism', in E. Seligman (ed.), *Encyclopedia of Social Sciences*, vol. VI. New York: Macmillan, pp. 203–10.

1962. *Feudal Society* (second edition). London: Routledge and Kegan Paul.

1967. *Land and Work in Medieval Europe*. London: Routledge and Kegan Paul.

Bloch, Maurice, 1975. 'Property and the End of Affinity', in M. Bloch (ed.), *Marxist Analyses in Social Anthropology*. London: Malaby Press, pp. 203–28.

Bloch, Maurice and Parry, J., 1989. 'Introduction: Money and the Morality of Exchange', in J. Parry and M. Bloch (eds.), *Money and the Morality of Exchange*. Cambridge: Cambridge University Press, pp. 1–32.

Bohannan, P. 1963. '"Land,", "Tenure" and Land-Tenure', in D. Biebuyck (ed.), *African Agrarian Systems*. London: Oxford University Press, pp. 101–15.

Boldyrev, B. V., 1994. *Russko-Evenkiiskii Slovar'*. Novosibirsk: Nauka.

Bracton, H., 1968. *On the Laws and Customs of England* (ed. S. E. Thorne), vol. II. Cambridge, MA: Harvard University Press.

Braroe, N. W., 1990 [1975]. *Indian and White: Self-Image and Interaction in a Canadian Plains Community*. Stanford, CA: Stanford University Press.

Brewer, J. and Staves, S., 1995. 'Introduction', in J. Brewer and S. Staves (eds.), *Early Modern Conceptions of Property*. London: Routledge, pp. 1–18.

Brubaker, E., 1995. *Property Rights in the Defence of Nature*. London: Earthscan.

*Cambridge History of Japan*, 1990. Vol. III: *Medieval Japan* (ed. K. Yamamura). Cambridge: Cambridge University Press.

1991. Vol. IV: *Early Modern Japan* (ed. J. W. Hall). Cambridge: Cambridge University Press.

Campeanu, P., 1988. *Genesis of the Stalinist Social Order*. Armonk, NY: M. E. Sharpe.

Canby, W. C., Jr., 1988. *American Indian Law in a Nutshell* (second edition). St Paul, MN: West Publishing.

Carlson, L. A., 1981. *Indians, Bureaucrats, and Land*. Westport, CT: Greenwood Press.

Carrier, A. H. and Carrier, J. G., 1991. *Structure and Process in a Melanesian Society: Ponam's Progress in the Twentieth Century*. Chur, Switzerland: Harwood Academic Publishers.

Carrier, J. G., 1992a. The Gift in Theory and Practice in Melanesia: A Note on the Centrality of Gift Exchange, *Ethnology* 31: 186–93.

1992b. 'Introduction', in J. Carrier (ed.), *History and Tradition in Melanesian Anthropology*. Berkeley: University of California Press, pp. 1–37.

1995a. *Gifts and Commodities: Exchange and Western Capitalism since 1700*. London: Routledge.

1995b. 'Maussian Occidentalism: Gift and Commodity Systems', in J. Carrier (ed.), *Occidentalism: Images of the West*. Oxford: Clarendon Press, pp. 85–108.

Carrier, J. G. and Carrier, A. H., 1989. *Wage, Trade, and Exchange in Melanesia: A Manus Society in the Modern State*. Los Angeles: University of California Press.

Catselli, R., 1974. *Kyrenia: A Historical Study*. Kyrenia: Flower Show Edition.

Chamberlain, B. H., 1971. *Japanese Things*. Tokyo: Tuttle.

Christodoulou, D., 1959. *The Evolution of the Rural Land Use Pattern in Cyprus* (World Land Use Survey Monograph 2). London: Geographical Publications.

Clammer, J., 1978. 'Concepts and Objects in Economic Anthropology', in J. Clammer (ed.), *The New Economic Anthropology*. London: Macmillan, pp. 1–20.

Cohen, F. S. (ed.), 1982. *Handbook of Federal Indian Law*. Charlottesville, VA: The Mitchie Company.

Comisso, E., 1991. 'Property Rights, Liberalism, and the Transition from "Actually Existing Socialism"', *East European Politics and Societies* 5(1): 162–88.

Coombe, R. J., 1994. 'Challenging Paternity: Histories of Copyright', *Yale Journal of Law and the Humanities* 6: 397–422.

1996. 'Embodied Trademarks: Mimesis and Alterity on American Commercial Frontiers', *Cultural Anthropology* 11: 202–24.

Cornea, A., 1993. 'Directocraţia Remaniază Guvernul', 22 (5) (16–22 March): 7–8.

Crocombe, R. (ed.), 1971. *Land Tenure in the Pacific*. Melbourne: Oxford University Press.

Cronon, W., 1983. *Changes in the Land: Indians, Colonists, and the Ecology of New England*. New York: Hill and Wang.

Dalton, D. M., 1996. 'The Aesthetic of the Sublime: An Interpretation of Rawa Shell Valuable Symbolism', *American Ethnologist* 23(2): 393–415.

Dalton, G., 1981. 'Comment' [Symposium on the Work of Karl Polanyi], *Research in Economic Anthropology* 4: 69–94.

Daniels, R. E., 1970. 'Cultural Identities among the Oglala Sioux', in E. Nurge (ed.), *The Modern Sioux: Social Systems and Reservation Culture*. Lincoln: University of Nebraska Press, pp. 198–245.

Davis, J., 1973a. *Land and Family in Pisticci*. London: Athlone Press.

1973b. 'Forms and Norms: The Economy of Social Relations', *Man* 18(2): 159–76.

1977. *People of the Mediterranean*. London, Routledge and Kegan Paul.

1992. *Exchange*. Buckingham, Open University Press.

1996. 'An Anthropologist's View of Exchange', *Social Anthropology* 4(3): 213–26.

Debo, A., 1986. *A History of the Indians of the United States*. Norman: University of Oklahoma Press.

Deloria, E., 1944. *Speaking of Indians*. New York: Friendship Press.

Deloria, V., Jr. and C. Lytle, 1984. *The Nations Within: The Past and Future of American Indian Sovereignty*. New York: Pantheon Books.

DeMallie, R. J., 1979. 'Change in American Indian Kinship Systems: The Dakota', in R. Hinshaw (ed.), *Currents in Anthropology: Essays in Honour of Sol Tax*. St Paul: West Publishing, pp. 221–41.

1984. *The Sixth Grandfather: Black Elk's Teachings Given to John G. Neihardt*. Lincoln: University of Nebraska Press.

1993. '"These Have no Ears": Narrative and the Ethnohistorical Method', *Ethnohistory* 40(4): 515–38.

1994. 'Kinship and Biology in Sioux Culture', in R. J. DeMallie and A. Ortiz (eds.), *Anthropology of North American Indians: Essays in Culture and Social Organization*. Norman: University of Oklahoma Press, pp. 125–46.

Department of the Environment, 1987. *The Government's Proposals for a Public Regulatory Body in a Privatised Water Industry*. London: HMSO.

Dias, R. W. M., 1985. *Jurisprudence* (fifth edition). London: Butterworths.

Dolgin, J., 1994. 'The "Intent" of Reproduction: Reproductive Tehnology and the Parent–Child Bond', *University of Connecticut Law Review* 26: 1261–314.

Dominy, M. D., 1995. 'White Settler Assertions of Native Status', *American Ethnologist* 22(2): 358–74.

Dore, R., 1973. *British Factory, Japanese Factory*. London: Allen and Unwin.

Douglas, M. and Isherwood, B., 1978. *The World of Goods: Towards an Anthropology of Consumption*. Harmondsworth: Penguin.

Dowling, J. H., 1968. 'Individual Ownership and the Sharing of Game in Hunting Societies', *American Anthropologist* 70(3): 502–7.

Dumont, L., 1970. *Homo Hierarchicus: The Caste System and its Implications.* London: Weidenfeld and Nicolson.

1977. *From Mandeville to Marx: The Genesis and Triumph of Economic Ideology.* Chicago: University of Chicago Press.

Earle, J. S. and Sapatoru, D., 1993. 'Privatization in a Hypercentralized Economy: The Case of Romania', in J. S. Earle, R. Frydman and A. Rapaczynski (eds.), *Privatization in the Transition to a Market Economy: Studies of Preconditions and Policies in Eastern Europe.* London: Pinter, pp. 147–70.

Edwards, J. and Strathern, M., n.d. 'Including Our Own', in J. Carsten (ed.), *Cultures of Relatedness.* In preparation.

Elias, N. and Scotson, J. L., 1994. *The Established and the Outsiders: A Sociological Enquiry into Community Problems* (second edition). Thousand Oaks, CA: Sage.

Endicott, K., 1988. 'Property, Power and Conflict among the Batek of Malaysia', in T. Ingold, D. Riches and J. Woodburn (eds.), *Hunters and Gatherers*, vol. II: *Property, Power and Ideology.* Oxford: Berg, pp. 110–27.

Engels, F., 1972 [1884]. *The Origin of the Family, Private Property and the State.* New York: Pathfinder Press.

Fabian, J., 1983. *Time and the Other: How Anthropology Makes its Object.* New York: Columbia University Press.

Feher, F., Heller, A. and Markus, G., 1983. *Dictatorship over Needs.* New York: St Martin's Press.

Feit, H., 1994. 'The Enduring Pursuit: Land, Time and Social Relationships in Anthropological Models of Hunter-Gatherers and in Subarctic Hunters', in E. S. Ellanna and L. Burch (eds.), *Key Issues in Hunter-Gatherer Research.* Oxford: Berg, pp. 421–40.

Fifoot, C. H. S., 1949. *History and Sources of the Common Law.* London, Stevens and Sons.

Finney, B., 1973. *Big Men and Business.* Canberra: Australian National University Press.

Firth, R., 1965 [1939]. *Primitive Polynesian Economy* (second edition). London: Routledge.

1972. 'Methodological Issues in Economic Anthropology', *Man* 7(3): 467–75.

Fisher, D., 1993. 'The Emergence of the Environmental Movement in Eastern Europe and its Role in the Revolutions of 1989', in B. Jancar-Webster (ed.), *Environmental Action in Eastern Europe*, pp. 89–113.

Fitzgerald, P. J., 1966. *Salmon on Jurisprudence* (twelfth edition). London: Sweet and Maxwell.

Forde, C. D., 1946. *Habitat, Economy and Society* (fifth edition). London: Methuen.

Foster, R. J., 1995. *Social Reproduction and History in Melanesia; Mortuary Ritual, Gift Exchange and Custom in the Tanga Islands.* Cambridge: Cambridge University Press.

Franklin, S., 1995. 'Science of Culture, Cultures of Science', *Annual Review of Anthropology* 24: 163–84.

Frazier, I., 1989. *Great Plains*. New York: Penguin.

Fuller, C. J., 1989. 'Misconceiving the Grain Heap: A Critique of the Concept of the Indian Jajmani System', in J. Parry and M. Bloch (eds.), *Money and the Morality of Exchange*, pp. 33–63.

Gazioğlu, A. C., 1990. *The Turks in Cyprus: A Province of the Ottoman Empire (1571–1878)*. London: Rustem.

Gearty, C., 1989. 'The Place of Private Nuisance in a Modern Law of Torts', *Cambridge Law Journal* 48(2): p. 214–42.

Gell, A., 1992. 'Inter-Tribal Commodity Barter and Reproductive Gift-Exchange in Old Melanesia', in C. Humphrey and S. Hugh-Jones (eds.), *Barter, Exchange and Value: An Anthropological Approach*. Cambridge: Cambridge University Press, pp. 142–68.

Getches, D. H. and Wilkinson C. F. (eds.), 1986. *Federal Indian Law: Cases and Materials* (second edition). St Paul: West Publishing.

Ghani, A., 1996. 'Production and Reproduction of Property as a Bundle of Powers: Afghanistan 1774–1901'. Paper presented at the Agrarian Studies Program, Yale University.

Gill, E., 1937. *Work and Property*. London: Dent.

  1983. *A Holy Tradition of Working*. Ipswich: Golgonooza Press.

Glazer, N. and Moynihan, D. A. (eds.), 1975. *Beyond the Melting-pot*. Cambridge, MA: Harvard University Press.

Gluckman, M., 1955. *The Judicial Process among the Barotse of Northern Rhodesia*. Manchester: Manchester University Press.

  1965a. *The Ideas in Barotse Jurisprudence*. New Haven, CT: Yale University Press.

  1965b. *Politics, Law, and Ritual in Tribal Society*. Oxford: Basil Blackwell.

  1968 [1943]. *Essays on Lozi Land and Royal Property*. Manchester: Manchester University Press/The Rhodes–Livingstone Institute.

Godelier, M., 1972. *Rationality and Irrationality in Economics*. London: New Left Books.

  1986. 'Territory and Property in Some Pre-Capitalist Societies', in M. Godelier, *The Mental and the Material*. London: Verso, pp. 71–121.

Goody, J. R., 1962. *Death, Property and the Ancestors*. Stanford: Stanford University Press.

  1971. *Technology, Tradition and the State in Africa*. London: Oxford University Press.

  1977. *Production and Reproduction*. Cambridge: Cambridge University Press.

  1980. 'Rice-burning and the Green Revolution in Northern Ghana', *Journal of Development Studies* 16, (2): 136–55.

  1983. *The Development of the Family and Marriage in Europe*. Cambridge: Cambridge University Press.

  1986. *The Logic of Writing and the Organization of Society*. Cambridge: Cambridge University Press.

  1990. *The Oriental, the Ancient and the Primitive*. Cambridge: Cambridge University Press.

  1996. *The East in the West*. Cambridge: Cambridge University Press.

Gray, K., 1991. 'Property in Thin Air', *Cambridge Law Journal* 50(2): 252–307.

1994. 'Equitable Property', *Current Legal Problems* 160: 157–214.

Gregory, C. A., 1980. 'Gifts to Men and Gifts to God: Gift Exchange and Capital Accumulation in Contemporary Papua'. *Man*, 15(4): 626–52.

1982. *Gifts and Commodities*. London: Academic Press.

Gudeman, S., 1978. 'Anthropological Economics: The Question of Distribution', *Annual Review of Anthropology* 7: 347–77.

1986. *Economics as Culture*. London: Routledge.

1995. 'Sketches, Qualms and Other Thoughts on Intellectual Property Rights', in S. B. Brush and D. Stabinsky (eds.), *Valuing Local Knowledges: Indigenous People and Intellectual Property Rights*. Corelo CA: Island Press, pp. 102–21.

Haigh, N., 1992. *Manual of Environmental Policy: The EC and Britain*. Harlow: Longman.

Hall, P. S., 1991. *To Have This Land*. Vermillion, SD: University of South Dakota Press.

Hann, C. M., 1980. *Tázlár: A Village in Hungary*. Cambridge: Cambridge University Press.

1993a. 'From Production to Property: Decollectivization and the Family–Land Relationship in Contemporary Hungary', *Man* 28(2): 299–320.

1993b. 'Property Relations in the New Eastern Europe: The Case of Specialist Cooperatives in Hungary', in H. G. DeSoto and D. G. Anderson (eds.), *The Curtain Rises: Rethinking Culture, Ideology, and the State in Eastern Europe*. Atlantic Highlands, NJ: Humanities, pp. 99–121.

1996. 'Land Tenure and Citizenship in Tázlár', in R. Abrahams (ed.), *After Socialism; Land Reform and Social Change in Eastern Europe*. Oxford: Berghahn, pp. 23–49.

Hardin, G., 1968. 'The Tragedy of the Commons', *Science* 162: 1243.

Harring, S. L., 1994. *Crow Dog's Case*. Cambridge: Cambridge University Press.

Harrison, S., 1990. *Stealing People's Names: History and Politics in a Sepik River Cosmology*. Cambridge: Cambridge University Press.

1992. 'Ritual as Intellectual Property', *Man* 27(2): 225–44.

1993. 'The Commerce of Cultures in Melanesia', *Man* 28(1): 139–58.

1995. 'Anthropological Perspectives on the Management of Knowledge', *Anthropology Today* 11(5): 10–14.

Hart, K., 1982. 'On Commoditisation', in E. Goody (ed.), *From Craft to Industry*. Cambridge: Cambridge University Press, pp. 38–49.

Hart T. B. and Hart, J. A., 1986. 'The Ecological Basis of Hunter-Gatherer Subsistence in African Rain Forests: The Mbuti of Eastern Zaire', *Human Ecology* 14(1): 29–55.

Hasselstrom, L., 1991. *Land Circle: Writings Collected from the Land*. Golden, CO: Fulcrum Press.

Henriksen, G., 1973. *Hunters in the Barrens: The Naskapi on the Edge of the White Man's World*. Toronto: Memorial University of Newfoundland.

Herskovits, M., 1965 [1940]. *Economic Anthropology: The Economic Life of Primitive Peoples*. New York: Norton.

Herzfeld, M., 1991. *A Place in History: Social and Monumental Time in a Cretan Town*. Princeton: Princeton University Press.

Hinton, W., 1990. *The Great Reversal: The Privatization of China, 1978–1989*. New York: Monthly Review Press.

Hirschon, R. (ed.), 1984. *Women and Property, Women as Property*. London: Croom Helm.

Hivon, M. (in press) 'The Bullied Farmer: Social Pressure as a Means of Resistance', in S. Bridger and F. Pine (eds.), *Surviving Post-Socialism: Local Strategies and Regional Responses in Eastern Europe and the Former Soviet Union*. London: Routledge.

Hoebel, E. A., 1966. *Anthropology: The Study of Man*. New York: McGraw-Hill.

Hohfeld, W. N., 1923. *Fundamental Legal Concepts*. New Haven: Yale University Press.

Homans, G. C., 1942. *English Villagers of the Thirteenth Century*. Cambridge, MA: Harvard University Press.

House of Commons Environment Committee, First Report Session, 1991–92, *The Government's Proposals for an Environment Agency*. HC (1991–92).

Howarth, W., 1988. *Water Pollution Law*. London: Shaw and Sons.

1992. 'Regulation, Operation and Management: The Functions of the Proposed Environment Agency', *International Journal of Regulatory Law and Practice* 1(1): 82–92.

Howarth, W. and McGillivray, D., 1996. 'Sustainable Management of Aquatic Ecosystems and the Law', in C. P. Rogers (ed.), *Nature Conservation and Countryside Law*. Cardiff: University of Wales Press, pp. 33–64.

Hoxie, F. E., 1984. *A Final Promise: The Campaign to Assimilate the Indians, 1880–1920*. Cambridge: Cambridge University Press.

Hume, D., 1962 [1739–40]. *A Treatise of Human Nature*, 2 vols. London: Dent.

Humphrey, C., 1983. *Karl Marx Collective: Economy, Society and Religion in a Siberian Collective Farm*. Cambridge: Cambridge University Press.

1989. 'Perestroika and the Pastoralists: The Example of Mongun-Taiga in Tuva ASSR', *Anthropology Today* 5(3): 6–10.

Humphrey, C. and Hugh-Jones, S. (eds.), 1992. *Barter, Exchange and Value*. Cambridge: Cambridge University Press.

Ingold, T., 1986. *The Appropriation of Nature: Essays on Human Ecology and Social Relations*. Manchester: Manchester University Press.

1994. 'From Trust to Domination: An Alternative History of Human–Animal Relations', in A. Manning and J. Serpell (eds.), *Animals and Society: Changing Perspectives*. London: Routledge, pp. 1–22.

1996. 'Hunting and Gathering as Ways of Perceiving the Environment', in R. Ellen and K. Fukui (eds.), *Beyond Nature and Culture*. Oxford: Berg, pp. 117–55.

Institute for the Development of Indian Law, n.d. *A Compilation of the Treaties, Agreements, and Selected Proceedings of the Treaties of the Tribes and Bands of the Sioux Nation*. Washington, DC: Institute for the Development of Indian Law.

Jacobs, N., 1958. *The Origin of Modern Capitalism and Eastern Asia*. Hong Kong: Hong Kong University Press.

Jancar-Webster, B., 1993. 'The East European Environmental Movement and the Transformation of East European Society', in B. Jancar-Webster (ed.), *Environmental Action in Eastern Europe*. London: M. E. Sharpe, pp. 192–219.

Jenkins, T., 1991. 'The Changing Face of Central and Eastern Europe and the Role of the Environmental Movement', *European Environment* 1(4): 1–4.

Jones, E. L., 1981. *The European Miracle*. Cambridge: Cambridge University Press.

Josephides, L., 1985. *The Production of Inequality: Gender and Exchange among the Kewa*. London: Tavistock.

Kames, Lord, 1796. *Sketches of the History of Man*, 2 vols. Basil (*sic*): J. J. Tourneisin.

Kiralfy, A. K. R., 1958. *Potter's Historical Introduction to English Law* (fourth edition). London: Sweet and Maxwell.

Kwon, H., 1993. 'Maps and Actions: Nomadic and Sedentary Space in a Siberian Reindeer Farm'. Unpublished doctoral thesis, University of Cambridge.

Ladbury, S. and King, R., 1982. 'The Cultural Construction of Political Reality: Greek and Turkish Cyprus Since 1974', *Anthropological Quarterly* 55: 1–16.

Lampland, M., 1995. *The Object of Labour: Commodification in Socialist Hungary*. Chicago: University of Chicago Press.

Landes, D. S., 1972. *The Unbound Prometheus*. Cambridge: Cambridge University Press.

Laroche-Gisserot, F., 1988. 'Pratiques de la dot en France au XIX$^e$ siècle', *Annales ESC* 43: 1433–52.

Lawrence, P., 1955. *Land Tenure among the Garia*. Canberra: Australian National University Press.

1984. *The Garia*. Melbourne: Melbourne University Press.

Lazarus, E., 1991. *Black Hills White Justice*. New York: HarperCollins.

Leach, E. R., 1961. *Pul Eliya: A Village in Ceylon*. Cambridge: Cambridge University Press.

Lee, R. B., 1969. 'Eating Christmas in the Kalahari', *Natural History* 14(22): 60–3.

1979. *The !Kung San: Men, Women and Work in a Foraging Society*. Cambridge: Cambridge University Press.

1982. 'Politics, Sexual and Non-Sexual, in an Egalitarian Society', in E. Leacock and R. Lee (eds.), *Politics and History in Band Societies*. Cambridge: Cambridge University Press, pp. 37–59.

1984. *The Dobe !Kung*. New York: Holt, Rinehart and Winston.

1988. 'Reflections on Primitive Communism', in T. Ingold, D. Riches and J. Woodburn (eds.), *Hunters and Gatherers*, vol. I: *History, Evolution and Social Change*. Oxford: Berg, pp. 252–68.

Lewis, E. H. (ed.), 1980. *Wo'wakita Reservation Recollections: A People's History of the Allen Issue Station District on the Pine Ridge Indian Reservation of South Dakota*. Sioux Falls, SD: Centre for Western Studies, Augustana College.

Linton, R. (ed.), 1963 [1940]. *Acculturation in Seven American Indian Tribes*. Gloucester, MA: Peter Swith.

Locke, J., 1956 [1670]. *The Second Treatise of Government*. Oxford: Basil Blackwell.

Loizos, P., 1981. *The Heart Grown Bitter: A Chronicle of Cypriot War Refugees*. Cambridge: Cambridge University Press.

Lowie, R., 1921. *Primitive Society*. London: Routledge and Kegan Paul.

Macfarlane, A., 1978. *The Origins of English Individualism*. Oxford: Blackwell.

1987. *The Culture of Capitalism*. Oxford: Blackwell.

1992/93. 'Louis Dumont and the Origins of Individualism', *Cambridge Anthropology* 16(1): 1–28.

1995. 'Law and Custom in Japan: Some Comparative Reflections', *Continuity and Change* 10 (3): 369–90.

Macpherson, C. B., 1962. *The Political Theory of Possessive Individualism: Hobbes to Locke*. Oxford: Clarendon Press.

1978. 'The Meaning of Property', in C. B. Macpherson (ed.), *Property: Mainstream and Critical Positions*. Toronto: University of Toronto Press, pp. 1–13.

Maddock, K., 1983. *Your Land is Our Land. Aboriginal Land Rights*. Harmondsworth: Penguin.

Maine, H., 1875. *Lectures on the Early History of Institutions*. London: Murray.

1876. *Village-Communities in the East and West* (third edition). London: Murray.

1890 [1861]. *Ancient Law* (tenth edition). London: Murray.

1901. *Dissertations on Early Law and Custom*. London: Murray.

Maitland, F. W., 1908. *The Constitutional History of England*. Cambridge: Cambridge University Press.

1911. *Collected Papers*, 3 vols. (ed. H. A. L. Fisher). Cambridge: Cambridge University Press.

1921. *Domesday Book and Beyond*. Cambridge: Cambridge University Press.

Major, I., 1993. *Privatisation in Eastern Europe*. Aldershot, Edward Elgar.

Malinowski, B., 1922. *Argonauts of the Western Pacific*. London: Routledge and Kegan Paul.

1935. *Coral Gardens and Their Magic*, vol. I. London: Allen and Unwin.

Manser, R., 1993. *The Squandered Dividend*. London: Earthscan.

Marcus, G. E. (with P. D. Hall), 1992. *Lives in Trust: The Fortunes of Dynastic Families in Late Twentieth Century America*. Boulder, CO: Westview.

Markham, A., 1994. *A Brief History of Pollution*. London: Earthscan.

Marriott, M. and Inden, R., 1977. 'Toward an Ethnosociology of South Asian Caste Systems', in K. David (ed.), *The New Wind: Changing Identities in South Asia*. The Hague: Mouton, pp. 227–38.

Marshall, L., 1976. *The !Kung of Nyae Nyae*. Cambridge, MA: Harvard University Press.

Marx, K., 1963. *Selected Writings in Sociology and Social Philosophy* (ed. T. B. Bottomore and M. Rubel). Harmondsworth: Penguin.

1964 [1857–8]. *Pre-Capitalist Economic Formations* (ed. E. J. Hobsbawm). London: Lawrence and Wishart.

1973 [1857–8]. *Grundrisse: Foundations of the Critique of Political Economy*. Harmondsworth: Penguin.

1974 [1857–8]. *Capital. A Critique of Political Economy*, 3 vols. London: Lawrence and Wishart.

Marx, K. and Engels, F., 1974 [1845–6]. *The German Ideology*. London: Lawrence and Wishart.

Matthews, A., 1992. *Where the Buffalo Roam: The Storm over the Revolutionary Plan to Restore America's Great Plains*. New York: Grove Press.

Matthews, D., 1987. *The Cyprus Tapes*. London: Rustem.

Mauss, M., 1990 [1925]. *The Gift: The Form and Reason for Exchange in Archaic Societies*. London: Routledge.

McCay, B. and Acheson, J. (eds.), 1987. *The Question of the Commons*. Tucson: University of Arizona Press.

McDonnell, J. A., 1989. 'Competency Commissions and Indian Land Policy, 1913–1920', *South Dakota History* 11(1) 21–34.

    1991. *The Dispossession of the American Indian*. Bloomington: University of Indiana Press.

McLaren, J. P. S., 1972. 'The Common Law Nuisance Actions and the Environmental Battle – Well Tempered Swords or Broken Reeds', *Osgoode Hall Law Journal* 10: 505–61.

McLaughlin, J., 1910. *My Friend, the Indian*. Boston: Houghton Mifflin.

Meek, C. K., 1949. *Land Law and Custom in the Colonies* (second edition). London: Geoffrey Cumberlege, Oxford University Press.

Millar, J., 1812. *An Historical View of the English Government*, 4 vols. London: Mawman.

Milsom, S. F. C., 1968. 'Introduction', in F. Pollock and F. W. Maitland, *The History of English Law*

Mitchell, J. and Goody, J. 1997. 'Feminism, Fatherhood and the Family in Late Twentieth-Century Britain', in A. Oakley and J. Mitchell (eds.), *Who's Afraid of Feminism?* London: Penguin.

Montesquieu, Baron de., 1949 [1748]. *The Spirit of the Laws*, 2 vols. London: Hafner.

Mooney, J., 1973 [1896]. *The Ghost-Dance Religion and Wounded Knee*. New York: Dover Publications.

Moore, T. G., 1961. 'The Purpose of Licensing', *Journal of Law and Economics* 4: 43–117.

Morgan, L. H., 1877. *Ancient Society*. New York: Henry Holt.

Morris, B., 1977. 'Tappers, Trappers and the Hill Pandaram', *Anthropos* 72: 225–41.

    1982. *Forest Traders. A Socio-Economic Study of the Hill Pandaram*. London: Athlone.

Morris, I., 1969. *The World of the Shining Prince*. London: Penguin.

Morvaridi, B., 1993. 'Demographic Change, Resettlement and Resource Use; Agriculture and the Environment; Social Structure and Social Change', in C. H. Dodd (ed.), *The Political, Social and Economic Development of Northern Cyprus*. Huntingdon: Eothen, pp. 219–68.

Murphy, T., 1993. 'Enterprise, Economics and the Environment in Eastern Europe', *European Environment* 3(2): 10–13.

Neale, W. C., 1962. *Change in Rural India: Land Tenure and Reform in Uttar Pradesh, 1800–1955*. New Haven: Yale University Press.

Nelson, P. M., 1986. *After the West was Won: Homesteaders and Town-Builders in Western South Dakota, 1900–1917*. Iowa City: University of Iowa Press.

Nelson, R. K., 1983. *Make Prayers to the Raven*. Chicago: University of Chicago Press.

Newark, F. H., 1949. 'The Boundaries of Nuisance', *Law Quarterly Review* 65: 480–90.

Nielson, L., 1993. 'The Right to a Child Versus the Rights of a Child', in
    J. Eekalaar and P. Sarcevic (eds.), *Parenthood in Modern Society: Legal and
    Social Issues for the Twenty-First Century*. Dordrecht: Martinus Nijhoff,
    pp. 313–21.
Nolan, P., 1988. *The Political Economy of Collective Farms*. Cambridge: Polity.
    1994. 'Introduction' in Q. Fan and P. Nolan (eds.), *China's Economic Reforms:
    The Costs and Benefits of Incrementalism*. London: Macmillan, pp. 1–20.
Norris, K., 1993. *Dakota: A Spiritual Geography*. New York: Tricknor and
    Fields.
Obst, E., 1912. 'Von Mkalama ins Land der Wakindiga', *Mitteilungen der
    Geographischen Gesellschaft in Hamburg* 26: 2–27.
Ogus, A. I., 1994. *Regulation Legal Form and Economic Theory*. Oxford: Clar-
    endon Press.
Ogus, A. I. and Richardson, G. M., 1977. 'Economics and the Environment:
    A Study of Private Nuisance', *Cambridge Law Journal* 36(2): 284–325.
One Feather, V., 1974. *Tiyospayes*. Pine Ridge, SD: Oglala Sioux Culture
    Centre, Red Cloud Indian School.
Osgood, C., 1936. *Contributions to the Ethnography of the Kutchin* (Yale University
    Publications in Anthropology 14). New Haven: Yale University Press.
O Rabote, 1932. 'O Rabote v Natsional'nykh Raionakh Krainego Severa',
    *Sovetskii Sever* 2: 47–8.
Otis, D. S., 1973. *The Dawes Act and the Allotment of Indian Lands* (ed. F. P.
    Prucha). Norman: University of Oklahoma Press.
Pannell, S., 1994. 'Mabo and Museums: The Indigenous (Re)appropriation of
    Indigenous Things', *Oceania* 65: 18–39.
Papadakis, I., 1993. 'Perceptions of History and Collective Identity: A Study of
    Contemporary Greek Cypriot and Turkish Cypriot Nationalism'. Unpub-
    lished doctoral thesis, University of Cambridge.
Parry, J., 1986. '*The Gift*, the Indian Gift and the 'Indian Gift', *Man* 21(3):
    453–73.
Parry J. M. and Bloch, M. (eds.), 1989. *Money and the Morality of Exchange*.
    Cambridge: Cambridge University Press.
Petchesky, R. P., 1995. 'The Body as Property: A Feminist Re-vision', in F. D.
    Ginsburg and R. Rapp (eds.), *Conceiving the New World Order: The Global
    Politics of Reproduction*. Berkeley: California University Press, pp. 387–406.
Peterson, N., 1993. 'Demand Sharing: Reciprocity and the Pressure for
    Generosity among Foragers', *American Anthropologist*, 95(4): 860–74.
Polanyi, K., 1944. *The Great Transformation*. Boston: Beacon Press.
    1957. 'The Economy as Instituted Process', in K. Polanyi, C. Arensberg and
    H. Pearson (eds.), *Trade and Market in the Early Empires: Economics in
    History and Theory*. New York: Free Press, pp. 243–70.
    1977. *The Livelihood of Man*. London: Academic Press.
Pollock, F. and Maitland, F. W., 1923. *The History of English Law*, 2 vols.
    (second edition). Cambridge: Cambridge University Press.
Popkov, Y. V., 1994. *Etnosotsial'nye i Pravovye Protsessy v Evenkii*. SO RAN:
    Novosibirsk.
Posey, D., 1990. 'Intellectual Property Rights and Just Compensation for
    Indigenous Knowledge', *Anthropology Today* 6(4): 13–16.

Posey, D. A. and Dutfield, G., 1996. *Beyond Intellectual Property.* Ottawa: International Development Research Centre.

Povinelli, E. A., 1993. *Labour's Lot: The Power, History and Culture of Aboriginal Action.* Chicago: University of Chicago Press.

Price, J. A., 1975. 'Sharing: The Integration of Intimate Economics', *Anthropologica* 17(1): 3–27.

Quesnay, F., 1962 [1767]. 'The General Maxims for the Economic Government of an Agricultural Kingdom', in R. L. Meek, *The Economics of Physiocracy: Essays and Translation.* London: George Allen and Unwin, pp. 231–64.

Ratzell, F., 1898. *The History of Mankind*, 3 vols. London: Macmillan.

Reche, O., 1914. *Zur Ethnographie des Abflusslosen Gebietes Deutsch-Ostafrikas auf Grund der Sammlung der Ostafrika-Expedition (Dr E. Obst) der Geographischen Gesellschaft in Hamburg.* Hamburg: Abhandlungen des Hamburgischen Kolonial-Instituts.

Reeve, A., 1986. *Property.* Basingstoke: Macmillan.

Reich, C., 1964. 'The New Property', *Yale Law Review* 73: 733.

Reid, C. T. (ed.), 1992. *Green's Guide to Environmental Law in Scotland.* Edinburgh: W. Green/Sweet and Maxwell.

Rein, J. J., 1884. *Japan. Travels and Researches.* London:

Richardson, G., Ogus, A. and Burrows, P., 1982. *Policing Pollution.* Oxford, Clarendon Press.

Ridington, R., 1990. *Little Bit Know Something: Stories in a Language of Anthropology.* Douglas and McIntyre.

Roberts, S., 1979. *Order and Dispute: An Introduction to Legal Anthropology.* Harmondsworth: Penguin.

Robertson, J. A., 1994. *Children of Choice. Freedom and the New Reproductive Technologies.* Princeton: Princeton University Press.

Rostow, E., 1960. *The Stages of Economic Growth: A Non-Communist Manifesto.* Cambridge: Cambridge University Press.

Ryan, A., 1984. *Property and Political Theory.* Oxford: Blackwell.

Ryavec, C., 1983. 'Legal System', in *Kodansha Encyclopedia of Japan*, vol. V. Tokyo, pp. 375–9.

Sahlins, M., 1963. 'Poor Man, Rich Man, Big-Man, Chief: Political Types in Melanesia and Polynesia', *Comparative Studies in Society and History* 5: 285–303.

1974. *Stone Age Economics.* London: Tavistock.

Said, E., 1978. *Orientalism.* Harmondsworth: Penguin.

Salisbury, R., 1962. *From Stone to Steel: Economic Consequences of a Technological Change in New Guinea.* Melbourne: Melbourne University Press.

Sansom, G. B., 1950. *The Western World and Japan.* London: Cresset Press.

1962. *Japan. A Short Cultural History.* New York: Appleton Century Crofts.

Sant-Cassia, P., 1982. 'Property in Greek Cypriot Marriage Strategies, 1920–1980', *Man* 17(4): 643–63.

Schneider, P., Schneider, J. and Hansen, E., 1972. 'Modernisation and Development: The Role of Regional Elites and Non-Corporate Groups in the European Mediterranean', *Comparative Studies in Society and History* 14: 328–50.

Schwimmer, E., 1973. *Exchange in the Social Structure of the Orokaiva*. London: C. Hurst and Company.

    1979. 'The Self and the Product: Concepts of Work in Comparative Perspective', in S. Wallman (ed.), *Social Anthropology of Work*. London: Academic Press, pp. 287–315.

Scott, C., 1989. 'Knowledge Construction Among Cree Hunters: Metaphors and Literal Understanding', *Journal de la Société des Americanistes* 75: 193–208.

Scott, J. E., 1995. '"Turning the Corner": Identity, Visibility and Legitimacy as Issues in Turkish Cypriot Tourism Development'. Unpublished doctoral thesis, University of Kent at Canterbury.

Sharp, H. S., 1988. *The Transformation of Bigfoot: Maleness, Power and Belief Among the Chipewyan*. Washington: Smithsonian.

Shirokogoroff, S. M., 1933. *Social Organization of the Northern Tungus*. Shanghai: Commercial Press.

Shmelev, N. and Popov, V., 1990. *The Turning Point: Revitalizing the Soviet Economy*. London: Tauris.

Sillitoe, P., 1988. Property Ownership in the New Guinea Highlands, *Research in Melanesia* 10: 1–11.

Simpson, A. W. B., 1961. *An Introduction to the History of the Land Law*. Oxford: Oxford University Press.

Skachko, A., 1930. 'Organizatsiia territorii malykh narodov Severa', *Sovetskii Sever Sbornik Statei* 2: 5-68.

Smith, A., 1976 [1776]. *An Inquiry into the Nature and Causes of the Wealth of Nations*. Chicago: University of Chicago Press.

Smith, H. N., 1978 [1950]. *Virgin Land: The American West as Symbol and Myth*. Cambridge, MA: Harvard University Press.

Smith, R. J., 1983. *Japanese Society*. Cambridge: Cambridge University Press.

Smith, T. C., 1988. *Native Sources of Japanese Industrialization, 1750–1920*. Berkeley: University of California Press.

Sorokin, P., 1928. *Contemporary Sociological Theories*. New York:

Spencer, J. R., 1989. 'Public Nuisance – A Critical Examination', *Cambridge Law Journal* 48(1): 55–84.

Spencer, J., 1995. 'Occidentalism in the East: The Uses of the West in the Politics and Anthropology of South Asia', in J. G. Carrier (ed.), *Occidentalism: Images of the West*. Oxford: Oxford University Press, pp. 234–57.

Spicer, E. H., 1961. *Perspectives in American Indian Culture Change*. Chicago: University of Chicago Press.

    1994. 'The Nations of a State', in K. Kroeber (ed.), *American Indian Persistence and Resurgence*. Durham: Duke University Press, pp. 27–49.

Staniszkis, J., 1991. 'Political Capitalism in Poland', *East European Politics and Societies* 5(1): 127–41.

Stark, D., 1992. 'Path Dependence and Privatization Strategies in East Central Europe', *East European Politics and Societies* 6(1): 17–54.

    1996. 'Recombinant Property in East European Capitalism', *American Journal of Sociology*, 101(4): 993–1027.

Starr, J., 1984. 'The Legal and Social Transformation of Rural Women in Aegean Turkey', in R. Hirschon (ed.), *Women and Property, Women as Property*. London: Croom Helm, pp. 92–116.

Stasiulis, D. and Yuval-Davis, N. (eds.), 1995. *Unsettling Settler Societies: Articulations of Gender, Race, Ethnicity and Class*. London: Sage.

Stec, S., 1993. 'Public Participation Laws, Regulations and Practices in Seven Countries in Central and Eastern Europe: An Analysis Emphasising Impacts on the Development Decision-Making Process', in A. Vari and P. Tamas (eds.), *Environment and Democratic Transition Policy and Politics in Central and Eastern Europe*. London: Kluwer, pp. 88–119.

Steele, J., 1995. 'Private Law and the Environment', *Legal Studies* 236: 238.

Stein, P. and Shand, J., 1974. *Legal Values in Western Society*. Edinburgh: Edinburgh University Press.

Stewart, D., 1854. *Collected Works* (ed. W. Hamilton), 11 vols. Edinburgh: Thomas Constable.

Stolojan, T. D., 1991. 'Romania', in P. Marer and S. Zecchim (eds.), *The Transition to a Market Economy*, vol. I: *The Broad Issues*. Paris: OECD, pp. 92–3.

Strathern, A. J., 1971. *The Rope of Moka*. Cambridge: Cambridge University Press.

1972. *One Father, One Blood*. Canberra: Australian National University Press.

Strathern, M., 1984a. 'Marriage Exchanges: A Melanesian Comment', *Annual Review of Anthropology* 13: 41–73.

1984b. 'Subject or Object? Women and the Circulation of Valuables in Highlands New Guinea', in R. Hirschon (ed.), *Women and Property, Women as Property*, pp. 158–75.

1988. *The Gender of the Gift: Problems with Women and Problems with Society in Melanesia*. Berkeley: University of California Press.

1996. 'Potential Persons: Intellectual Rights and Property in Persons', *Social Anthropology* 4(1): 17–32.

Suslov, I. M., 1927. 'Okhota u Tungusov', *Okhota i Pushnina Sibiri* 1: 44–9.

Swain, N., 1985. *Collective Farms Which Work?* Cambridge: Cambridge University Press.

Tanner, A., 1979. *Bringing Home Animals: Religious Ideology and Mode of Production of the Mistassini Cree Hunters*. St John's: Institute of Social and Economic Research.

Testart, A., 1987. 'Game Sharing Systems and Kinship Systems among Hunter-Gatherers', *Man* 22(2): 287–304.

Thompson, E. P., 1968. *The Making of the English Working Class*. Harmondsworth: Penguin.

1977. *Whigs and Hunters: The Origin of the Black Act*. London: Peregrine.

1991. *Customs in Common*. London: Merlin Press.

Thunberg, C. P., 1796. *Travels in Europe, Africa and Asia*, 3 vols. (third edition). London: Rivington.

Tocqueville, A., 1956 [1856]. *L'Ancien Régime*. Oxford: Blackwell.

1968. *Journeys to England and Ireland* (ed. J. P. Mayer). New York: Doubleday.

Tönnies, F., 1955 [1887]. *Community and Association*. London: Routledge and Kegan Paul.

Turing, H. D., 1952. *River Pollution.* London: Edward Arnold.

Turner, C. J. W., 1941. 'Some Reflections on Ownership in English Law', *The Canadian Bar Review* 19: 342–252.

Vasilevich, G. M., 1969. *Evenki: Istoriko-Etnograficheskie Ocherki (XVIII-nachalo XX v.).* Leningrad: Nauka.

Verdery, K., 1983. *Transylvanian Villagers: Three Centuries of Political, Economic and Ethnic Change.* Berkeley: University of California Press.

1991. 'Theorizing Socialism: A Prologue to the Transition', *American Ethnologist* 18(3): 419–39.

1994. 'The Elasticity of Land: Problems of Property Restitution in Transylvania', *Slavic Review* 53(4): 1071–109.

1998. 'Fuzzy Property: Rights, Power, and Identity in Transylvania's Decollectivization', in M. Burawoy and K. Verdery (eds.), *Ethnographies of Transition.* Forthcoming.

Vestal, S., 1989 [1932]. *Sitting Bull: Champion of the Sioux.* Norman: University of Oklahoma Press.

Vogel, D., 1986. *National Styles of Regulation.* London: Cornell University Press.

Wagoner, P. L., 1994. *Ambivalent Identities: Processes of Exclusion and Marginalization* (Occasional Paper 25, MacArthur Scholar Series). Bloomington: Indiana University Press.

1997. 'Surveying Justice: The Problematics of Overlapping Jurisdictional Domains in Indian Country,' *Droits et cultures,* 33(1): 21–52.

Watson, J. L. (ed.), 1980. *Asian and African Systems of Slavery.* Oxford: Blackwell.

Weber, M., 1961 [1920]. *General Economic History.* New York: Collier.

Weiner, A., 1976. *Women of Value, Men of Renown: New Perspectives on Trobriand Exchange.* Austin: University of Texas Press.

1980. 'Reproduction: A Replacement for Reciprocity', *American Ethnologist* 7: 71–85.

1982. 'Sexuality among the Anthropologists: Reproduction among the Informants', in F. J. P. Poole and G. Herdt (eds.), *Sexual Antagonism, Gender and Social Change in Papua New Guinea.* Special issue of *Social Analysis* (Sydney) 12: 52–65.

1992. *Inalienable Possessions: The Paradox of Keeping-While-Giving.* Los Angeles: University of California Press.

Wellenreuther, R., 1993. *Siedlungsentwicklung und Siedlungsstrukturen im ländlichen Raum der Türkischen Republik Nordzypern.* University of Mannheim: Materialien zur Geographie.

White, R., 1991a. *The Middle Ground: Indians, Empires, and Republics in the Great Lakes Region, 1650–1815.* New York: Cambridge University Press.

1991b. *It's Your Misfortune and None of My Own: A New History of the American West.* Norman: University of Oklahoma Press.

Whitehead, H., 1986. 'The Varieties of Fertility Cultism in New Guinea: Part I', *American Ethnologist* 13: 80–99.

Wiessner, P., 1982. 'Risk, Reciprocity and Social Influences on !Kung San Economics', in E. Leacock and R. Lee (eds.), *Politics and History in Band Societies.* Cambridge: Cambridge University Press, pp. 61–84.

Williams, G., 1967. 'Control by Licensing', *Current Legal Problems* 20: 81–103.

Williams, N. M., 1986. *The Yolngu and Their Land: A System of Land Tenure and the Fight for its Recognition*. Canberra: Australian Institute of Aboriginal Studies.

Wittfogel, K. A., 1957. *Oriental Despotism. A Comparative Study of Total Power*. New Haven: Yale University Press.

Woodburn, J. C., 1972. 'Ecology, Nomadic Movement and the Composition of the Local Group among Hunters and Gatherers: An East African Example and Its Implications', in P. Ucko, R. Tringham and G. W. Dimbleby (eds.), *Man, Settlement and Urbanism*. London: Duckworth, pp. 193–206.

1979. 'Minimal Politics: The Political Organisation of the Hadza of Tanzania', in P. Cohen and W. Shack (eds.), *Politics in Leadership: A Comparative Perspective*. Oxford: Clarendon Press, pp. 244–66.

1980. 'Hunters and Gatherers Today and Reconstruction of their Past', in E. Gellner (ed.), *Soviet and Western Anthropology*. London: Duckworth, pp. 95–117.

1982a. 'Egalitarian Societies', *Man* 17(3), 431–51.

1982b. 'Social Dimensions of Death in Four African Hunting and Gathering Societies', in M. Bloch and J. Parry (eds.), *Death and the Regeneration of Life*. Cambridge: Cambridge University Press, pp 187–210.

1988a. 'African Hunter-Gatherer Social Organization: Is It Best Understood as a Product of Encapsulation?', in T. Ingold, D. Riches and J. Woodburn (eds.), *Hunters and Gatherers*, vol. I: *History, Evolution and Social Change*. Oxford: Berg, pp. 31–64.

1988b. 'Hunter-Gatherer "Silent Trade" with Outsiders and the History of Anthropology'. Unpublished paper delivered at the Fifth International Conference on Hunting and Gathering Societies, Darwin, Australia.

1995. 'Als Jäger und Sammler diskriminiert, Die Hadzabe wollen in Tanzania anerkannt werden', *Pogrom: Zeitschrift für Bedrohte Völker* 185: 15–17.

# Index